$4.95

D1535113

THE RESPONSIBLE CHURCH

THE
RESPONSIBLE
CHURCH

Selected Texts of Cardinal Suhard

Compiled by
Olivier de la Brosse, O.P.

FIDES PUBLISHERS, INC.
NOTRE DAME, INDIANA

First published in this edition, 1967, Geoffrey Chapman Ltd

This book was originally published in French under the
title *Vers une église en état de mission*
by Les Editions du Cerf, Paris, 1965

This abridged translation was made by Patrick Hepburne-Scott

Nihil obstat: R. D. Desmundus Leahy, D.D., Ph.D., L.S.S.,
          censor deputatus
Imprimatur: H. Gibney, Vicarius Generalis

This book is set in Period Old Style, 11 on 13pt.
Made and printed in Great Britain.

CONTENTS

COMPILER'S PREFACE

Fr Bouëssé, who was a student under Abbé Suhard in the major seminary at Laval, was for some thirty years the Cardinal's intimate friend and confidant, and is now his biographer. All who had known the Cardinal entrusted his personal papers, letters, souvenirs, and other private and public documents concerning him, to Fr Bouëssé.

I wish here to thank him most warmly for giving me such full access to these archives, allowing me to draw on them for the biographical material and some unpublished papers, from which I have been able to compose the introduction and the explanatory passages of this collection.

My thanks are also due to Mgr Brot, to Mgr Lalande, to Frs Hollande, Augros, Le Sourd and Depierre, to Mlle Jordan, and to all whose personal recollections and generous advice have enabled me to complete this work.

O.B.

INTRODUCTION

Looking back on Cardinal Suhard's work as Archbishop of Paris from 1940 to 1949 one is astonished at the personal transformation he underwent and at the missionary impetus he gave to the priests working in his diocese during those ten years. From Paris his influence spread throughout the rest of France and to many other countries.

What caused this typical pastoral priest, with his roots in tradition and the land, to realize that the Church could no longer wait for men to come to her but must plunge boldly into the heart of the earthly city? After a lifetime wedded to sure, well-tried methods, how was he able to launch and maintain missionary activities in such a new and audacious style? What influences turned this discreet, conscientious bishop into the 'Father of the Mission'?

Here is a man who served his curacy at the age of seventy! But under what influence? By what miracle of grace? There were some who were perfectly sure they had the explanation: this earnest but ordinary priest was bowled over in 1943 by the revelations of Abbé Godin, and was suddenly made aware of the extent to which his immense diocese had ceased to be Christian. A sudden conversion; a psychological reversal; the pastor becomes an apostle.

The truth is more striking and more simple than this. Suhard certainly read *La France, pays de mission?*[1] at the beginning of the most fruitful period of mission in his life. But for such a challenge to produce a clear and immediate response, the man must have had a missionary soul, an infinite

[1] English translation *France Pagan?*, London, 1949.

desire to make Christ known. He must have possessed resources of intelligence, courage and resolution equal to such a
task, if the mission was to be started. The soil must have been
prepared for the seed to germinate so quickly. Before that
date, in fact, he must already have proved himself an apostle.

As we set out on our search for the 'missionary secret'
which filled the soul of this man, we shall see that the turning-
point of 1943 was really only a stage in a life already long
devoted to proclaiming the good news of the kingdom.

THE DAYS OF CHRISTENDOM

ROOTS IN THE LAND AND CHRISTIAN TRADITION

Emmanuel Suhard was born on 5 April 1874, at Brains-sur-
les-Marches, in the department of Mayenne. He never knew
his father, who died a month after his son's birth, but was
brought up by his mother in the little farm of Isodière,
which was a heavy burden for a woman on her own. A
purely feminine education, in that silent, gloomy house, made
the child into a recluse, quiet and well-behaved, rather too
meek, a timid boy with little outward self-expression. It was
not till 1882, when Emmanuel was about eight, that Jeanne
Suhard decided to send him to the school at Brains, run
by the Brothers of Ploërmel. The child went there every day,
accompanied by the big farm dog, which growled whenever
anyone came too near his master. There he was a studious
pupil, rather clumsy and awkward, who played, as one of his
schoolfellows said, 'only at saying Mass and having processions'. The parish priest of Brains thought his intelligence
very moderate, his natural gifts limited. At the time of his
first communion the child confided in him his desire to be a
priest. 'That boy Manuel?' rudely retorted the curé to
Jeanne Suhard. 'He's far too stupid! They'll never make a
parish priest of him!' ('And indeed,' the Cardinal commented

later, 'I was too stupid to be a parish priest, but they made a professor of me!')

At Chalon-du-Maine, there was a little 'presbytery school' kept by Abbé Réveillard. He took the boy in charge and gave him his first Latin lessons (1886-7). At fourteen, Emmanuel went to the junior seminary at the town of Mayenne, and came under the thumb of a new master, M. Quentin. Still timid and awkward, in his old-fashioned clothes, the child looked rather like Charles Bovary. He was often teased, and it hurt him. But as he was always top of his class in religious instruction, for three years he never left the 'table of honour' in the refectory, where custom forced him to sit next to the superior.

In October 1892 he entered the major seminary at Laval. There he was the pupil and spiritual son of Abbé Daligault, a remarkable priest, traditional and simple, whose maxim, 'We must act like the saints', he used later to repeat. At the end of his philosophy year his studies were interrupted for a year by military service, which had recently been imposed on the clergy (1875). As this period was spent at Laval, he was able to keep in touch with his teachers. No one, of course, could have been less military in temperament than Private Suhard. Full of good will, but not in the least fitted for sports or the profession of arms, the young peasant was incapable of marching in step or wearing his uniform properly. Once, at an inspection, his exasperated colonel shouted: 'Suhard! Get off parade! You make me ashamed!'

This trial did not last long. On his discharge he profited by a bursary, offered to the diocese, to be sent to the French seminary in Rome, there to pursue his studies at the Gregorian University. His teachers there were Wernz, De Augustinis and, above all, Billot, whose teaching and ideas so thrilled him that he would waylay him in the corridors and track him down to his room. This was a period of solid and intense work, which won him two doctorates (theology and philosophy) and a licentiate (canon law), to which the University spontaneously added its gold medal. From this Italian period he carried away not only his nostalgia for the light of Rome but that solid attachment to the pope and the central institutions of the Church, which were to be so characteristic of his teaching at Laval. His theological thought always bore the impress of that Roman training, steeped in the theses of the First Vatican Council. 'The Church is, above all, the pope,' he used to say, 'and so wherever the pope is, there must needs be the Church.'

Ordained priest on 18 December 1897, Emmanuel Suhard said his first Mass the next day in St Mary Major. He returned to France in July 1899 and was then able to sing his first High Mass in his native village, in the presence of his mother. In September he went to the major seminary at Laval, there to begin a teaching career which was to last for thirty years.

'DOCTOR BECAUSE'

This nickname, aptly given him by his pupils, described a man who was athirst for reasons. He must understand, he must explain, he must hand on. His teaching, a simple reproduction of what he had learned in Rome, had no striking originality, but, said his hearers, it was plain, solid and well worked out. In charge of the philosophy course from 1899 to 1912, he gave lectures in logic, psychology and metaphysics, inspired by the great lectures of Mercier of Louvain, whom he wholeheartedly admired. Then from 1912 to 1928 he went on to theology, teaching the treatises on the Trinity, grace, the incarnation and the sacraments. If the first-year seminarists did not always understand, that was the fault of the law, not of the professor, for the lectures were in Latin! Too prudent, too respectful of tradition to break the established rules, he sometimes had to resign himself sadly to preaching in the wilderness. He was not one of those (in the next generation, I grant) who could get round the difficulty by explaining to their critics that 'the form may be in French, but the substance is in Latin'. But having no desire to perpetuate a state of affairs which reduced teaching to an exercise in style, he hastened to dictate summaries and supplements to the lectures, in French.

In substance as in form, then, Abbé Suhard's teaching remained 'obstinately traditional', but the man himself had broad ideas, for which he was sometimes blamed. His colleagues felt rather hurt at seeing him acting as sole spiritual director for two-thirds of their pupils, nor was Bishop's House unaware that many priests of the diocese had chosen him as their adviser. Busied all day with visits and consultations, the professor worked late into the night, but never gave up his early rising or his unfailing attendance at the community offices. On Sundays he would join his old students, now priests, to give them a hand in their parishes, or would take a day's duty for a convent chaplain in Laval. Thus he learned to consider work for priests as a fundamental ministry and became convinced that the priesthood is an essential part of a country's spiritual life.

This role of direction, confessions and discreet, generous help was intensified during the 1914 war. Discharged from the army in September, the Laval professor prized the honour of at least maintaining faithful and deepening relations with those who were mobilized. His finest letters of direction date from this period. Through the confidences given him he learned to know men, their concrete situations, the difficulties of their daily lives. With the absent seminarists he formed relations which were never broken. In December 1917, when the post of superior was left vacant by the death of Fr Poirier, Abbé Suhard's influence in the seminary and indeed in the diocese was so well-known that all agreed in seeing him as the obvious successor. But such was not the

opinion of the Bishop, Mgr Grellier, who, mistrusting this
'man of broad ideas', nominated to the post a certain Fr C.,
a worthy oddity of no culture, instinctively attracted to everything mediocre, and rejoicing in the nickname of 'Daisy'.

With this new superior Abbé Suhard (appointed canon in
1919: 'It's my consolation prize!') had to face the problems
of the return of the ex-servicemen to a house which had become, for them, stifling and shabby. We can scarcely imagine
what the atmosphere of a provincial seminary, ruled by a
man of gifts, must have been like after the war. Some
examples must be quoted. Suhard tried, in the governing
body, to raise the question of scientific studies. He thought
the standard too low: what should be required? 'To enter
the seminary,' replied Fr C., 'I think it is enough for them
to know the four operations of arithmetic.' To leave the
seminary, it seemed, even less was required. Four seminarists,
all ex-servicemen, were kept back from major orders because
they had finished off a carafe of wine, left unwanted on the
corner of a table in the refectory. This was the period when
a man could be expelled for a few puffs at an illegal
cigarette, for visiting a friend's room, for reading a 'dangerous' paper. 'My dear children', the superior was for ever
repeating to these young men who had been four years at
the front and known the life of the trenches. 'My dear children, a bad paper in the hands of a cleric—what a scandal!'
When Canon Suhard tried to open the windows on the stuffy
atmosphere of this house, Bishop's House in the Rue des
Tuyaux was promptly informed. And so, in spite of the
wishes of the Laval clergy, Mgr Grellier always refused to
appoint the professor as vicar general. It was all quite clear:
'Suhard is too broadminded.'

So Canon Suhard grew older, meekly, humbly, remote
from honours. He attended to his work, to his Sunday duties.
He kept on revising his lectures, hearing confessions, giving
direction and advice. Every year, during the summer vaca-

tions, he allowed himself only a fortnight's holiday away from the seminary. He was now past his fiftieth year. Many who had been his friends in Rome were now bishops, or vicars general at least. The good Canon Suhard stayed on as professor at the major seminary! Was he happy? Did he mind? Too timid and too humble to show his feelings, he was not unaware of the ostracism to which he was subject, but went on working, 'quite calmly, quite simply', as St Vincent de Paul would have said.

Those around him never knew that in 1926 he had secretly avoided being nominated to the bishopric of Sées. 'I think it is a mortal sin to want to be a bishop', he confided one day to his old pupil, Fr Bouëssé. God knows, he desired nothing, he was incapable of intrigue. But the consistory did not give up its plans. On 28 June 1928, during an examination session, someone plucked at his sleeve: he was appointed Bishop of Bayeux and Lisieux. This time it was in vain that Canon Suhard wrote to Rome to decline the honour and the charge: scarcely had his letter arrived when a firm telegram came back: 'No refusal except on medical certificate.' But what doctor could convince the authorities that this son of the soil, six foot tall and broad-shouldered, frugal, sleeping five hours a night, was unfit to undertake the charge of a diocese? He had to accept. On 6 July the apostolic bulls were signed by Pius XI, and a new stage of his life began. He was now fifty-four.

IN FIDE ET LENITATE

The little world of the diocese was soon astir. Compliments and friendly advice, sincere or ambiguous, poured in. 'Poor M. Suhard, you have never been on the administrative side, so you'll find it hard to know what to do!' 'Very likely, my dear colleague, but at least I know very well what not to do: I've heard plenty of complaints.'

The summer of 1928 was occupied with receptions, with making contacts and with preparations for the consecration. The bishop-elect began a heavy correspondence with his vicars general, his future clergy and the diocesan administration. In honour of the Saint of Lisieux, he fixed his consecration for 3 October. Early in August he retired to the Trappist monastery at Port-du-Salue, to meditate in the presence of God on the charge laid on him by the Church. During these days of retreat he used the *De moribus et officio episcoporum* of St Bernard, that other violent man who had learned to overcome his gentleness. When he wanted to explain his motto, *In fide et lenitate,* he would translate it according to circumstances: if he spoke of the bishop's charge, it was 'in faith and kindness', but if it was question of his relations with his priests, then it was 'in mutual trust and gentleness'.

The consecration took place in Laval cathedral. At the evening function the address was given by Fr Janvier. On 10 October the new bishop drove to his diocese, which received him officially the next day. His first step, his first visit, was a pilgrimage. The humble Carmelite sister, his contemporary, who had entered religion while he was starting at the junior seminary, and died shortly before his ordination, she who was to be the inspirer and patroness of all his missionary work, surely deserved his first homage as bishop. From St Thérèse he drew his faith and gentleness, but also his apostolic ardour and crucifying poverty. In his new dignity he had so little property and personal effects that all the expenses of his installation had to be met out of the diocesan budget. One of the vicars general grumbled in jest, 'We mustn't have bishops like this too often!'

Thus, under the protection of St Thérèse, began the brief Norman episcopate. Those were halcyon days for himself and his clergy, according to those who shared them.

The diocese of Bayeux was still, in fact, within one man's

powers. The bishop could know his priests personally and have relations of cordial collaboration with everyone. His ministry, being essentially pastoral, involved much travelling: confirmation tours, opening Church schools, Catholic Action activities, visits to convents. The Benedictine and Carmelite nuns, the Sisters of the Holy Family and the Little Sisters of the Poor, all received personal visits from their bishop at this time. Except to pay his *ad limina* visit to Pius XI in November 1929, he practically never crossed the borders of his diocese. Two years thus passed quickly by.

On 18 June 1930 a telegram reached Bishop's House: Mgr Suhard was transferred to Reims.

This nomination marked the end of a period in his life which we may call 'the days of Christendom', for the diocese of Reims is very different from the peaceful diocese of Bayeux and far more profoundly dechristianized. Mgr Suhard's life was henceforth to be identified with the history of 'the mission' in France. We shall explore its stages in the course of the passages I shall quote: the experiment of the rural districts, the foundation of the Mission de France, and then the nine, short, crowded years during which, as Archbishop of Paris, faced with the problems of an enormous diocese, the Cardinal attempted the impossible, in order that the word of God, despite all difficulties, should be heard.

This book is not a biography, and it is he, this pastor and apostle, who will speak to us on the spirit of the apostles who are not content to be only pastors—on the spirit of mission.

URGENCY OF MISSION

The passages composing this collection have been chosen for their connection with a single governing idea: the way in which the Cardinal came to feel the need for a missionary Church. What did the word 'mission' mean to him? What

response did he try to make and what means did he try to
employ, that the mission might be carried out?[2]

THE URGENCY OF THE MISSION

As I said above, the Cardinal's concern for a generous, fruitful and supernatural apostolate was present in his life from
the time when he was professor at Laval. But he became increasingly aware of the real dechristianization of the country,
and therefore his ideas on the choice of missionary means
developed accordingly. This awareness became, with the years,
more and more lucid, relentless and definite, and yet, in spite
of his being 'haunted', as he said, by the thought of the
general apostasy of the masses, it seems that his knowledge
of it was never quite complete. As a man of the West, a peasant of a Christian land, his heart always preserved a little
corner of illusion, of a dream, even when his judgement of
situations was desperately lucid.

But he felt the urgency of the mission in varying degrees
in the different periods of his life. In his letters of direction
to the Laval seminarists, the dominant idea is that it is
necessary to be an apostle, because that is what a priest is
for. The priest cannot be satisfied with giving the sacraments; he must represent Christ, make him known, reverenced
and loved, and to that end he must be fully a 'man of the
Church', so that other men in their turn may discover Christ
in his person and his life.

But before 1914 priests in France were still numerous, and
the country people still practised their religion. The apostolate therefore consisted chiefly in a priestly life which was
worthy, devoted and generous, with no need to resort to new

[2] The reader should therefore not expect to find here certain spiritual
writings and famous passages on the role of the priest and the bishop.
Priority has been given to the missionary texts. Passages more directly
concerned with priestly spirituality will be found in other publications.

or revolutionary 'methods'. If we are truly priests, that should be enough. The priest's best apostolate is his teaching of doctrine and the example of his life.

But in the years between the wars the dechristianization of the countryside advanced more rapidly. Priests decreased in number and a new wave of anticlericalism succeeded the truce of the Union sacrée.[3] From this time, in his writings as professor at Laval and then as Bishop of Bayeux, a new phrase often occurs: the 'apostolate of conquest'. Even before the birth of Catholic Action, with its vocabulary full of military terms, he used the expression spontaneously. The Church must be 'conquering', she must take part in a 'crusade', in a spirit of love and gentleness, of course, for a 'peaceful conquest' which does not, however, exclude struggle. The Bishop now readily saw the world and the Church in juxtaposition: the Church must penetrate the world, conquer it and subject it to Christ. The use of all these words is very definite in the early years of the Reims period. It was then, for the first time, that Mgr Suhard found himself at grips with a vast and complex diocese. It was then that he took detailed stock of a state of dechristianization which could no longer be dealt with by accustomed methods, but demanded a pastoral method renovated by a 'mission'.

A LEADER WHO LISTENS

How did this pastor come to learn about it? First of all, he knew how to see, to observe and to reflect on what he had seen. He moved about the diocese, visited the parishes, made many contacts in all circles. At night he noted down his observations in order to impart them to his staff or his council. He proposed new measures. As a former professor he knew

---

[3] Union sacrée is the term describing the attitude of good will towards the clergy after the 1914-18 War, as a result of their fine war record.

too well the importance of doctrinal formation not to wish
to give his priests the benefit of it. His first measure was at
Reims: the reorganization of a seminary which was in the
throes of a crisis. Very soon came the creation of a 'third
year', as he called it: a periodic session of some weeks,
designed for the young priests in the parochial ministry. In
his scale of apostolic priorities the training of the priest
always held the first place.

Secondly, he listened a great deal. He knew *how* to listen,
with keen and kind attention. Always respectful of the
speaker, he yet would not hesitate to interrupt him with precise questions, bringing him back to essentials. In this way
he quickly acquired a wealth of information on the state of
the diocese. Above all, it was his priests whom he received;
they could approach him at any time, on any problem, apostolic or personal. They knew it and made full use of it. Later
on, in his office at the archbishop's house in Paris, one of his
intimates surprised him at the clock, a finger on the dial:
'What are you doing, your Eminence?' 'What am I doing?
Stopping my clock. Today I am receiving my priests, and
when I am receiving my priests I don't want to know the
time!' An interview with Abbé Hollande, about the Mission
de Paris, lasted eleven hours, after which, as the victim remarked, 'he was so kind as to dispense me from my breviary!'
Parish priests, curates, Catholic Action chaplains, seminary
principals or professors, diocesan missionaries—they could all
bring the bishop their problems, their ideas, their pastoral
worries, their projects, their desires. Through them he came
to know the actual situations, the work being done, or left
undone. For each, he knew how to find words of encouragement and understanding, and also 'instructions', for he knew
himself to be their head as well as their father. Through his
priests, all his life long, the Cardinal discovered the reality
of a world without God.

But many lay people too could knock at his door: Catho-

lic Action militants, leaders of Catholic activities or movements, ambassadors and politicians, employers and workmen,
Jocists[4] or students of all ages, intellectuals, ordinary parishioners (with a preference for the poor and humble): all knew
that they would be welcomed and given a hearing. Through
them, the problems of life, of work and of society got through
to the Archbishop.

From his own reflection and these numerous contacts, Mgr
Suhard thus became aware of the large-scale dechristianization of his diocese and the urgent need of missionary enterprises. He discovered, first of all, that a new society was
being built up, without God: it no longer felt the need of
the one thing necessary, it was building itself on its own
values, in which the supernatural had no part. At Laval and
during the First War, he had already understood that
atheists, or rather 'anticlericals' and the indifferent, existed.
But gradually, through the exercise of his office, he came to
see that atheism was in process of becoming the normal state
of the civilization in which he lived. Men were no longer
simply 'against God' or 'against his priests'; they were organizing themselves without him. God no longer had a place
in the life of man. Between the atheist and the believer
there was not only a difference of personal reaction towards
God or the Church; there was a difference of worlds. The
atheist was not merely one who did not believe in God, but
one who had faith in another world, another mystique, one
who looked for another salvation, which was not that of the
Church. The massive atheism of the world was no longer
simply a lack: it had become a positive and living reality.
It built itself and existed by itself, no longer troubling to

[4] The JOC and the JOCF are the men's and women's branches of the
Jeunesse Ouvrière Chrétienne (corresponding to the Young Christian
Workers), which has turned into the names 'JOC' and 'Jocist'. There are also
the JAC (Agricole), the JEC (Etudiante) and the JIC (Indépendante), with
similar derivatives.

struggle against a God who seemed now to be an eternal
absentee.

'THE ANXIETIES OF MY PEOPLE'

Through the lips of those who spoke to him the Bishop
heard also the appeals of that world, in their infinite variety,
and all the more despairing because they knew not to *whom*
to appeal. The misery of the poor, the social injustice, the
instability of men's minds, the disappearance of the last cer-
tainties, the deprivation of freedom, all the desires to live, with
no knowledge of life's purpose—all this reached him in a
throbbing, confused murmur and sounded in his ears till it
became an obsession.

'Yes, my friends, I know your troubles ... I know your
situation, through my priests and through all those fervent
Christians who tell me every day of your anxieties, but also
of your courage and your goodness. Through their eyes and
ears, I see you and I hear you. I know who are the victims
of a civilization which, without design, has in some aspects
become inhuman. ... There are some non-Christian philosophers who say that life is absurd. That is a sad thing for
a bishop to hear, but what makes him even sadder is that a
single one of the souls entrusted to him should be crushed
by despair.'[5]

As the Church's man, Mgr Suhard also learned that she,
'the handmaid of men', lived among them in fact as a
stranger. She was not known; how then could she be loved?
Her speech, her customs, her ideas, her reactions, all separated her from a world which regarded her with ironical
curiosity, when it regarded her at all. Her ways of thought,
her incomprehensible rites, the jargon of Churchmen, the
burden of her traditions, all this, he was told, weighed her

[5] Saint-Séverin is a church in the Latin Quarter of Paris, famous as a
'mission community'.

down and prevented her from living in step with the world. He himself sadly noted: 'At the day of judgement the Lord will not ask me how many ceremonies I have presided over, but whether I have done everything possible to save souls'.

And yet, with too great a respect for customs, for 'what must be done', for the value of traditions, he was still attached to a certain 'ecclesiastical style'. With the passing of the years, and notably in Paris, he came to understand what an obstacle this placed before the eyes of a new world. In December 1938, talking with Abbé Lalande about the criticisms levelled at the Vatican for its luxury and its remoteness from the problems of the masses (criticisms which came from non-Catholic circles, but also from Catholics), he suddenly exclaimed, in passionate and almost prophetic tones:

'We too are remote from them! We are ten centuries behind, handicapped by ten centuries! They have shut us up in a regular mould, they have made *bourgeois* of us! Sooner or later, by the very evolution of events, we shall be forced to return to the simplicity of the gospel. We have adopted the bad habits of governments, especially we higher clergy. When I go in my car to the workers' quarters, I am ashamed, and still more when someone arranges my cloak, or my cape. It is to help me, of course! But if they only thought what an impression it gives! But they don't see, do they?'

'THE WALL TO BE LEVELLED'

The Cardinal saw it. He understood that the working class (not alone, but notably) no longer knew what the Church was, and indeed *could* not know. 'There is a wall separating us from the working class, there is a moat.' This 'wall to be levelled', this 'moat to be filled in', recurred daily in his conversation from 1943. We must *go* to the masses, since they no longer come to us. We must show them another face, a new face, of the Church.

How deep did this sense of missionary urgency penetrate, with the Cardinal? It haunted him, as he often said. Yet even in his latter years some parts of himself were not completely penetrated by that pitiless light of the truth. He had 'presided over too many ceremonies', addressed too many vast, attentive congregations, heard too many Christians chant their faith in mass functions, for him to be totally persuaded that he had before him only a tiny percentage of the inhabitants of his diocese. He still let himself be deluded by the magic of full churches. In September 1945, when Abbé Le Sourd handed over his papers as private secretary to Abbé Lalande, he told him: 'We can and must help him to discover the truth; for example, by comparing the number of occupied chairs in a parish church with the population of the quarter, and saying to him: "They are *all* your subjects, your Eminence".' On Sundays, when he drove off to preside at some ceremony, a Lenten station or a Way of the Cross, his secretary would show him the long queues waiting outside the cinemas: 'These are becoming the new churches!' He had difficulty in realizing it, he hesitated before answering: 'How right you are!'

THE DEMANDS OF TRUTH

Though this realization was not complete—but what leader's soul is big enough to bear the whole truth?—it was deep and true enough to make this man, so prudent and reserved, take the boldest measures or at least encourage them. By temperament, no doubt, he was not a founder or an inventor of new formulas. He had too much feeling and love for tradition, for what had once been successful, to take the initiative in certain breaks with the past. But he could authorize, encourage and support experiments which he himself would never have thought of launching. The Superior of the Mission de Paris once said: 'He crystallized currents rather than created new things.' That the Church should have a certain manner of being present to the world, in a 'style of mission', was something he would never have discovered for himself, either in principle or in detail, but he had too much sense of the real and the true not to believe those who had seen and told him, and not to support their efforts. He willingly allowed himself to be invaded by the problems, and refused to shut his eyes when the light became too painfully violent.

Fr Augros, for example, wrote: 'While the Cardinal was convinced of the need for the seminary of the Mission de France, he did not see, to start with, what it ought to be, just as he did not see, to start with, what the Mission de Paris ought to be. In either case he left us to find out, only watching lest anything in the way of audacity might unite men's minds in an attitude of opposition, or compromise orthodoxy, but allowing a free hand to whatever seemed to respond to his expectation or to the problem raised.'

When he thought that an enterprise was inspired by the Holy Spirit, he threw into the balance all the weight of his authority as bishop, to ensure its success. On the other hand, he could never allow one to refuse to see a thing face to face or to evade one's responsibilities. He then judged others—and sometimes most cruelly—by their faithfulness to the demands of the apostolate.

One of those close to him notes: 'I have never heard such severe criticisms, especially when the pastoral charge was not well performed. On reflection, it is clear that his love of the person never lessened, but the demands on conduct were immense. He mercilessly condemned all whom he thought to have fallen asleep.'

His phrases were clear cut and abrupt, whether they concerned his close collaborators, his subordinates or his fellow bishops. These are taken at random from his diary: 'X ... used some unfortunate expressions which revealed great naïvety and no doubt a certain ambition.' 'Visit to Y . . . , not very interesting, and still less consoling. When personal interest overshadows everything else, there is little hope of using men.' At the end of an episcopal assembly he observed: 'In general, the declarations were without value, because without energy'; then charity prevails: he erases this and writes 'The declarations were without effective conclusions'.

When one of his colleagues is proposed for nomination to the council of the Mission de France, he rejects him with a word: 'Him? Oh, he would never understand!' And another day: 'What needs founding now is Catholic Action among the bishops!' Finally, was this line from *Essor ou déclin de l'Eglise?*[6] a familiar sally, or a gloss, or a note slipped into the text?—'That Christians have been behindhand in ideas may be a fact, but it is no virtue.' Good secretaries, they say, can imitate even the style of those they serve.

This Churchman, who so clearly understood the urgency and immensity of a missionary movement in France, this 'timid man possessed by the Holy Spirit' (as Canon Hollande defined him), what did he hold a missionary movement to be, and what, in his mind, were its principal means?

WHAT IS THE MISSION?

To the Cardinal, the origin of the spirit of mission is simply the spirit of Pentecost. When the apostles had been given the task of evangelizing all nations (Matthew 28:19), God gave them the Spirit of strength and light. On that day, the Church began to live, at the moment when she began to preach the gospel. It was the same vocation and the same act: to exist means, for the Church, to carry out her mission.

Her whole subsequent history is merged in her missionary work. Radiating out from Jerusalem, she rapidly made her

[6] English translation, 'Rise or Decline of the Church?' in *Pastoral Letters of Cardinal Suhard*, New Life, London (no date), from which quotations are taken.

presence felt in the Roman world. When that world collapsed, she was able to 'pass to the barbarians', knowing well that it is her nature to plant the faith brought to her by the God-Man, wherever men live.

The Cardinal, brought up on Bossuet, instinctively finds the phrase for it: the mission is 'the very task of Christ', developed, renewed, continued throughout the ages. Christ came into the world to bring the light of his truth: to impart that light is the mission of the Church. Like Christ himself, she brings to the world, in time, the promises of eternity: mission is, in her case, a service, an organization, for the supply of the faith.

It is also, by its own nature, a service of charity, or rather, in charity. To the Cardinal, being a missionary meant giving oneself, for thus it is imitating Christ, and therefore putting into practice a law of life which is fundamental for every Christian. The love of God came into the world as a gift which men cannot keep for themselves, but must pass on to all their brethren. The mission is, in charity, the actual gift of charity.

MISSION AND REDEMPTION

But the purpose of this gift to the world is to renew it, to transform it into a world in the image of God, according to his will and his laws. The mission is real only if it transforms and animates the whole world from within. A phrase often on the Cardinal's lips was 'To be a missionary is to be a redeemer'. The mission exists only for a redemption, since the mission imitates the very attitude of Christ, whose motive in being incarnate was to save the world, in order to bring it back to the Father. *To save the world*; that was the task of Christ, and therefore of the Church, and to save it integrally, in all its parts, its hopes, its values:

'Modern inventions, which have increased at an ever-grow-

ing pace, cannot be for Christians just another news-item or a
mere scientific discovery. *They have their value as pointers*,
and they must henceforth be integrated into the Christian's
apostolic vision of redemption. For they are something more
than empty symbols: they are making a new universe. And
this is the universe we are called upon to save.'[7]

This, as I see it, rapidly defined on the basis of these passages, is the Cardinal's conception of the missionary spirit:
the redeeming work of Christ, continued by the Church.

From this we can understand his insistence on the unity
which must be preserved in missionary action. Mission is
not primarily a rupture, a refusal, on principle, to conform,
nor is it an uncontrolled enthusiasm. 'The real apostle is not
a critic.' His position is not primarily on the fringe of the
Church, and certainly not against her; he represents the
essence of her activity: to impart to those who are ignorant
of it a message of salvation, which has been deposited with
her only in order to be handed on.

The Cardinal lays down that the foundation of the missionary spirit is, quite simply, the spirit of the Church or,
more precisely, the spirit of faith. And this can be extended
to the level of corporate action, as well as to the individual
missionary. The missionary spirit of the Church consists, in
fact, in recalling, in season and out of season, that the gift of
God is first and foremost a supernatural gift.

'It is not the aim of Christianity to establish a just social
order. Its aim is to cause us to share in the divine life, to
communicate with God; that is its ultimate aim and at the
same time its supreme value. That has value in itself, and
we do not need to try to justify it by anything else. Christianity too has value in itself, independently of its human
repercussions. The communion with God which the Church
inaugurates here on earth cannot be regarded as a means to

---

[7] *Le prêtre dans la cité*, p. 1. English translation, 'The Priest in the Modern
World' in *Pastoral Letters*, p. 105.

procure some human progress. Not to desire God for himself is to despise the divine gift.'[8]

But this gift is handed on to men by other men. They act, then, in the name of God alone, and their action as missionaries must be based on their possession of the Spirit:

'Only God can bring about conversion, and we cannot emphasize too strongly that the apostolate is essentially a work of God. It is God's love giving itself to the world by Christ and the Church. Being an apostle means, therefore, opening oneself to the gift God makes, so as to be able, as a humble instrument of his work, to communicate it to the world.'[9]

If the missionary wants to transmit, not an adulterated doctrine, but a really supernatural Christianity, he must first of all try, with all his might, to be a saint. Being present to God comes before being present to the world: the latter finds its real meaning in the former. 'The primacy of the spiritual' —that was another classic expression, a 'master-word', of the Cardinal's. He liked to remind Benedictine nuns that their contemplative life had a missionary dimension. One day at Vanves he admitted that the very name of 'missionary Benedictines' enchanted him: he saw in it a whole progamme of 'presence to the world'. In the same spirit, he gladly accepted the offer of Fr de Féligonde, who wanted to found a priory of Benedictine monks in charge of a parish, at l'Hay-les-Roses. He held that nothing solid was done in missionary action which was not first based on a strict and deep spiritual life, and on loyalty to the traditional forms of prayer in the Church. But this prayer, of course, even if traditional, must never become a form of escape. It commits one to action, because it is the source and food of action:

'To have recourse to God is not only to pray to God; it is also to take God's cause in hand and strive to defend it;

---

[8] *Lettre de carême* (Lenten pastoral letter), 1945, p. 59.
[9] '*Rise or Decline* . . . ?', p. 39.

it is to carry out, as far as in us lies, what we know to be God's will.'[10]

Missionary action, being based on the supernatural, is in the second place a collective action, for the preaching of God's word has not been entrusted to individuals but to a family, which has become a people. So the Cardinal wished his missionaries, even the most isolated, the most 'parachuted', as it were, into pagan territory, always to be attached to a 'team', not only for their own support, but also to show by their membership in a cell of the Church that they were the envoys of a community.

CANDID SYMPATHY

Only on these conditions can the missionary, filled with the Spirit of Pentecost and acting in the Church's name, walk boldly in a world where the gospel is not heard. He must approach this world with a sympathy which is sincere but candid. Sympathy first of all, because in order to carry on the mission it is important to be well and truly in the world. For this, one must love it as it is, be prepared to enter it and live in it without reserve, without backward looks or vain regrets for the good old days of Christendom. Sympathy, too, because the world is made of men created in the image of God, because it *is* the work of God and still hymns his praise even if it ignores and rejects him. Sympathy, because the message of the gospel is a brotherly message; the men whom the missionary addresses are his brothers, though they may not know it. But sympathy must be candid and even critical, because prudence and realism oblige him not to approve everything in the world, where it is his business to make known and accepted 'the folly of what we preach' (1 Cor. 1:21), and the eternal contradiction of the cross. The mission is a task of salvation, but that salvation comes through

[10] *Pastorale de carême*, 1944, p. 13.

the cross, and the mission is accomplished only if the cross is accepted. In a word, the missionary spirit is a *gift of sympathetic presence* in the pagan world, lucidly conscious of its values and its defects; human enough for the world to see in the missionary a brother according to the flesh and to recognize him for one of themselves; supernatural enough for the world not to stop short at that but to accept, from this Christian brother, the message of the cross.

Therefore, for the mission to be real, to be really *present in the world*, and not to pass by, even fraternally, *beside it*, it must honestly recognize the legitimacy of the world's tasks. The Church can no more save the world without it than she can save herself without the world. In a footnote to *Rise or Decline of the Church?* the Cardinal quotes Gilson:

'The Church's task is not to preserve the world as it is, even if it has become Christian, but to keep it Christian, so that it never ceases to become something other than it is.... The Church's task is not to prevent the world from passing away, but to sanctify a passing world.'[11] She must therefore be present in all fields, in all circles, must accept its tempo, work with it at its own speed and rhythm. While the working class must be the first to benefit from the mission, the mission must not confine its efforts to it alone; there will have to be a mission for students, a mission for the learned and the research workers. 'The first apostolate, at the crossroads where we stand, is the apostolate of thought. The Church is at a turning-point such that she can lose everything or gain everything, according to the spirituality she asks humanity to adopt.'[12]

To intellectuals the Cardinal would say: 'Do the work of the mission by your work of thinking'; and in all circles he would return to this theme: place yourselves inside human structures, so as to animate them from within. 'Do not aban-

[11] Adapted from '*Rise or Decline*', p. 61, n. 56.
[12] '*Rise or Decline ... ?*', p. 35.

B

don what is human.'[13] To research workers he would say: 'Your way of being missionaries is first of all to give form and purpose to the human knowledge you acquire'. For the workman, his mission will be in the midst of his professional work, face to face with all the values of his class. We do not go out of the world in order to evangelize it; the first law of the mission is the law of incarnation, and of 'redeeming incarnation'.

This was the missionary task which so haunted him by its urgency, and the need for which is identified with the future and life of the Church. We must now inquire through what men and by what means the Cardinal wished to see it carried out.

MISSIONARY METHODS

PRIESTS IN THE CITY

When he considers the means at the Church's disposal for penetrating the mass of paganism, the Cardinal thinks first of his priests. He was himself a priest in every fibre of his being. His spirituality was nurtured on St Francis de Sales, Bossuet, the French school. He believed in the redeeming and therefore missionary value of the priesthood in itself. It was primarily on the priest, mediator between God and man, that he counted for 'reconciling two worlds'.

He wanted his priests to be saints. Only in so far as they were invaded by the presence and the love of God could they be fully endowed with the missionary spirit. To a seminarist at Laval he wrote: 'Do your utmost to be a saint, for in the first place that is the whole end of man, and in the second place you are, by your state of life, a converter of souls. But it is only saints who convert. Make your holiness shine out from the conditions of life which are made for

[13] *Ibid.*, p. 49.

you, and which you have to live out. Never doubt that your holiness is contained in them. Yes, it is found in the integral, conscientious, supernatural and devout accomplishment of your daily, professional task.'

He wanted his priests to be young! From his first days at Rheims he knew how to enlist dynamic fellow-workers and to trust important responsibilities to men still young. In Paris he remarked to one of his intimates: 'Priests who are fit for the most important responsibilities should be able to reach them at the latest by the age of forty-five', and he added that it was the duty of superiors to think about preparing them for this if they wanted to avoid grave disappointments. In practice he placed great trust in 'new men' if he thought them capable of bearing such responsibilities, but always on one condition, that they must be thoroughly trained and theologically prepared for their work. 'It was no small thing,' he said of his own case, 'that I had to teach theology for some thirty years.' As an old teacher he believed in ideas. He knew their compelling force, their importance for giving direction to the life of an apostle. A man is no less a missionary for having first wished to be sound and sure. 'The priest who is devoted to doctrinal study is both saved and saving', he noted one day. He did not think that the seminary at Lisieux ought to form 'pure intellectuals', but he wanted his missionaries at least to leave it with a taste for the life of the mind and the conviction that the world of thought is not foreign to the world of action. He insisted on this all the more because the missionary in his turn must be a *former* of others:

'The world can only be saved by the presence of Christians in the different fields, and of Christians who are leaven in them. Now these Christians will only exist and be effectively present if they are themselves formed by priests conscious of their task and steeped, not only in their direct ministry, but in their indirect ministry as "formers of apostles". Hence the necessity for our seminarists and young priests to be keen to undertake this role and to train themselves for it, by being involved in the temporal sphere, but convinced of the primacy of the spiritual.'[14]

But the Cardinal also wanted his priests to be energetic and strong, with abilities and human qualities which should make them acceptable in their surroundings. This would require time and effort and a suitable training. It would need the spirit of sacrifice, a certain aptitude, or rather a profound desire for renunciation and openness to others: a man is not a priest for himself but in order to impart Christ. The priest 'in the city' is a man of the world, and must have the virtues which make men of action: the gift for struggle and effort. The story is told how one Wednesday at the archbishop's house in the middle of his council meeting, he suddenly burst out:

'Gentlemen, a parish priest in the suburbs has called on me, to ask for a parish in Paris. Why? "Your Eminence, in my district I am on my own; in Paris I shall have two curates." "And what will you do when you have two curates?" "I shall be able to rest," he says. "Rest? But the Church is not a farm you can let out! If you need to rest, there is the Marie-Thérèse!" '[15]

Certainly, the missionary priest according to Cardinal Suhard's heart could not be a waverer, a craven or a weakling. Best of all, he should be not only a man but a leader. One evening in May 1948, alone and ill, under treatment in a clinic in St Germain-en-Laye, he made a note on this point in his diary:

'As the hours drag by, I admit to myself that the finest thoughts, even those which seem the most fruitful, produce no results unless they are put into practice. In the way of

[14] *Journal*, 7 March, 1948.
[15] The Marie-Thérèse Infirmary is the house of retirement for the priests of Paris.

practice, speeches count for little, isolated actions are worthless. It is souls that count, above all the souls of young men, who are formed by convictions, who mature them, who make them clear to themselves and then, in the work of an apostolic ministry, do their best to carry them out. And in carrying them out, become workers for the gospel and *leaders*.... Leaders! How few they are! And how fruitful their presence is! Wherever one of them is found to be present, a revival begins and strengthens and spreads. May our seminaries prepare such workers ... and such leaders!'

When the Mission de Paris was founded, he finally defined his idea of the missionary priest: 'devoted, holy, wise, apostolic, dedicated to reconciling two worlds'. For this work he wanted men who were firm and resolute, ready to run certain risks. For example, on the subject of the first worker-Jesuits, in a conversation with Fr de Gorostarzu, after emphasizing the solid formation required, he added: 'Even danger would not excuse the abandonment of a work which is as indispensable to the Church as the apostolate of the first Christian generation.'

UNITED FOR ACTION

Under these priests, or rather, with them, there must be layfolk, those 'Christians of action,' as he loved to call them. He wanted them to be thoroughly steeped in their faith, not only generous and devoted, but competent in every way. Good will, he considered, was no substitute for human and professional worth. 'I do not believe in the action of a man whose life cannot be an example.'[16]

Finally, priests and laity must work as a team. 'In our days, individual work is no longer possible: only teams produce anything, even in intellectual matters. If St Thomas came back, he could no longer produce his *Summa theologica*

[16] Address to railway workers, 1948.

by himself: it would be the work of a team.' At Reims his country districts were reanimated by deanery teams; in Paris, he always insisted on work done in common, rejecting individualism and isolation. As to the precise methods which priests and laity could choose for carrying out the mission, it could truly be said that to the Cardinal, a convinced empiricist, all methods were good, provided that they were honest and that nothing was hidden from him: he must be given a faithful account of the experiments undertaken. A missionary method may be bold, provided it guards the necessary prudence and accepts the supervision of those in charge.

'One of my worries,' he admitted about some missionaries, 'is that they hide some things from me. They don't tell me everything. How do they expect me to support them?' But if collaboration was frank and honest, that support was given, on his part, firmly and without recall. 'If I make some remarks to you here, in your house, or in my office, take note of them. If I give the impression of disavowing you elsewhere, it will really be because I am forced to it: carry on, keeping me informed.' There was something of the Norman in this man of the Mayenne: when difficulties were too great to be overcome by frontal attack, he would smile and give the advice 'Like the water, get round the stone. . . .'

As another example of this empiricism, in 1941, when the foundation of the seminary of the Mission de France seemed to be hanging in the balance, he gave Fr Augros no precise instructions as to what the seminary should be. At most he knew what it should not be. The positive programme was vague: 'Form priests not only for the countryside but for the urban populations too.' In 1947, on the subject of the Mission de Paris, he remarked: 'There must be no doctrinairians in it. There have been, and it was a pity.'

THE MISSIONARY'S FREEDOM

But when the ground seemed firm, when the experiments were honest and the reports accurate, he did all he could to obtain for his missionaries the permissions and 'faculties' they needed. It must not be forgotten that it was due to his patient, repeated requests that the concessions concerning the eucharistic fast and evening Masses, obtained in Paris from 1947 to 1949, were granted to the priests and communties of the Mission de Paris, being later extended to all the faithful and then to all dioceses. In these matters, his loyalty to the pope was not inconsistent with a war of attrition against the Curia; in private he would sometimes declare: 'Act first, report afterwards.'

We may note here, on this question of missionary methods, his strong sense of the universal. Before belonging to a diocese or a parish, the Christian belongs to the Church. Before being concerned with the interests of his diocese alone, the bishop must think of the universal mission. He would readily have applied to the Church that saying of an English statesman: 'Any problem which is not first stated in universal terms, on a world scale, is badly stated and therefore insoluble.' Thus, for example, while he was the real founder of the Mission de France, it is still in principle the creation of the whole episcopate of France, it is still in principle the creation of the whole episcopate of France, at the service of the whole country. In the same spirit of universality, in 1945-6 the Cardinal formed very close contacts with the German and Belgian bishops, through the Superior of the Mission de Paris. From Belgium, in particular, he received a delegate of the episcopate who came to Paris to learn about the experiment of the worker-priests. We now know that the bishops of Münster and Paderborn, about the same time, had sent their professors and seminarists to do a period of work in the mines of the Ruhr, in order to learn more about the phenomena of dechristianization, and had informed the Cardinal about these activities.

'We can do nothing apostolic in France,' he said a little later, 'if we are not in touch with other countries. Otherwise, if we go too far ahead, we shall be *sawn off* one of these days.' It is also known that the idea of a secretariat of the French episcopate, responsible for co-ordinating missionary efforts on a nation-wide scale, was launched by him in the hope of encouraging general apostolic action.

THE PARISH AND THE MISSION

There is obviously great variety in the methods of the mission. The Cardinal once summed them up thus: 'The charity of Christ, piety, devotedness and total self-surrender; prudence which does not exclude boldness, doctrine and discipline. But we must proceed, in more precise fashion, to the organisms of the Church to which the Cardinal entrusted the care of missionary work. There were, in general, three: the parish, Catholic Action and specialized institutions.

Later in this book passages can be read in which the Cardinal defines and encourages the work of the 'missionary parishes', the prototype of which he saw, no doubt, in Fr Michonneau's parish at Petit-Colombes. The parish must not only be the home of the faithful, the community assembled together; it must rather 'go out from itself' and from its structures in order to meet the pagan world, which it does not normally reach. The parish must not only be an institution for protecting and safeguarding acquired positions, but must shed abroad from itself—beyond its walls, its movements and societies—the faith which it must communicate by an effective presence to the world in which it lives.

It is well known that the first attempts towards an opening at Petit-Colombes had consisted in making the text of the liturgy more acceptable to the faithful. One example will

enable us to measure the advance which has been made since
then and to remember the suspicion in which all such attempts
were then held. On 11 August 1944, in an introductory letter
to an enquiry conducted by a vicar general of Paris, the
diocesan ceremoniarius wrote:

'Translations of the liturgical texts are always forbidden,
even when hymns in the vulgar tongue are authorized....'
And in his actual report, the vicar general specially remarked,
on the subject of funerals:

'The Chant des Adieux[17] cannot, I think, be allowed, at
least during Mass. Although adopted by the Scouts (but also
by the Eclaireurs[18] and the Protestant Scouts), this hymn
is of Scottish and Protestant origin. It cannot be said of it,
what is rightly alleged of the French or Latin adaptations of
certain of Bach's chorales, that they are Rhenish airs of the
later Middle Ages, before the Reformation. The Chant des
Adieux is of exclusively Protestant origin.'

The weight of routine: the difficulty of renewal.... The
Christian world is never ripe enough to welcome anything
that changes its habits.

The second institution approved by the Cardinal was
Catholic Action, duplicating the action of the parish, or
rather extending it to make it truly missionary. We shall see
the part he took as Bishop of Bayeux and then Archbishop
of Reims in developing that 'action of the milieu on the
milieu'. He never ceased to encourage and support it, even
after he had launched specifically missionary institutions. He
sometimes showed a certain irritation when some JOC chaplains found it difficult to understand the object of these new
creations.

Chief among these is the Mission de France, which is
really the Cardinal's work.

'I am more and more convinced,' wrote Fr Augros, its first

[17] The Chant des Adieux is a hymn sung to the tune of Auld Lang Syne.
[18] The non-sectarian branch of the French Scouts.

Superior, 'that this seminary, apparently founded by a decision of the French episcopate on 24 July 1941, originated in fact from the charismatic inspiration and peasant obstinacy of Cardinal Suhard. His colleagues trusted him.' The passages I shall quote later excuse me from dwelling on it here.

If he was not by himself the founder of the Mission de Paris, at least the Cardinal understood at once, when he heard Abbé Godin, the idea involved in it and the scope of the project. Without his patient, obstinate pressure, the proposals put to him would never have seen the light and would not have later survived.

Finally we should remember the number of societies, movements and institutions of missionary type, with the origin or development of which the Cardinal was connected. The mere enumeration of them would involve a regular inventory of the Church's action in France between 1940 and 1950.

Instead, we shall quote the Archbishop's own words. His style in places has dated, but it often retains a peculiar savour. The warm, sonorous words carry their message far, like the slow strokes of a church bell, in the calm of the evening. The language is that of a peasant, in simple, direct words, saying quite simply what they have to tell us. The tone is heavy and slow, like the pace of a team of oxen returning from the day's work. These passages, in words already old, are the work of a peasant who ploughs deep, going over and over the same furrows, constantly turning again, sowing the same ground. They are the work of a teacher, bent long over his pupils' exercises, never ceasing to 'exhort ... unfailing in patience and in teaching' (2 Timothy 4:2).

Many of the fruits now seem to us ripe and ready for the plucking; then they were only seeds, germinating in the obscurity of a thick, heavy soil, or fragile young shoots, beginning to show green in the mildness of spring. One man sows, another reaps, but their joy remains the same: they are workers in the Lord's field.   Olivier de la Brosse

TEXTS

1. THE PERIOD OF CATHOLIC ACTION
(Bayeux and Reims)

The missionary outlook of the Bishop of Bayeux is well illustrated by this significant anecdote. In May 1929 Abbé Leroy, a late vocation, on the eve of being ordained subdeacon called on Mgr Suhard and asked his permission to leave the diocese in order to join the African missions. The bishop listened attentively, then answered:

I need not tell you how dear my diocese is to me. It is the portion allotted to me by the Lord. I give it all my life. But my diocese is only a part of the Church. The Church is therefore infinitely dearer to me. Need I say more? If I thought that your going would be more useful to her, I should answer at once: 'Go, you may leave us.' But in your case, I think that you will serve her better by remaining here. There is a whole region around Caen where our big factories are. The people there really do not know Christ; they live apart from him. It is a real mission in our midst! To me, it is something that haunts me. Every day ... every day ... every day, I think of all those unfortunates. I need missionaries. I must have apostles.

Abbé Leroy could understand such language, and he went on to carry out a ministry among the working class in the diocese.

WHAT IS FAITH?

And yet this diocese, so dear to him, and which he regarded as the field of his apostolate, was one which Mgr Suhard scarcely had time to tour. On 18 December 1930 came the news of his transfer to the see of Reims.

The first letter he addressed to his new flock (12 February 1931) was entitled 'The maintenance and increase of Christian faith'.[1] It is the 'programme-speech' of his pastoral activity in the Marne and the Ardennes: the spreading of the faith by the then new methods of Catholic Action.

Faith! At once the basis of Christianity, the foundation of our hopes, the source of our salvation! 'Faith is the assurance of things hoped for, the conviction of things not seen' (Heb. 11:1).

Faith! The source of all that is solid and enduring! Nothing stable can be built apart from Christ, corner-stone of the human building which is crowned by grace.

Faith! The inspirer of everything beautiful and great brought forth by the thought of men, and by the works of their hands!

I want my first contact with you to be made on this supernatural ground; I want my first words to your souls to be in praise of Christian faith, an appeal to the spirit of faith which should animate your lives.

The spirit of man (who can deny it?) needs truth, needs to possess it, to taste it, to rest in it. But who will offer him this truth? What helping hand will put him in reach of it, so that he may perceive it and feed on it: so that, satisfied with it, he may attach himself to it, be fixed in it and there find rest?

History, which gives God's answer, tells us, for to satisfy this desire, which he had planted in his creature, God himself, the supreme Truth, has made himself known to man. He has spoken to him! From the dawning of the world his voice has made itself heard, clear and luminous, definite in affirmation.

In the course of time came the prophets, who echoed him in the midst of a dark and unheeding world.

Then came the Christ, who filled out the work with all the light which proceeds from the divine Word, with all the

[1] Extracts from Pastoral Letter 1, 'Le maintien et l'accroissement de la foi chrétienne (12 February 1931).

simplicity belonging to a God made man, who became one among men, Immanuel with men.

The Apostles followed, witnesses to the ends of the earth of the truths they had heard, sowing them in men's souls and becoming their authorized interpreters.

The Church came, inheriting that teaching and, under the safeguard of God's help, she presented it as she had received it, without diminution or exaggeration, her special mission being to preserve and explain it.

To give authority to their words, the Church, the Apostles, Christ and the prophets produced their letters of credence. By their preaching and their writings, above all by their lives and their deaths, they proved the truth of what they taught, and to such witnesses men gave their belief. They rightly thought that it was not too much to give them the entire adherence of their minds; that every truth taught by such masters ought to be accepted on the authority of the guarantors, and that to reject any one of those truths was as insulting to God as to reject them all, since each of them, even the loftiest and most obscure, comes to us by the same path, which is the authority of God, summoning us and imposing itself on us.

Relying on these principles, every honest and sincere man is readily persuaded that with all the power of his mind and all the ardour of his soul he must entrust himself to a word which carries in itself the sign of the divine.

FAITH AND HAPPINESS TODAY

And now, dearest brethren, admire the wonderful fruits produced by this certitude! In that light, the believer leads a life which is, strictly speaking, divine. Favoured with God's friendship, made his adopted son, fellow-heir of Christ and a member of his Mystical Body, he moves in a divine sphere, he is nurtured on a food which is the very body of the Son of

God, he uses the instruments which are the sacraments of Christ, at his entry into life he receives an investiture which is the seal of Christ, he relies on hopes which are Christ's promises.

In this light, too, he appraises himself and appraises the beings around him at their deep and true value. For he sees them, not as nature reveals them to him, nor as they appear to human view, but as God judges them, as God wills them to be, and as he, the believer, is bound to help them become. And to judge them in this way, believe me, is not to be under an illusion! Even from the human point of view, it is to judge sanely, it is to keep oneself in that perfect equilibrium which puts everything in its place and banishes all excess.

Thus understood, faith is necessary to salvation: 'Without faith,' says St Paul, 'it is impossible to please him [God], for whoever would draw near to God must believe that he exists and that he rewards those who seek him' (Heb. 11:6).

The truth is that our salvation consists in union with the holy Trinity, union which begins here among obscurities and symbols and will be perfected in the light of eternity. But would this union be possible, if we had not given the assent of our whole being to the world revealed by God? 'That which we have seen and heard,' says St John, 'we proclaim also to you, so that you may have fellowship with us, and our fellowship is with the Father and with his Son Jesus Christ' (1 John 1:3).

We must add that faith, necessary for future happiness, is no less necessary for happiness in the present. Experience proves it. The man who has missed the goal assigned by God to his being and activity never finds true happiness outside God. For a moment, perhaps, he may think himself happy among the pleasures with which he tries to drown his cares, but the illusion is soon dispelled!

But ask yourselves from whom those cries, those outbursts of hatred, those cursings against life come, if not from those who, along with their faith, have been robbed of Christian hope? Why these waves of pessimism, that premature disenchantment, that bitterness on the part of bewildered young people, on whom all seemed to smile, who seemed so happy, but sadly confess the unhappiness which overwhelms them, the torment which gnaws them? What lamentable fruits of unbelief! They have confined their paradise of happiness within earthly limits. Having touched these and been wounded by the contact, finding no contentment of heart, they have plunged into a despair from which there is no escape.

Marvel, in contrast, at those Christian souls who have been smitten by trial but, instead of cursing, bless Providence! How many young men and girls, renouncing human joys, go to seek happiness and find it where less perceptive eyes could only see sadness and sacrifices! The fact is that these believers' souls are in possession of a divine promise. They know that God cannot deceive them, that what crucifies nature exalts it in the sight of God. They know that Jesus is near them, watching over them, and when the tempest roars, safe in Peter's bark they watch undaunted the rising of the waves.

THE BASIS OF ACTION IS THE SUPERNATURAL

The writer then traces the picture of Christian lives inspired by faith. He shows their effectiveness even on the human planes of justice, friendship and mutual help, and asserts the power of that faith in Christ, which is the support both of personal life and of social structures. He then shows that the impact of faith in the world depends largely on its dissemination by Christians:

But faith, the assent of minds to the divine truth, depends to a great extent on its being spread, and on how it is presented. The bishop's first task is therefore to provide for its dissemination and to cause it to bear its fruits.

Truth, in fact, only deploys its action and attains its end if the minds attracted to it submit to this attraction, and if it becomes truth admitted and recognized: in a word, conviction.

Now we must not forget that once the truth has become the conviction of a mind submitting to it, it is for that mind a gift of God. It is he who not only reveals it but, by his grace, makes it attractive and luminous, who incites the mind to seek it and who, once it is known, makes the mind taste its sweetness and discover its practical applications for daily life.

Further, if faith is to be established in souls, God must act by his prevenient grace on those souls and turn them to himself. You will understand, then, that the first care of my apostolate is to provide, for myself and my priests, abundant and effective help from God. My first appeal, then, will be an appeal for prayer!

Having asked my priests to be above all things men of prayer, having imposed on myself the duty of setting them an example, I turn to our religious communities, whose value I feel so fully in the sight of God, because it is they who draw down God's grace on the world. I appeal to pious souls, whom I ask to devote their supernatural activity to this end. I appeal to pastors, directors of Catholic activities, heads of organized groups, and I say to them: 'Let the foundation of all your action be the supernatural! As the final object of your action, choose the supernatural! As your hope of success and first means of action, choose prayer!'

Having then defined the respective roles of clergy, seminaries, houses of religious education and the press in this work of spreading the faith, the new Archbishop of Reims reminds them that 'the sphere of faith extends beyond pure ideas. For, while it is the rule of right thought, it is also a rule for right living.... It governs all situations and resolves, by way of authority, all the problems of life.' He recalls the role of faith in the field of social justice and its relations with charity, ending his message with an appeal to all forms of Catholic Action.

THE APOSTOLATE OF CATHOLIC ACTION

These aims of February 1931 were developed in the whole series of pastoral letters which the Archbishop of Reims addressed to his diocese twice a year, in Lent and on the Feast of Christ the King.

In those days, Catholic Action seemed something of an innovation and sometimes rather disturbing. The pope himself, of course sanctioned and encouraged it, but these new notions of a 'mandate of the laity' or 'participation in the mission of the hierarchy' were often imperfectly understood, and their very principles met with loud and obstinate opposition in certain circles and among some of the clergy. The Archbishop therefore found himself obliged to explain patiently and at length, to those who could not or would not understand, the profoundly traditional meaning of these seemingly new words. He did it by following the development of a human life, considering one by one, from 1932 to 1938, the education and Christian formation of young children, Christian instruction and the general principles of Catholic Action, the education and Christian formation of schoolchildren, the participation of priests in Catholic Action, the Christian formation of young men and of girls, the participation in Catholic Action of men and of women, the problems of the Christian family and finally the relations between the traditional parish and the new methods.

Many of these pages, which at the time seemed advanced from the pen of a bishop, are now dated. From year to year they often repeated themselves and they are of unequal value. Yet they cannot be completely passed over in silence, for they are evidence of the spirit of enterprise and apostolic feeling in a man who was never satisfied with seeing the various organizations of his diocese functioning correctly, but wanted to breathe new life into them and was not afraid to employ the methods best adapted to that end.

THE ROLE OF THE LAITY[2]

It is not merely tomorrow, but today, and over all souls, that Christ must reign.

To this end, while everyone must be personally devoted

[2] Extracts from Pastoral Letter 10, 'L'Enseignement chrétien et l'Action catholique (15 October 1932, for the Feast of Christ the King).

to Christ, he must also be devoted to gaining for him the souls of others, to becoming his apostle, to carrying out what is now called 'Catholic Action'. This term Catholic Action sounds to you like a new phrase, and indeed it is chiefly Pope Pius XI who has used it and accredited it. But while the term is new, the thing it stands for is ancient, for it is nothing else but the Christian apostolate of the laity in society. Now, while this apostolate has been greatly intensified in our time, at the instance of our great pope, it has in fact always existed in the Church.

Yes, there have always been apostles among ordinary Christians, for there have always been among them souls in love with Christ. Is it possible to love someone without wanting to impart to others the love which consumes one? If that is true of all created love, how much more is it true of the love of Christ which, being divinely inspired, yearns to be spread without limit.

Providence, however, seems to have disposed that the number and fervour of these apostles should now be constantly on the increase. This must needs be so! For at the same time the official apostles of Jesus, the priests, are becoming even fewer. The task laid upon them becomes even heavier and harder. For among those masses returning to paganism many circles are obstinately closed to them. At all costs, then, the laity must come to the aid of the exhausted priests, they must supplement them, extend their influence, go in themselves where the priests can no longer penetrate. That is the task to which, for the last ten years, Pius XI has constantly been urging them. That is the task to which I, too, never tire of calling you and to which I invite you still more solemnly today: to become, once for all, apostles of Christ, Catholics of action!

How will you become so? First, of course, by thinking, speaking and acting in a Christian way. There is something infectious in the example of a Christian. It was by the sight of their lives, even more than by their preaching, that the early Christians converted the world. 'We do not speak so much as act—*Non multa loquimur sed agimus*,' said the Bishop of Carthage, St Cyprian. But the fact remains that individual action is necessarily limited, whereas in association with other efforts its power is doubled. Alone, one tires and is discouraged. With others, one feels the strain less and maintains a better morale. Isolated individuals are only like grains of sand, but grouped, led by heads who can look higher and farther, applied to a combined operation, they constitute an army.

It was this word *army*, a *Catholic army*, that Pius XI used more than once to describe the Catholic Action movement.

Individualism, in fact, which in itself is not without value and can be made use of, even in Christian activities, cannot be pushed to excess without some danger. For the success of the movement it is essential that all convinced Catholics resolutely join one or other of these movements, not, as too often happens, as purely nominal or decorative members, but as members who are active and devoted.

Active and devoted: yes, but also subject to the hierarchy, disciplined and dependable workers.

Understood in this sense, Catholic Action cannot fail to bear its fruits. It cannot fail to further the reign of Christ in souls and in society. '*Ecce rex tuus venit tibi mansuetus* —Behold thy king cometh to thee, humble . . .' (Matt. 21:5). That is true, it is a very gentle king who comes to us. He it is of whom it is said 'to obey him is to reign'.

Obeying him, in fact, we shall reign over our passions, we shall be freed from their tyranny and from the disorders they produce and we shall have the peace which is the tranquillity of order. Imagine all the influence of Christ and the gospel banished from the world; what chaos, what anarchy there would be! Imagine, on the other hand, that their influence spread and ruled everywhere: it would mean order, tranquillity, peace and happiness!

THE ROLE OF THE YOUNG[3]

Through membership of our organizations, young people must become *apostles*. Christianity and the apostolate have been two mutually necessary terms, ever since Christ, our head and our model, united them in his person, thus making the apostolate of conquest one of the conditions of holiness. The formed Christian, then, can only be a Christian, a Catholic, of *action*!

There is more to it than that. The form taken nowadays by human activity is such that it divides men into 'citadels', and makes these citadels, based on occupation, into impenetrable blocks, to which no one can gain entry, let alone freedom to act, unless he forms part of the block, unless he 'belongs' to it. Formative action for the young must therefore make them not only apostles but 'apostles of the milieu', of that milieu in which they are called to live: the milieu of the family, of work, of leisure, the intellectual milieu or that of the middle class, and so on. The Pope says: 'The worker will be converted by the worker, the employer by the employer, the professional man by his fellow professional.'

Through membership of our organizations, young people must learn the theory, and still more the practice, of an 'integral catholicism'. There is, of course, a parcelled-out, fragmentary catholicism, consisting mainly of badly understood rites and routine practices, but alongside it there is a catholicism which I should readily call 'totalitarian', one which, with all the brightness of its doctrinal precision and the essential marrow of its life, gives out to souls the whole reality of its divine power. It is this catholicism which makes

[3] Extracts from Lenten Pastoral Letter 18, 'La formation chrétienne des jeunes gens' (2 February 1934).

the Christian 'one who lives in Christ and at God's service'; one in whose life the essential rites of prayer, divine office and the sacraments play a basic part as supports of that life, but one to whom the supreme thing, dominating all the rest, is 'the presence of God, united to the soul and giving it life', the presence of divine charity, maintaining that union and making it fruitful. That is the catholicism we must teach our young people! In this light, and in this light alone, they will grasp the living reality of Christian charity, with its many urgent applications; in this light they will understand that as we, the baptized, form one body with Christ as our Head, so the true spirit of the Christian is the spirit of love—or better, 'the gift of self to others for the love of Christ'. And it is in this light that they will become ardent apostles of Christ: 'those who will make their brothers Christians'; those who, in order to conquer, will learn the real secrets of love; those who will go into action only with the God who inspires and supports them, and who for that reason will be the victors of tomorrow!

An élite for the masses
Finally, through membership of our organizations, our young people must, of their own accord, 'join the ranks of an élite, an élite of conquest'! An élite in the first place, for it is the élite which attracts and is followed. But also an élite of conquest, 'an élite for the masses', not formed for its own sake, or to remain in an enclosure, the comfort and joy of its chaplain, but an élite devoted to the apostolate of the masses, one which is drawn to this apostolate in its own milieu, and which tries, in this milieu, to form a social environment more in conformity with the gospel, more basically Christian. That is the formula which suits the young, the only one, in fact, which fully suits them.

Now, as has been said, what places a man among the élite is not his wealth, nor his position, nor a specially advanced education, but his moral conscience, his professional worth and, for us Christians, his profound faith, his burning charity and his aptitude for the apostolate. To form this élite, therefore, we must give our militants the virtues which make 'the man before all': honesty, courage, obedience, patience and generosity. In their homes, they must be the best sons; in their jobs, the best workers; in society, the best citizens. Then, on the basis of these natural virtues, each must stand up proudly as a true Christian, one who prays, who loves, who suffers, and through all his hard toil, as a man diligent in his place of work, and as a Christian undaunted in his sphere of action, smiles and is always an optimist. Such a man is an ardent apostle of Christ, and that is the proudest conquest of our youth organizations! And that conquest will be decisive. Through it will be attained that goal which our young people aim at, that which every apostle ought to aim at: to rebuild the ancient edifice of Christianity on its foundations and to consolidate it.

So we address our young people and we say to them: the hour is critical! In the chaos in which the world struggles, every man looks for a saviour. Who will it be? A man? Perhaps, rather than a man, it will be a group of men, an enlightened and resolute élite which, with accurate and objective views on the world and the evils from which it suffers and the causes of those evils, will pool individual efforts to apply the remedy. Now it is you, the youth of today, who will form that élite of tomorrow. You are that élite! So get ready!

SPEECHES ON BECOMING CARDINAL[4]

Mgr Suhard was as much concerned for the Christian formation of his people as for the high quality of his priests. One of his first pastoral decisions had been to reform the organization and

[4] Extracts from the brochure published for the occasion at Reims, Imprimerie du Nord-Est, 1936 (no pagination).

curriculum of his major seminary, and two years later he planned to help the clergy in their duty of teaching and preaching. On 18 October 1935 the diocesan bulletin published a plan of sermons for the year for the use of parish priests, an innovation soon imitated by other dioceses.

On 20 November the Archbishop received the telegram announcing his nomination as cardinal. He had then to go to Rome, for the first time since his *ad limina* visit in 1929, in order to receive the red hat in the consistory of 16 December.

Arriving on the 6 December, he stayed at the French seminary, where he had once been a student. He took the opportunity of his stay in Rome to visit his old professor at the Gregorian University, Father (formerly Cardinal) Billot, who had been 'retired' from his dignity by Pius XI in a particularly stormy scene because of his attachment to the tenets of Action Francaise,[5] and had since been mouldering in a Jesuit retreat-house some distance from Rome. This gesture of loyalty made Mgr Suhard late for his audience with Pius XI, and when the Pope enquired the reason for this unpunctuality, he replied simply: 'I went to visit Fr Billot.' The Pope was annoyed but did not pursue the matter.

MEN OF THE CHURCH

The festivities associated with the creation of a cardinal of the Roman Church involve a certain number of toasts and speeches. Mgr Suhard bowed to the conventions of this sort of thing, but was able to use them in order to explain his own idea of the role of the Churchman faced with the tasks of the apostolate. The following words were spoken on 19 December at the French seminary, on the occasion of the delivery of the biretta.

How could I fail to be filled with the sense of my responsibilities? As a man of the particular Church to which I am attached, and a man of the universal Church to which I am vowed by my new title, in union with the pope, head of all the Churches, how could I fail to realize that I could only undertake my responsibilities if I were truly a 'man of the Church'?

Now to be a man of the Church means, in the first place,

[5] The royalist movement associated with Charles Maurras, condemned by Rome in 1936 until its submission in 1939.

to give men's minds the truth which sets free, which enlightens, which itself gives the true life. To be a man of the Church means to do the work of the apostolate, the apostolate of conquest and of preservation, the apostolate of Catholic Action. It means to display in one's person and work the true face of catholicism, the face of goodness and beauty, of attractive gentleness and compelling strength. It means, moreover, to serve one's country—our country, France. And, of course, to serve our country is not to cease to serve the Church, for since the baptism at Reims it has been France's mission, through space and time, to carry out the deeds of God!

We may well say of the most exalted dignities what Bossuet says of those springs of living water, that they are placed higher only in order to spread their fertilizing action over a wider area.

'To shine, not to flash!' is the motto which befits all, both great and small, and which enables us to see that we are all equal in God's service. May this motto, gentlemen, be always mine!

TO SERVE IN CHARITY

The Roman ceremonies were followed by these in which, from 30 December, the city of Reims showed its pride and joy on the Cardinal's return. To the compliments and speeches of homage he replied by reminding his hearers of the real meaning of the dignities in the Church: to be in the service of the poor and humble, which is not so much an honour as a duty.

But what you expect from me is not a stream of sentiments: it is a statement of what ought to be a cardinal's programme of life. That programme is short and can be expressed in a few words.

I was speaking just now of responsibilities and duties. The dignity to which I have been raised places me higher, I feel, only so as to enable me to give the universal Church and my own particular Church a broader and deeper service. To serve her in charity, that is, by giving myself!

Giving myself, my friends, means in the first place offering myself to all and for all as conciliator and peacemaker: seeking not to deepen the ditches which separate men but to build bridges to unite them; and to bring about *rapprochements* which I shall believe to be always possible and desirable, provided principles are respected: making it my ambition not to dominate by power and intimidation but to attract by kindness and gentleness to all, holding that as all men are brothers in Christ, all must be able to know, to understand and to love one another.

Giving myself also means making myself accessible to all, to the strong and the weak, the rich and the poor, especially to the weak and humble, for as Christ has taught that he is their friend and brother, he has assigned to me a fatherhood over them, the honour of which I cannot decline.

Giving myself means teaching the truth and refuting error: speaking to those who are baptized, so that they may grow in the knowledge of God and the practice of virtue, and to those who are not, so that they may learn that religion means safety and happiness for them and the guarantee of peace for society; recommending, propagating Christian teaching in all its forms.

Giving myself also means intensifying pastoral action, parochial, Catholic and social, throughout the extent of the diocese and in every place. We know from experience that the harvest is great. We know too, unhappily, that it is in danger of being lost for lack of hands to gather it. To make good this lack, I cannot fail to make earnest appeals to lay apostles and to those who recruit the ranks of the clergy.

Finally, giving myself means taking on myself the care, imposing on myself the charge, of those who are called 'the poor, the orphans and the sick'. Are they not the favourites of Christ? Has not the Church in all ages covered herself with glory by protecting them?

My brethren, I understand my duty in this respect all the better, for in these hours of crisis the poor are more deserving of pity; all the better, too, because by performing my duty I am acting not only on the life and health of men's bodies, but on the eternal interests of their souls, since a minimum of well-being is necessary to man if he is to persevere and save his soul; all the better, finally, because at this season of the year the liturgy reminds us that when Christ came into the world he appeared first to the shepherds, and that he began his earthly mission by announcing that the gospel is preached to the poor.

It is a vast and difficult programme, my breathren, which calls for all the power and the grace of God and for all your collaboration, if it is to be progressively applied.

May I be able to work, and may you be able to help me, in that spirit which I have tried to make the rule of all my conduct in your midst; 'the spirit of faith and kindness—*in fide et lenitate* (Sirach 45:4).

2. FIRST MISSIONARY EXPERIMENTS THE RURAL DISTRICTS

(REIMS, 1934-6)

At Reims, the Cardinal did not confine himself to encouraging the activities of Catholic Action. He was equally concerned with the dechristianized parts of his diocese and tried to find a practical and appropriate solution to the problem of the religious indifference of the country people.

Since 1933 the Bishop had toured the country parishes of the Marne and the Aube sufficiently to judge how paganized they were. During a pastoral visitation he had observed the 'pitiable state' of the churches in Champagne and the complete isolation, the inhuman solitude of certain country priests. He had seen empty churches turned into dovecots, presbyteries in ruins, priests with nothing to do in parishes which had become too small and deserted by the drift from the land. In one of these worm-eaten presbyteries, in a region where seven parishes together numbered scarcely a thousand souls, he had met an old priest, solitary, without work, embittered and growing worse. For twenty years he had not administered a single baptism; every morning he said his Mass to empty pews and could no longer remember by heart the words of absolution. Spending all his days in digging his garden, the old man had become so used to his poverty and decline that he refused the Bishop's offer of a place in a house for retired priests.

Mgr Suhard pondered long on how to restore life to these disinherited parishes. He hoped to find a solution by regrouping some priests of the same deanery, so as to provide jointly for the service of the surrounding parishes. The idea seems very simple now, but at that time it was opposed by a body of obstinate diehards, who made it extremely difficult to carry out.

First of all he had to find a man ready to make the first experiment. He called in Abbé Georgin, a young chaplain to the JOC and JOCF, whose enthusiasm and courage he knew. This is the chaplain's account of how the Archbishop, in a conversation, presented his plan:

For priests to have a normal ministry, they need at least
a thousand parishioners, otherwise they have not enough
pastoral work, nor enough to live on. Before ten years are out,
the boundaries of the parishes must be revised. There is
something wrong in the administration: we have no right to
leave things as they are. The clergy are badly distributed.
We have got to set up districts, that is, groups of parishes in
charge of a priest whose duty it will be to organize the pastoral ministry, so that all may receive equally the benefit of
his activity. You are going into a forest! I know what I am
asking of you. You will have a tough job. You are going to
do the hacking down. You will make some clearings. But one
man ploughs and sows, another reaps.

In October 1934 Abbé Georgin set to work and tried to build
up the first 'rural district'. Thus the community of Châtillon-
sur-Marne became the prototype of those priestly teams whose
principles were adopted ten years later by the Mission de France
in the Aube and the Yonne.

The objections and misrepresentations of the administrative
staff of the diocese prevented Mgr Suhard from giving 'his missionary' the title and powers of dean-in-charge of Châtillon until
1936. But during those two years he kept up a correspondence,
from which I quote two extracts. In reply to the Abbé's good
wishes for Christmas in 1934, the Bishop replied from Reims,
in a letter dated Christmas Day. Some of its terms already anticipate the words of realistic hope addressed in 1944 to the Superior of the Mission de Paris, another enterprise conceived in
hope and hard work.[1]

My dear Father,

I am very moved by the contents of your letter, by your
first successes and also, unhappily, by your trials. You are
really doing God's work and I cannot doubt that the attempt
you are making to form a district will be successful. You will
thus be the founder of a great and noble work, which should
be decisive in the diocese, not only because it must last, but

[1] Correspondence with Abbé Georgin, unpublished. From Fr Bouëssé's
papers.

because it will indicate a method of the apostolate which, if it is understood, can bear fruit. It is important to begin well. I am not indifferent to your troubles and difficulties, my dear son, and I wish I could cure them. God will help you, but you know, too, that as you are upsetting the work of the devil, you have got to reckon with him. That is inevitable. Thank you again for your good wishes. Not one of those I received went so straight to my heart as yours. I give you my fatherly blessing.

Opposition, criticism, obstacles, were certainly not lacking. But the community of priests at Châtillon obtained results enough to disarm many of the critics. From Reims, again, at Christmas 1936, the Cardinal replied to the dean's good wishes, congratulating and encouraging him. He ended his letter with this passage, in which for the first time we meet a phrase which was to become famous: *pays de mission*, missionary country:

Let us beg, for ourselves and for all the clergy, the true missionary spirit. To be the true missionary of Christ: in these words there is a whole programme ... which, as I see it, is the true programme of salvation. You, dear Father, are in the way of carrying it out. Who knows whether the experiment you will have made on your soil, which is truly 'missionary country', may not prove to serve other similar regions? We can at least pray for it to the divine infant in the crib. . . .

In the years that followed, such teams were in fact planted in other areas and other parishes. Justice was then done to that first attempt which had been so much criticized in its beginnings. And when Abbé Georgin, passing through Paris in 1945, was invited to lunch by the Archbishop, he was able to tell him, in a letter of thanks:

I was particularly pleased to be able to tell you of the happy results obtained by the priestly community of Châtillon, thanks to your initiative, and to inform you, too, that these results and spiritual advances were progressing, with almost giant strides, in that once unpromising and disinherited countryside.

Today I can only thank you for giving me the honour of undertaking a mission like that, pretty hard and difficult at first, but now so fruitful and consoling!

I am persuaded that the method was the best and that you were truly inspired by the Holy Spirit to propose it to us. I only regret one thing, that I was too often unequal to that magnificent task, to which in your kindness you had called me.

ACTIVE APOSTOLATE AND CONTEMPLATIVE APOSTOLATE

'If St Thérèse of the Child Jesus was chosen to be the patron of the missions, it was not because the missionaries were fond of her, or because she was popular, but because she knew how to combine the contemplative life with an intense desire for missionary activity' (to the Benedictine Missionary Nuns of the Priory of St Bathilde at Vanves, 14 November 1940).

At Reims as at Bayeux, a great part of Mgr Suhard's pastoral work was devoted to religious communities. At clothings, anniversaries or professions, the bishop used to visit contemplative, teaching or nursing nuns, diocesan communities and those of the religious orders.

Some of those 'few words', which nuns know so well how to extract from visiting priests, in his case sometimes assumed the dimensions of regular exhortations or spiritual conferences. Here he speaks to contemplatives about the apostolate, and to an active congregation about the evangelization of the poor.

PRAISE THE LORD AS APOSTLES[2]

Dear Daughters,

I want to speak to you today about the apostolate. My reason is that you have a mission to perform; directly, you

[2] Spiritual conference to the contemplative nuns of the Bayeux diocese, 10 May 1930 (Fr Bouëssé's papers). Published in *La Vie Spirituelle*, no. 412, December 1955, vol. XCIII, pp. 506-10.

have the duty of praising God, but even in this duty of praise I perceive a very important role which belongs to each one of you, the role of the apostolate to souls. When we speak of the apostolate, we think instinctively of a type of religious community quite different from yours: of those religious who work at teaching, or in the missions to the heathen, or even at ministering to lepers, for there are religious who devote themselves entirely to that ministry. It is especially to such orders that no one's mind turns and yet, weighing things up, I venture to say that the apostolate to souls is not the peculiar property of anyone, but that it pertains to all the orders, and also that the order to which you belong essentially includes the apostolate.

In the first place, the apostolate is not peculiar to any religious order, because it is impossible to conceive an order which is other than apostolic. When our Lord called souls to him, he made them apostles: that is obvious in the case of the Twelve. The gospel tells us that he called to himself twelve fishermen, 'whom he called apostles'. The same can be said of the seventy-two disciples whom Jesus sent to preach the gospel, as also of St Paul and of all the saints who carried on such a fruitful apostolate. All were called to exercise the apostolate; things could not have happened otherwise. When we consider the role that our Lord assigned to himself when he came into the world, there was no possible way of carrying it out but that of the apostolate.

When God calls a soul to himself, he entrusts him with a mission of apostolate, which is simply the mission to make him known to souls, to glorify our Lord, to spread the reign of God on earth. I would dare to say that the more a religious has this mentality rooted in her spirit, the better religious she is. This might, I know, prompt some objections, because the world does not understand these things, but you must show that you have this apostolic spirit, and sow around you the good seed you have in you.

It is there that we have to look for the apostolate in its true form, and not to be tied to facts in too down-to-earth a manner. The apostle is one who introduces the kingdom of God to souls; in so far as he enlarges the kingdom of God he carries out the apostolate. This spreading of the kingdom of God does not depend solely on human means. They are necessary, of course; miracles are not the ordinary way, and in this earthly life our Lord showed us that the real way to make God known is to speak about him. But besides this outward word there is the inner word, and for the outward word to be active the inner word must first penetrate into the souls themselves. And that is how the religious life must exercise its apostolic activity, if the inner word of God is to be effective. Ask God, then, that the missionary's word may not be in vain, but effective, obtaining a perfect response in souls. It is by prayer, by sacrifice and by all the supernatural means that this apostolate is carried out. You see, then, how you have an apostolate to carry out.

But in order to carry it out, certain conditions must be fulfilled. First, you must think about it. If you perform your duty externally you will find in it a spiritual gain for your soul, especially as regards the prayer in choir, but if you take care to observe that this prayer, sung or said, is a sort of permanent supplication, to obtain the success of your apostolate, if you think about it often, your praise will have a real efficacy which otherwise it would not have. I do not think there is any more consoling thought than that; so you must think about it.

Then you must have the true dispositions of the apostle, for certain inner dispositions are necessary. First, the disposition of zeal; whoever has not felt that ardent desire cannot carry out the apostolate. The disposition for sacrifice, too, for you know that the apostle must suffer: 'The servant is not above his master.' You cannot conquer souls except through sacrifice: you must therefore have in you that disposition for sacrifice.

The apostle is one who is not only zealous but also at God's disposal, for I think there is no better disposition in an apostolic soul than that. It is, moreover, the disposition recommended by St Paul, who knew all about being an apostle. He said to Timothy, in effect: 'As for you, man of God, be equipped for every good work'; therefore be equipped to accomplish, not what pleases you, but what is right, whatever is good, according to wisdom and order.

St Paul also adds that one must be a workman who need not be ashamed, that is, one who gives all his attention to following the line traced for him by God. For it is only Christ who is the true apostle: all we are only his lieutenants, and we shall be so the more, the more we are in the hands of God, the more ready we are to run counter to our own will in order to follow more directly the will of God.

This is the disposition to obedience, which is far more than obedience itself, for there is a merely material manner of obeying. The spirit of obedience is worth more, for it is that disposition which places the soul in the hands of God. How often, I am sure, you must have read those passages in the Old Testament which express this fundamental truth, that God does not need our immolations and our sacrifices. No, he can do without them. God needs them only in so far as those sacrifices are the formal expression of our submission to his will. I think there is no more holy disposition than that: to will or not to will just what God wills or does not will—that is the fundamental disposition of the apostolic spirit. The apostle is the man of Christ, the man who has brought his will into conformity with the will of Christ.

With these dispositions, your praise will acquire a quite different tone. That *opus Dei* which is your outward sacrifice will have value in proportion as it is the outward expression of the inmost sentiments of your soul, and if that is what it is, how much more meritorious it will be from the apostolic point of view! You will have fulfilled the first condition of the apostolate. By this means, your activity will be great in God's sight. I say 'in God's sight', for the world will not understand it. Let the world talk, but do your best to contradict it. You will give it a flat contradiction if you are truly apostolic in your duties and if, praying to God, you have learned to pray to him in those apostolic and supernatural dispositions.

You know what scripture says: he who does good to an apostle will receive an apostle's reward. You will have reinforced the apostle's action; you will have turned a poor human action into a divine action. This happens, of course, without our knowing it; we do not know to what extent we are acting in this way, but if we have been apostles, we shall have part in the fruits of the apostolate. In my ministry I rely a great deal on those prayers offered in our convents. Be sure that you will have your part in the apostolate in so far as you have been penetrated with the love of God; then you will be able to accomplish the work for which you are destined, in a truly apostolic spirit. So be it!

LET THE GOSPEL BE PREACHED TO THE POOR![3]

Have you ever thought, my brethren, of the effect produced when a new house of the Little Sisters of the Poor is founded. Whether it is in some forgotten corner, or in the beauty of the countryside, or in the overcrowded quarters of a suburb, it makes no difference. There, through this foundation, a shelter is raised where the aged poor are welcomed with a smile, cared for and comforted, and finally led to God and

[3] Extract from a speech at Glaire, 13 July 1939, for the centenary of the foundation of the Little Sisters of the Poor. Unpublished. Historical archives of the archbishopric of Paris.

sanctified by nuns, sometimes quite young nuns, who you would think were their mothers.

It is a shelter which is an arsenal of holiness, in which every day and at every hour of the day and night, the Little Sister is led, through her duties, to produce acts of virtue; to give herself to God in the persons of the poor; to advance, by charity, into intimate union with Christ; to climb by the path of renunciation towards that perfection of the heavenly Father which our Saviour shows us as our ideal and our programme.

It is a shelter which produces the most wonderful effects of Christian charity, thanks to that almsgiving which only awaited the providential occasion of the poor needing help and the diligent, discreet hand of the collector.

It is a shelter which is a home, a home which warms and gives light! In this house, charity abounds in all its glory. It is impossible to see a Little Sister, at the bedside of the sick, or accepting the meanest tasks in the service of the poor, or serenely begging their daily bread from door to door, without being deeply moved by it, without being stirred up to greater love of our neighbour, who can call forth such devotion in certain souls. My brethren, on all sides we hear anguished appeals to moral forces. But do we know that these moral forces are simply the forces of the gospel? But the gospel would, as we know, remain a dead letter to many, it would never be accepted by some men who are still ignorant of it, it would never penetrate certain milieux to which it ought to bring the maxims of life, if it were not already being lived in their sight, if some souls filled with its spirit were not presenting it to them in its lovable, attractive, human form! So let us thank God that, alongside other testimonies whose heroes we salute, he has raised up the humble Little Sister who, because she practises the gospel at every moment of her life, reconciles to it those who admire her in silence and soon, perhaps, may wish to imitate her.

God is everything

The value of a benefit is measured by the part God has taken in it. For it is he who gives its worth to every activity, and the more his action is apparent in a work, and the less it has been helped by human elements—or rather, the more the human elements harmonize with the divine—so much the more precious is that work. It is the grain of mustard which becomes a great tree. It is the little flock to which victory is promised. The things of small account, which should be called the things which are not, those are the things which are chosen for the great designs! So says the Apostle Paul, the interpreter of Christ.

Now with the Little Sisters of the Poor, for a hundred years God's action has been everything. Human elements count for nothing!

God is everything in a foundation whose foundress is a little working woman of the people, without education, without money, without any means but her devotion, her trust and her virtue.

God is everything in the beginnings, where even the foundress's virtue is not used, where she is excluded from the government of the house, reduced for nearly thirty years to the humblest role, especially set apart for sacrifices and prayer.

God is everything in every house they have founded, where poverty is strictly the rule, and Providence alone must provide the most urgent and indispensable needs.

God is everything in these houses, where all storing up is forbidden, and alms alone are the means of livelihood.

And God, my brethren, is most effectively all! For it is a thing unheard of that any house ever lacked necessities, and it is a regular experience that the help arrives in the nick of time, and that even by means of a miracle God often gives to his poor not only what is necessary but comforts too!

Finally, God is everything to the Little Sister. Littleness, that is her motto. Littleness means, no doubt, the willingness to refer everything to God, but it is also the will to forget oneself and let oneself be forgotten, in order to leave room for God. It is the will to become quite insignificant, quite annihilated, in order to win the hearts of the poor, who, we know, will never be won over by an air of domination but are always open to courtesy and kindness. It is, above all, the will to be annihilated in order to win the heart of God who, as we know, resists the proud but is irresistibly drawn to the humble. We know too that it is in the practice of charity and humility together that he comes into a soul, acts in it and operates through it and for it!

Thus for the last hundred years not only has God's work been done here, but God himself is the great worker, who governs all, *'Quia manus Domini fecit hoc*: the hand of the Lord has done this' (Is. 41:20).

If this has been for the good of the Little Sisters, it has also been for our good. There is nothing on earth so precious as to know how to manage one's life. He best manages his life who knows that he can always count on God. 'Men of little faith, why do you doubt?' He best manages his life who, when he has laboured and toiled, remembers that above all he must count on God: 'Without me you can do nothing.' He best manages his life who, when he has laboured and toiled, leaves to God the glory of success. To work for self is always disappointing. To work for God is always rewarding.

For this, too, we must give thanks.

The service of the poor

The value of a work, my brethren, lies in its power to expand. A work is great which extends and prospers.

For a hundred years we have seen proof of this. The mustard-seed has become the great tree. One after another, the nations have sheltered under its shade. Everywhere it has its admirers and friends; not only among the old people who have been helped, and their families, but in all quarters where they are known: rich or poor, believers or non-believers, Catholics or non-Catholics.

Everywhere it has adapted itself. Everywhere, seeing the acts of devotion abounding in it, souls have been inspired with a holy emulation. In the service of the poor, they have found a joy above all human joys. And everywhere they have made the poor believe in the charity of Christ, which has been shown to them with such touching simplicity!

It is recorded in the gospel that when John the Baptist, in the prison where Herod had confined him, heard of the works of Christ, he sent two of his disciples, who asked him: 'Are you he who is to come, or shall we look for another?' Jesus replied: 'Go and tell John what you hear and see: the blind receive their sight and the lame walk, lepers are cleansed and the deaf hear, and the dead are raised up, and the poor have the good news preached to them.'

'The poor have the good news preached to them'—that is the sign of his coming.

The preaching of the good news to the poor did not, of course, have to wait for the birth of Jeanne Jugan's Order. Before her time, many attempts had been made, and not without success. But to make herself poor in order to evangelize only the poor, to choose them from among the most failing, the most needy, the least attractive to human nature, to consecrate to these poor aged men and women all the fibres of her soul, all the riches of her heart and finally to make herself small in order to win them for Christ: that, without question, was the sublime originality of her apostolate.

We all, my brethren, wish the kingdom of God to be established on earth. As Catholics of action, we want to work for this coming. For pity's sake, then, let us not forget the condition laid down for this coming of the kingdom: that the poor must have the good news preached to them!

And since this house, this institute, has accepted the burden of this divine programme, let us thank God for the gift he has given to this world, so sick with egoism, with hate, with love of enjoyment and revulsion from the unpleasant; the gift of having trained here—as it were in an incomparable training college—teachers of true charity. Let us attend their school, let us learn from them that the secret of putting things to rights is not to get worried, not even to work with ardour, but to give oneself generously to the full extent of one's powers: better still, to give oneself in pure unselfishness.

In the early days of her foundation, someone who knew Jeanne Jugan only under her family name asked her one day what he ought to call her in future. 'Humble servant of the poor' was her instant reply.

'Humble servant of the poor': what a wonderful name! Her daughters have taken another, which is even lovelier: 'Little Sisters of the Poor'. My brethren, in this name of 'Sisters' let us see something not just connected with the religious life, but also something of fraternal tenderness. May they and Jeanne Jugan be blessed in God for giving to the world such an example and such a lesson.

3. PARIS, THE DECHRISTIANIZED DIOCESE — THE DEPORTEES

In the night of 8-9 April 1940, Cardinal Verdier died. He had ruled the diocese of Paris with authority and good sense, mingled with an optimism and a humour which were legendary with his clergy, and had performed his task in a peculiarly difficult time. On that same 9 April, in fact, German troops invaded Denmark and Norway, and it was clear that on the French front the offensive would soon be opened.

The Holy See had little hesitation over the choice of his successor. The apostolic nuncio began his consultations at the luncheon following the funeral ceremonies, asking the advice, among others, of Mgr Rolland-Gosselin. The Bishop of Versailles (according to another French bishop), after weighing up the professional abilities, merits and even the eccentricities of the various cardinals, replied: 'If I had to ask for advice, I should go to Cardinal Suhard.'

The journalists thought so too, for one of them, announcing that Pius XII was about to appoint a new archbishop of Paris, accompanied his article with the note: 'In our picture, Cardinal Suhard.'

So it was no surprise to anyone when on 11 May the papers officially announced the nomination which the Cardinal himself had learned on the 8th, during a confirmation luncheon in his diocese. His reactions and state of mind during those days of May 1940 are now known to us from his private diary: [1]

On this *Thursday, 8 May* (Appearance of St Michael), Mgr Delmont brought me the official news of my appointment to Paris. I was quite overwhelmed and wrote to H.E. the Nuncio, begging him to *place his choice on someone worthier*. Arriving at Buzancy the same day, I wrote another letter, which was more urgent than the first and might appear importunate.

[1] From Cardinal Suhard's private diary, 8 May 1940, folio 36.

This *Friday, 9 May,* on return to Reims, I learn that the Holy See insists on my acceptance, which is approved by the Government.

Saturday, 10 May, the official notice of my nomination is promulgated. There can be no more hesitation. Cost what it may, I must accept. And to ensure success I must make the resolution 'to be a saint'. That is the real secret. O God, how far I am from such an ideal! What a long way I have yet to travel! Yet I must reach it. Help me, O my God!

11 May 1940, the day after my nomination as Archbishop of Paris, on the feast of Pentecost. I feel all my weakness in God's sight. Five million faithful to rule. More than two thousand priests to direct. The most complex interests to be faced.... An immense work of apostolate to organize. I am instinctively inclined to be afraid. But I do not want to be afraid! This work is God's work. I am only his instrument. So the one end to pursue is to be a good instrument. And the best of all instruments will be the *holiest....* To be a saint! That, then, must be the sole objective. I ask the Holy Spirit to inspire me, and above all to remind me constantly of that maxim: 'To be a saint, so as to be a good Archbishop of Paris!'

At the same time he gave a broadcast address to the faithful of his new diocese, assuring them of his devotion and asking for their support: [2]

I have just learned the news of my nomination by the Holy Father to the Archbishopric of Paris. At once my thoughts turn to that great diocese, the heart of France, and to him who was its beloved, incomparable head, Cardinal Verdier.

I admit that I feel afraid of the burden which has been laid on my shoulders: to rule such a diocese, to succeed such a shepherd! If, in spite of that, I have bowed to the will of the Supreme Pontiff, it is because in the gravity of

[2] *Semaine religieuse de Paris,* no. 4506 (18 May 1940), p. 452.

the present time no one has the right to stand down, when it is a question of service.

I feel very weak. But I rely on the prayers of my new flock—I earnestly request them—I rely on the blessing of the Supreme Pontiff, whose wishes I am carrying out; above all I rely on God, who is all my strength and all my hope.

It is with keen regret that I shall leave this lovely diocese of Reims, that long-suffering and glorious cathedral, the cradle of France, that people and its leaders, whose good will and loyalty have given me, for ten years, nothing but comfort and joy. But, looking only to my present duty, I firmly assure Paris, and France too, that I am entirely devoted to them. I go to them with all the fervour of my soul as priest and father, with all the generosity of which I am capable. To the priests, too, who devote themselves so zealously to the evangelization of Paris and its suburbs, and so many of whom are with the forces, I hasten to say that I bless them with all my heart.

In these critical hours through which we are passing, may God guard our beloved country and lead it, through all the sacrifices and all the tears, to victory. Each of you in his post, and I myself in that which has been assigned to me, will work for that, regardless of our sufferings!

However, the letter of 11 May in which Mgr Beaussart, the Vicar Capitular, officially announced the news to the people of the diocese showed the favourable attitude of his future fellow workers and described very fairly the moral and spiritual characteristics of their new pastor: [3]

Cardinal Suhard arrives in Paris preceded by a reputation which has already won the hearts of his new flock. Our great capital with its suburbs, the bubbling crucible of intense life, the centre of so many national and international affairs, the home in which the most diverse and opposed movements of ideas, and the most paradoxical manifestations of intellectual

[3] *Ibid.*, p. 444.

life meet, cross and clash; the unique city in which the superficial or prejudiced view largely sees frivolity, pleasure or vice, but in which is also found—and our foreign friends have often expressed their admiration for them—the most amazing resources of charity, devotion, enthusiasm for great causes and the most ardent cells of sanctity; this Paris of ours has an infinitely sensitive heart. It gives itself when it encounters goodness. Now this, we are assured by the best judges, is the dominant trait of our new archbishop.

If to this we add the high virtues of profound piety and wisdom—drawn from meditation on the great problems of philosophy—of moderation and balance given to the soul by long contact with God in prayer, with souls in spiritual direction and with the delicate business of diocesan administration, we can see that His Eminence Cardinal Suhard will worthily continue in Paris the work of concord and peace accomplished by his predecessor, that 'ministry of reconciliation' which is supremely that of the bishop.

The archbishop's first task, before it could be reconciliation, had to be one of conciliation pure and simple. France's military and political situation was critical, and the Reynaud Government expressed the desire to make contact with the Cardinal as soon as possible. Leaving Reims by car on the morning of 15 May, he arrived in Paris during the day and the same evening visited the President of the Council. From this interview emerged the letter to Pius XII, begging him to use all his influence with Mussolini to prevent Italy entering the war on the side of the Germans.

The second attempt at conciliation required of the Cardinal had to do with Franco's Spain. The 'pilgrimage' to Our Lady of the Pillar, which he undertook on 17 May with Mgr Feltin and Mgr Courbe, included unofficial approaches to secure Spain's neutrality. This journey, which ended on 22 May, coincided with the return to Paris of Marshal Pétain, Ambassador to Madrid, so the French bishops did not meet him.

While the Cardinal was taking official possession of his palace (29 May), then of the Metropolitan See (1 June), and speaking at length to the people of Paris assembled for the consecration of the nation to the Sacred Heart in the basilica of Montmartre, events moved rapidly. The capitulation of the Belgian army,

Italy's entry into the war, the general collapse of the French lines, all followed during a few days, during which, as provisional administrator of the Reims diocese, the Cardinal had to make a short journey, on roads blocked by the 'exodus', to the towns of the south-west, where his former flock had taken refuge in large numbers. He was back at his residence in the Rue Barbet-de-Jouy on 11 June, having spent the whole day, all the way from Poitiers meeting columns of refugees abandoning the capital. On the 14th the German army marched down the Champs-Elysées. On the 17th the armistice was signed.

These were the circumstances in which the Cardinal had to begin his ministry in Paris. He devoted the months of June and July to visiting numerous institutes, parishes and religious communities. From 26 to 29 July he was shut up in his palace by a German search-party, the Occupation authorities hoping to find in the archives some traces of 'collusion between Archbishop Verdier and freemasonry'!

Among his first governmental acts in the diocese we may incidentally recall the decision by which on 6 September the Cardinal authorized, and even encouraged, those priests who so desired to adopt community life in their parishes

In the context of these first months of his time in Paris we can better understand the force and meaning of the words in which, at the solemn ceremony of enthronement in Notre-Dame on 6 October, he endeavoured to revive the courage of his people.

OUR REASONS FOR HOPE[4]

Our reasons for hope lie first of all in God, whose loving heart inclines towards all the afflicted.... God, whose goodness, as Bossuet says, visits us by the way of trials, and who is never nearer to us than when we are under the winepress of suffering! 'The Lord knows those who are his,' says St Paul, and the Lord had them before his eyes when he said 'Blessed are the poor'. We know that the hour of the great crucifixions of mankind was the hour of the great disillusions . . . , the hour of the great manifestations of truth and the revelations of God's redeeming omnipotence.

We hope in God who wills to save France and who, though

---

[4] *Semaine religieuse de Paris*, no. 4517 (12 October 1940), pp. 650-2.

he allows this trial, cannot allow it to be irreparable. The history of France is the history of the deeds of God. . . . He has assigned to our country a place of honour in the world, the place of the 'eldest daughter of the Church', charged with the duty of defending her and of blazing the trail for her missionary conquests. These are truths which were magnificently recalled from this very pulpit by Lacordaire, and later by Cardinal Pacelli, who is now Pius XII.

We have another motive for hope in what Paris has done for the Church and for Christendom. Paris! It is almost a truism to call it the 'head and heart of France', but it is none the less profoundly true! By its geographical position, by all the life of the country which flows into it and is concentrated there, by the attraction it has for the most distinguished minds, drawing them and keeping them here, by all its tradition and history, Paris is to France what the brain is to the human organism. It anticipates and sums up in itself the feeling and impulse of the country. It thrills for the country. It glows and throbs with all her generosity. It draws all our people in her train.

On a special level, is there any nobler edifice than that which is constituted by the Christian life in our capital? Splendid work of God's achievement, to which all eyes were drawn!

Our reasons for hope, my brethren, are in the work which I intend to carry out with you. It is our common task! We live, we must admit, in an age of transition in which, having looked at the past with the sorrow it calls forth, we must think of the future. And in that future, if we are to save France, we must depend on God and depend on ourselves. . . .

On God, from whom we beg the miracle which saves! But that miracle, let us recognize, is not one which will destroy the obstacle, abolish the suffering and at once bring joy and ease in living. No, for God does not grant that kind of miracle, and it would be unworthy of us to ask for it. But the miracle we ask is that which makes the trial bearable and gives us the strength to bear it; the miracle which will enable us to find in the trial itself the secret of overcoming it; the miracle which, when nothing will be easy and there will be long days without joy, will provide Frenchmen with an inexhaustible energy; the miracle which will show them the implacable discipline without which men slide inevitably into anarchy and ruin; the miracle which will show them that all this must be overcome, because life is stronger than death, and because France can and must live.

Yes, my friends, we must depend on ourselves! We must say to ourselves that this work 'will either be done by us or not done at all'! For what has to be done is to remake the French soul, to give it back its vitality and its character. Such a remoulding can only come from an effort springing from the depths of our souls as Frenchmen.

What we have to know, in addition, is that this effort must begin with a clear and objective vision of things—a vision of truth, clear of all illusion and error, a vision on which all today stake their hope and their life.

What we have to know is that this vision must be a diligent examination, in which each one questions himself, asking himself, if not what part he has played in that decadence, at least the part he must play in putting it right, and finding out what resources he can dispose of, perhaps what sacrifices he must undergo, in order to help.

What we have to know is that nothing in this change will be easy or immediate, and that our only chance of success for this change lies in patience, knowledge and the courage to wait.

During these first months of his ministry, the Cardinal was taking the measure of his new field of apostolate, but he also began to realize the extent to which Paris and its surroundings were de-christianized. The disproportion between the means at the Church's disposal for Catholic Action and the tasks needing to be done, together with the absence of many priests as prisoners of war after June 1940, drove him more and more to reflect on ways of penetrating the pagan masses.

On 12 November, speaking to the junior seminarists who came to be re-settled at Conflans after withdrawing for a year to Fontgombault Abbey, he put before them this ideal for the priestly life of tomorrow:

If we do not succeed in giving back to men the Christian meaning of life, there can be no hope of restoration. The apostles of the days to come will have two characteristics: the spirit of sacrifice, and personality. In the first place, a sacrificed life, a life which is hard and poor. The cross demands a discipline for which enthusiasm is no substitute; it must involve work, obedience and unavoidable privations. In the second place, personal worth. To help in rebuilding the earthly city, the priest of tomorrow must be prepared to take the initiative, must have a ready ear for souls and for situations, must adapt himself so that the Church may be ever young. Education, especially classical education, tends to form priestly personalities; to that end, it must be steeped in a true and solid piety. Piety will always be the main characteristic of the priest, and what the world expects of him.

Both at Bayeux and at Reims he had always sought direct, confident and frequent contact with his priests. The clergy of Paris had noticed, too, that one of the new Archbishop's first phrases, in his broadcast declaration in May, had been one of thanks and encouragement for their own efforts. The first real contact between the clergy and the Cardinal took place at the pastoral retreat in September, at the seminary of Issy.

Drawing up the conclusions of these days of retreat, he had emphasized the 'adaptation of the priestly life to the present conditions of the apostolate', and given as his pastoral directive 'the doing of a work of light, a work of goodness, a work of practical effect'. He had stressed the importance of the parish, of Christian teaching and the works of Catholic Action, and shown his anxiety about recruitment for the priesthood.

OUR TRUE RICHES[5]

And we, gentlemen, my dear sons, of what spirit are we? For we too are called to a mission of salvation. We too must prepare to make it succeed. We too have made the promise. How shall we keep it?

We shall keep our sacred promises if, like Mary, we aim at the heights, if we try spiritually always to climb, climb to her, climb to God. Only there shall we rule: we shall rule ourselves, we shall rule the world we have to conquer. There God's friends are to be found, the only powerful friends, the saints. There, every day, we must climb, for if we do not climb we shall tend to go down. We shall be drawn down to the things beneath, those which lower and diminish, which drag down to the abyss.

PRIESTLY RESPONSIBILITY

We shall keep our promises if we guard the sense of our responsibilities: our pastoral responsibilities of the present and of the future. We are essentially men in charge. It is on our faithfulness in assuming and bearing our responsibilities that we shall be judged.

Should not we, who are deacons, priests, bishop of the capital, have a more acute sense of those responsibilities? Are we not in constant touch with the masses? Does not this contact condition our ministry? The masses who believe, and those who do not; the crowds who fill our churches and those who never enter them; the crowds who welcome us as their pastor and father, and those who are indifferent. All these crowds, in various ways, are in our charge. We are responsible for them all. As we see them passing before our eyes, how can we help thinking of the trepidation which seized St Paul at the sight of the unbelieving Athenians?

[5] *Semaine religieuse de Paris*, no. 4524 (30 November 1940), pp. 827-8.

How can we fail to feel the conviction that we are bearing the burden of a world?

Gentlemen, we must think about this burden. Kept within due bounds, the impression left by that thought is a healthy impression ..., a beginning of conquest! The apostle who is steeped in it realizes the true meaning of his life, which is the meaning of an absolute 'belonging' to his neighbour, a total gift of himself. He is convinced that those men have a void in their souls and are to be pitied who have never heard the *misereor super turbam* ('I have compassion on the crowd') of Jesus (Matt. 15:32), who have never been haunted by the souls in danger who are calling for help. He is convinced that those above all are to be pitied who no longer realize the true value of souls in the field of the apostolate; they are capable of any flinching, any desertion.

THE SENSE OF EFFORT

We shall keep our promises if we bear in ourselves the sense of effort. We have to win souls, to conquer them! When we have won them, we have to offer them to God. Now for such a task, only one thing counts: effort! our daily effort, our personal effort, our professional effort! For if this success requires a divine element, it also requires, on pain of failure, a human element: all that is human in us, all that is best on the human level, tact, delicacy, penetration, foresight, and above all, devotedness. It was in toil and suffering that Christ redeemed the world, and in toil and suffering the apostles of all times have laid the foundations of the Church and kept them unchangeable!

We shall keep our promises if, recognizing our nothingness, we trust ourselves to God. Our nothingness.... Above all what matters is that we should be strong, and we shall only be strong if we possess the truth, if we are kept in the truth. Now the truth is that despite all our efforts we can do nothing by ourselves, all our sufficiency is from God. The truth is that it is by honestly admitting this insufficiency of ours that we find in God the strength we need. The truth is that it is by admitting to ourselves this insufficiency that we can soundly judge the tasks imposed on us; seeing in these tasks the responsibilities they involve rather than the honours attached to them; seeing especially that to desire the responsibilities is always presumption, and to seek the honours is vanity and sin. The truth, in short, is that relying on God, on prayer which opens the path by which we come to God, on his priesthood and on the filial abandonment which is in the logic of the priesthood, the priest has never any reason to be afraid, or to doubt or to be discouraged. There is no situation, however difficult, from which he does not emerge with honour. It is the glory of the Catholic clergy to possess this strength and to use it. And it is in proportion as they know how to use it that our priests will everywhere appear as the 'counsellors of the nations' and will be their guardians and defenders in tragic days.

These are our true riches: the riches which are the foundation of our hopes and of that optimism of conquest which will be the salvation of our country.

THE CHAPLAINCY TO THE WORKERS IN GERMANY

At that time, dechristianization (which the Cardinal described in a sermon in Notre-Dame in 1942 as 'the scandal of modern times, which constitutes the worst of all evils') was only one evil among many. Or rather it was aggravated by a new evil: the forced exodus to Germany of a large number of French workers, who were deprived in that exile of all spiritual help.

The *Service du travail obligatoire* (STO), or compulsory labour force, presented an extremely thorny problem from the end of 1941. The occupying power, with the aim of weakening the French economy and strengthening its own economic potential in industry and agriculture, organized (on the pretext of an 'exchange' of prisoners of war) a mass removal of the French work-

ing population to its own centres of production. The workers
thus requisitioned were placed at the disposal of more than 3,700
German factories (figures of 1 December 1943). Abbé Rodhain,
chaplain to the prisoners and then to the 'free workers', in his
reports to the Assembly of Cardinals and Archbishops of France
(the ACA), placed their number at 350,000 in January 1943. In
April of the same year it stood at 600,000 and at 800,000 in July.
Before the end of the year it had certainly passed the million
mark.

This population of French workers included many Christians
and even 'militants', but not a single priest accompanied them.
The occupying power systematically refused to allow chaplains to
the workers of the STO, in spite of the requests made to it from
January 1942. From February 1942, when he was instructed to
organize this chaplaincy, until 25 November 1943, when Bruneton
head of the French labour force in Germany, informed him of the
final refusal of the occupying power to allow official chaplains to
the STO, Abbé Rodhain negotiated in vain.

The departure of priests for Germany was therefore clandestine,
in direct opposition to the orders of the occupying power. When,
on 1 January 1943, Cardinal Suhard, in his archbishop's office,
gave his blessing to Fr Adrien Bousquet, first clandestine chaplain to the workers, he was setting in motion the great missionary
enterprise which was to take priests out of the traditional parochial structures and to plunge them, in the favourite phrase of
that time, 'full into the very stuff of mankind'.

In addition, the Cardinal spared himself no pains to obtain an
official status for the chaplains, as witness this letter to the head
of the French Government, Pierre Laval, dated 6 February, in
which he explained the situation and the solutions he requested: [6]

Mr President,

I am voicing the anxieties of the cardinals, archbishops
and bishops of both zones in submitting to you the following considerations:

At a time when the number of French workers in Germany
exceeds the population of several of our dioceses put together, it is our duty to provide for their religious needs.

The great majority of these French workers are Catholics.
From more than 1,300 German factories they have asked for
chaplains. In many camps they are far from any place of

[6] From Fr Bouëssé's papers.

worship, and although in certain towns they have found churches, they ask for French priests. Some, in fact, have already died without the consolations of their religion, to the great distress of their families. The whole episcopate voices the anxiety of these families, who see their fathers or sons leaving without a priest, whereas convicted prisoners, even those condemned to death under common law, have the right to the help of religion.

Further, these families very justly point out that to leave these young men without the spiritual support to which they are accustomed is to leave them open to all sorts of propaganda, including that of the Communists.

We therefore approach you, Mr President, by means of this letter to ask you to propose a solution to the German authorities; the clergy will not hesitate to bear their part of the burden which weighs on the working class.

We propose that, as chaplains to serve the French workers in Germany, there should be sent either priests who are prisoners in the Oflags, sent for this purpose on leave from imprisonment, or else priests sent from France.

It is perfectly understood that these priests would have a religious mission, for which we take full responsibility, all political activity being excluded. They would be nominated by us and appointed in full agreement with the German authorities. They would have the necessary faculties to exercise their ministry, including facilities for moving about in the regions assigned to them. They would perform their mission in the framework of the rules of the Reich concerning foreign workers, and according to our directives, conveyed to them through Abbé Rodhain, whom we have already appointed to represent us in this question of the workers' chaplaincy.

I venture to count on your good will, Mr President, to obtain for us, as soon as possible, an effective solution to this grave and urgent problem.

I have the honour to remain ...

On 15 February the Cardinal sent a message of encouragement to a fresh contingent of workers being sent to the STO, but several sentences were forbidden by the censors.

As the authorization to send chaplains officially had still not arrived, it was then decided to step up the secret departures. On 2 and 3 March, in the Rue Barbet-de-Jouy, a score of priests, volunteers for this mission, gathered round him to receive their instructions before going to the German factories. During the meeting, which also included lectures on the economic and social position in Germany, and on life in the prisoners' camps, Fr Evrard, a young Dominican, noted down the Archbishop's words. As he spoke very slowly, punctuating his words and repeating some phrases, the following notes may be taken as practically *verbatim*.[7]

Approaches have been made to the French and German authorities with a view to constituting a chaplaincy to the French workers of the STO in Germany. In a letter to President Laval we have suggested that some priests who are prisoners in the Oflags, or priests from France, personally chosen by the Cardinal-Archbishop of Paris, should be appointed by the French authorities, with the agreement of those of Germany, to carry out a priestly mission to these workers, excluding all political activities. We have pointed out the reasons for this mission: many of the young workers are Catholics; some of them have asked for chaplains, and many families have expressed the same desire, complaining of these workers' isolation.

Some priests have already asked to enlist as workers. The existing Canon Law would seem to be opposed to such enlistment. On the other hand, it is uncertain what the exact situation might be. If there were requisition, for example, all difficulty on that score would cease.

Things would be quite different if they could be appointed as chaplains. We have already asked for priests from the officer-prisoners to be sent to the workers, and we may hope that a certain number of these may soon be distributed

[7] From Fr Bouëssé's papers.

among them. But it would be a good thing, in spite of the
scarcity of priests in France, if a certain number could be
sent directly from our country: the gesture would be appre-
ciated by the families and would prove to them that the
bishops were not unmindful of their lot.

YOUR MISSION

What sort of mission would these priests have? It would be
one of great responsibility, because of the role they would
have to fill.

1. *A mission of salvation* for the souls of the workers, who
are subjected to the repercussions of the international drama.
Moral support and mutual help; the worst danger is isolation.

Can we hope that the conditions imposed on the priests
will allow of this contact? They will not be given permission
to enter the working sites, but only to put themselves at the
disposal of the workers, in the parish churches; a notice
would be posted in those working sites where there are
French workers. To begin with, they would obviously have
to put up with the conditions available.

They would have to help the workers to overcome the
moral dangers and all the abuses which arise from isolation,
and the intellectual dangers, Marxist or totalitarian ideologies,
which may infiltrate the sites. This mission will be carried on
directly to those who approach the chaplain, and indirectly
to all the others. There is immense scope here.

2. *To represent the Church there*, where the Church is
particularly committed. To the workers, to other Frenchmen
(prisoners, commandos), to the Germans who will observe
your conduct, for example the German clergy, who will wish
you well, but may judge the French workers. Again, to represent the Church in the face of Nazi and Communist
ideologies, and of events which may take very varied forms.

Never forget that the situation may change considerably
from day to day.

3. *To represent France and make her respected,* in a particularly painful situation. To keep respect for France very
high. There is a worthy manner of bearing trials: the workers
may not always understand this. The prestige of France, the
prestige of the Catholic faith: two points of which the
workers must continually be reminded and which form part
of the chaplain's responsibilities.

4. To safeguard, in this situation, the *Catholic Action* of
the French Church. You all know the important place of
Catholic Action in our Church's life. That activity is already
being shown in a foreign land; this is something characteristic
of our people's exile and captivity, a fact of great importance.
Even more than in time of peace, the real strength of
Catholicism is to affirm our faith, to show it, to live it, dis-
creetly but publicly. So, carry on Catholic Action there, with
devotion and zeal, but also with the wisdom and discretion
required by the situation.

In this field of Catholic Action, what will you be able to
undertake? That will depend on the precise situation and the
powers granted to you. Prudence, first of all, before you can
govern events! In all cases, abstain from any sort of political
manifestation.

5. *To prepare for the future.* Periods of shocks are the
prelude to revival. See how, even in these trials, there are
resources for the future! The great thing is to profit from
the period of trial in order to make this revival as wide and
as effective as possible, and no one knows better than the
workers what the trial means.

The future may be decided first in Germany. The attitude
of the Christian workers can have considerable influence,
which may even affect the leaders. The young men will
return and they will play an important part in the recon-
struction of the country.

YOUR RESPONSIBILITIES

What will your responsibilities be? They will be in proportion to your mission and the means of your activity. These means must be carefully prepared.

1. *Christian loyalty.* Frankness in the exercise of your ministry. It is one thing to have a personal opinion, another thing to display it publicly. You have a spiritual mission; 'dissidence' has nothing to do with it. Do not forget, too, that a priest is never isolated; he is always dependent on the hierarchy. In the exercise of this ministry there is no place for any deviation in a pro-German or anti-German direction. Systematically exclude any *openly* dissident policy. Otherwise you would do better to renounce what might be possible as priestly ministry.

2. *Wisdom and prudence.* No needless zeal, but always encourage and support the workers! You must not arouse in them a feeling of opposition to the work they have to do. It is a question of tact. The success of your mission depends first of all on your devotedness. Share their life, bear all their difficulties and sufferings.

3. *Priestly bearing.* You will be a spectacle to all. Live with frank, enlightened piety. There is room for a certain austerity, imposed by circumstances. Never forget that France is in mourning.

Dignity. As you are, so will you be respected, even by the Germans.

In conclusion, your business is essentially to prepare for the future. That task will appear to you in a favourable aspect! Lasting, effective work in the spiritual sphere does not go well with euphoria. Easy work leaves no fruitful trace, nor does violence. But to work hard, in suffering, is to work securely. Your mission will enable you to 'realize' for yourselves the problem of suffering, of trial. After these days there will be others still more difficult. To overcome the present trial is to be ready to overcome those of the future.

It is clear that the Cardinal's idea at this time was simply to provide the presence of some priests among the French workers of the STO. He was still thinking of the work of priests in the factories only in terms of a practical solution to the problem of sending them to Germany. As they could not go as chaplains, they had to go as labourers. If the worker-priest of 1946 originated largely from the labourer-priest of 1943, the latter, in the Cardinal's mind, was not so much a stable member of the working class as a chaplain temporarily attached to it. In this there was nothing theoretical, simply the response to a situation.

About this time he received from Abbé Bousquet, working as a fitter in the Berlin area, his first reports, full of realism and enthusiasm. His activities, he wrote, included the celebration of Mass four times a week, Catholic Action meetings almost every night, and several hours of confessions. He had already administered three baptisms in February, four first communions in the next month, and on 7 March he had collected the Berlin 'militants' in retreat. Admitting that they were all leading 'a very hard physical life', he still continued: 'These are the happiest hours of my priestly life'.

It is in the context of these first days of the secret chaplaincy, in its atmosphere of intense apostolic activity, that we should read the following pages of his private diary, dated 20th March 1943: [8]

My mind is more and more haunted by the thought of the dechristianized masses. We take note of a fact—the mass of our population no longer thinks itself Christian. Between them and the Christian community there is a gulf . . . which means that to reach them we must go out from ourselves to them!

That is the real problem. So far our efforts have been almost fruitless. Even our ordinary Catholic Action owns itself powerless. It is an action on 'Catholic milieux' at the lowest level of belief. It is not Catholic Action on 'pagan milieux'.

So *The house trembles* and is in danger of collapsing

[8] From Cardinal Suhard's private diary, 20 March 1943, folios 197-9.

unless we consolidate it by infusing faith into these pagan souls. They are the majority. Tomorrow they will be the ruling power, primarily because they are the majority, and then because they are liable to be captured by a mystique which will galvanize them and give them power. Finally, because we cannot expect the governing milieux to act effectively on them.

To consolidate it, nothing less is needed than an intense Catholic Action, organized and strong. Above all, we need a *missionary Catholic Action*. For we must reach them 'in their milieu', with their habits, their good qualities and their faults, along with their *opposition* to everything that *constitutes the Christian community*, and their distrust of it. In addition, we have to infuse into them the Christian mystique, in the manner which can reach them and which they can understand.

For such Catholic Action we need priests who are devoted and convinced, who are also priests of real character.

Devoted and holy, because this is a work which God will make fruitful only by employing ministers who are adequate, comprehensive. The minister's action is here of the first importance. He must be a *'missionary to a pagan people'*.

They must be specially applied to this work, for they have to be trained *outside the Christian community*. Therefore they must be the special missionaries of Christ.

—They must be wise.

—They must be *apostolic*.

—They must be devoted to reconciling two worlds.

If we are to have these priests one day, we must now have generous seminarists, who can surrender themselves, who believe in the action of conquest and do their utmost to achieve it.

A deep doctrinal training, for the subject is important. Our task is to restore a world to rights, hence apostolic formation, formation for wisdom and prudence, formation for a special

missionary life, with an outlook on the Christian world ...
which must not be neglected.

If we are to have such seminarists, there must be directors
and superiors who are themselves convinced and, in the service of that conviction, give direction, create an atmosphere,
give teaching and direction which are steeped in that spirit.

HAS THE PRIEST THE RIGHT TO BE A WORKER?

The day after the Cardinal wrote these lines, Abbé Rodhain
presented new arguments to the ACA for intensifying the newly
started movement, for giving it, if necessary, fresh justification
and for taking stock of the first results. Concerning the need for
the presence of chaplains and the manner of that presence—
manual labour—he declared emphatically: [9]

The spread of Catholic Action in certain German factories
is proudly claimed, and I should be the first to quote with
joy the letters which tell of it. But already we can guess at
possible deviations. The militants have certainly given proof
of successful boldness and providential initiatives. But in a
few months, when the propaganda of ideas will be more
apparent, when they are faced with these doctrines of force,
faced with these mystiques which from some aspects are
humanly so advantageous, will they be able to detect what
is pernicious in them? Their apostolic formation has been
effective for influencing their own milieu, but have they
enough doctrinal training to be able to judge the orthodoxy
of what is put before them? For this reason above all, their
leaders will need to have by them priests with a solid theological training.

Then again, in our sermons we honour St Paul the tentmaker, St Vincent de Paul voluntarily becoming a galley-
slave, St Francis Xavier embarking in disguise, Fr de Foucauld living like a Tuareg, and thousands of missionaries
who have adopted the same method of the shepherd putting

[9] From Fr Bouëssé's papers.

himself among the sheep, in the same condition as theirs. And we argue from this to the apostolic spirit of the Church.

Now at this moment there are more than 600,000 Catholics beyond the Rhine without a single priest. While, for the last fourteen months, permission to send them official chaplains has been continually put off, Protestant pastors, on the other hand, have gone as labourers and are already ministering there.

Several dozen priests have volunteered to go there in the same condition as the missionaries mentioned above, and like the Protestant pastors already at work. They knew that this sort of life—already shared in the same conditions by more than 1,200 priests, prisoners of war, under forced labour —is bearable, provided that the candidates are carefully chosen. They believe that this type of life is hard, therefore apostolic and therefore to be desired.

At the same time, others besides the first chaplains of the STO had taken note of that 'hard type of life', not in order to share it or even to wish it well, wholly apostolic though it was, but to try to have it forbidden. It was unseemly, they suggested, for a priest to work with his hands.

The opposition was strong enough to have its representatives even on the Archbishop's council. It had, therefore, to be reckoned with. It was with the idea of 'guarding his rear' that the Cardinal consulted Fr Le Blond, professor at the Gregorian University.[10] The Jesuit's reply to this consultation is an important document in the history of the workers' mission.

Can a priest, without breaking Canon Law, go to Germany as a voluntary labourer, in the absence of official chaplains,

[10] In the discussion in which he was opposed by certain members of his Council, the Cardinal in fact overstated the weight of this 'theological consultation in Rome'. Fr Le Blond was not in Rome; he had returned from captivity after two years in Germany, but still appeared on the register of the Gregorian University, where he had taught before the war. So the Cardinal, to carry his point, rather forced the note when he said 'We have advice about this from someone in Rome'. The person who gave me this information commented: 'But I do not dislike this wisdom of the serpent in this child of the light!'.

or because the number of those who may be allowed is insufficient?

Yes, certainly. Canon Law, in effect, forbids clerics to practise unbecoming occupations (c. 138), or those which, though not unbecoming, are incompatible with the clerical state (c. 139. 1), or those which consist in 'business and commerce' (c. 142). Now:

1. Even if it were granted that manual labour is incompatible with the ecclesiastical state, one could justify the action of the voluntary labourer-priest by applying the theory of the indirect intention.

2. It is difficult to admit that manual labour is an unbecoming occupation, for that would run counter to the present practice and the tradition of many religious orders, to the example of St Paul and the still higher example of our Lord. On the contrary, in the milieu in which the labourer-priest will live, his work will be a source of edification.

3. To receive *payment* for work is not contrary to the ecclesiastical state (e.g., professors, teachers) and the *negotiatio œconomica* is allowed by all the canonists.

There is therefore no canonical obstacle to the departure of volunteer priests, assuming that the question of their powers will be regularized, apart from privilege, with the ordinary of the place.

It is desirable that the volunteers should be sound in health, both physical and moral.

This brief document, with its firm and clear statement of the position, enabled the Cardinal to overcome the last scruples. Some more priests left at the end of March, with the authorization of the ACA.

Abbé Rodhain could not complain of a lack of generosity, for on 7 April he declared to the archbishops at their next meeting: 'Sooner than have forty excited curates, I should prefer to see in Germany twenty chaplains, full of good sense and dogmatic theology, becoming the discreet advisers of our Catholic Action militants.' Excited or discreet, but certainly clandestine, by August there were twenty-five priests, chosen from some two hundred volunteers, making the Church present in the German factories. Through them the chaplaincy to the workers had become a fact. But more than that, with them began a new way for the gospel to penetrate the working masses, and also a new kind of priest. Besides the names of Bousquet, Giraudet, Manche, Perrin and Dillard, one would have to quote many others. But instead of giving a roll of honour, I shall quote one of them: Pierre de Porcaro, writing from Leipzig in the autumn of 1943: [11]

'UNTO THE ALTAR OF GOD'

7 October 1943. After some pretty trying weeks, faced with the incomprehension of the majority, the contempt of certain strayed souls or the hatred of some madman, the Lord again lavishes his joy on me. I have long hesitated to tell you the reason. Tonight this seems to be the only way in which I can express my gratitude to you. I feel myself surrounded by so many prayers, I know or guess so many kindnesses! In return, I can only give you a little of myself, since, except for my prayer, I have nothing else to offer.

My joy is rather like that of Christopher Columbus. But also, by the grace of our Lord, I have just made a discovery which you will think, perhaps, is rather late: I have discovered the model factory prayer. When I enter the factory gates on the stroke of six in the morning, I say, *'Introibo ad altare Dei'* ('I will go in to the altar of God'). Yes, the saw, the truck of coal to be unloaded, the trailer to be loaded with five tons of cinders, etc. are really the altar on which we offer ourselves together: him and me, with all of you. On this altar I have learned to understand the devotion of our Jocists to Christ the worker. There are still some, I fear, who are shocked at the conjunction of these two words: they would prefer Christ in a dinner-jacket! And yet, like us, he wore the dungarees of his day, whatever they may have been.

[11] From Fr Bouëssé's papers. Abbé de Porcaro was later arrested and deported to the camp at Mauthausen, where he died shortly before the end of the war.

And till he was thirty he was a working man, a real one, who must sometimes have cut his fingers, just like us, with the saw. This devotion is one of the elements which will perhaps enable us to see an end to the barriers between the working class and the Church.

Then I go on to the terrible *Judica me, Deus*: Judge me, O God. Yes, judge me. Are you satisfied with my work yesterday? Did I carry out my mission? Did I play my part properly? Were you recognized in me? 'And honour my cause.' That is not hard for you, for it is your own. I have no cause of my own, only that for which you sent me. *De gente non sancta,* from all this people, dead to grace, impious in its lusts, blasphemous in its speech. 'Deliver me from the unjust and deceitful man', who in the darkness tries to hurt me, whose hate I can feel, as once you did. If I were alone I should be afraid and throw it all up, but 'thou art God my strength', and I want to remember it this morning, while perhaps the sky is dark, *dum affligit me inimicus*: 'while the enemy afflicts me'. *Emitte lucem tuam,* 'Send forth thy light': you who are light from light, the true light which lightens every man coming into the world, word of light coming to scatter the darkness and give light to all the souls who sit in the shadow of death; *et veritatem tuam*: 'And thy truth', the Spirit of truth promised long ago, who must extend and found his empire. Guided all through this day by that light, quickened by that Spirit of truth who will make my day true, I shall be able to stand again, tonight, on 'your holy mountain, before your tabernacle'. Then I shall go up to the true altar where I shall find 'God who gives joy to my youth', who keeps for me the eternal youth, the eternal beauty of the Spirit. Then 'why are you sad, O my soul', this morning? Why this anguish of soul which weighs down my groaning body? Why do even you, Lord, hide yourself or reproach me for my lack of generosity? 'Why do you disquiet me?' All this forms part of your plan. The source of

D

true joy is in suffering.... One thing suffices: 'Hope in God';
that little flower of hope has such an intoxicating scent that
it shuts out the foul smells surrounding you. So with what
faith, what trust and what love I then sing my *Gloria Patri*!

But all this, you see, loses its charm when it is written
down. It has to be lived. Imagine the surroundings: the
roar of machinery, a chap barking out orders which we
can't understand, trucks full of cardboard crossing or collid-
ing, a machine which refuses to start and gets more curses
than oil. In dungarees, without socks or shirt. The silence
in the din. And in a corner, working away, these thoughts,
followed by the hymn *Veni Creator*! That's an amazing life!

I don't want to preach a sermon. This isn't a sermon, its
just life. At bottom, we are rather on a cross of light. That
cross is no *ersatz*, believe me! Those ten hours in the factory
are not always great fun, and I'm often longing for Saturday
noon. But the light is so bright, so warm, so intoxicating
that, in short, everything is fine.

20 October. I am well into my sixth month now. On the
whole I don't think it has been time lost. But the more the
weeks pass, the more startling, is the separation between good
and evil. The life here involves such struggles, our poor
young men live in such an atmosphere. Some of them have
tried vaguely to react, but the seed had fallen on stony
ground or among thorns and they have fallen back, often
lower than before. Others remain hermetically sealed and,
I fear, become the most persuasive apostles of evil. The black
market is disgusting, so is the immorality. Happily, among
all this an élite is being formed. Our beloved Catholic Action
has done good work. What admirable souls it has forged, all
haunted by the thought of souls to be saved!

Next Saturday, to my great joy, I administer my third
baptism!

Saturday, 23 October. I have just read that thought of P.
Prin: 'God, who makes the crosses, also makes the shoulders,

and he is unequalled in the art of proportions'. How true
that is! We could add that these crosses are not made of
dead wood, but of still living wood, and its flowers are
watered with blood from the shoulders....

The reverse side of the medal. The delegate to the Berlin
youth, here, in the presence of the camp delegates, prohibited
the JOC, which is, he says, an antisocial movement! And
our regional delegate announced that he would break up all
existing movements (the JOC being especially aimed at). Unable to do anything, they find that destroying (or trying to
destroy) is as good as working. Poor little things! They
think they are charged with a mission and are able to halt
the preaching of Christ by his apostles. *Non possumus non
loqui* ('We cannot but speak'). I am public enemy number
one! Much froth and spitting. It is really very funny to see
young monkeys playing at being grown men. Ought we not
to be, in Claudel's words, 'the man who holds out a candle
to give light to a whole procession'? Pray to our Lord that
I may be a living candle which is consumed in giving light,
and can still be held out to give light to the procession of the
apostles.

It was not only in German factories, however, that the struggle
against the apostolate in the working world was raging. In Paris,
on 3 August, Abbé Guérin, national chaplain of the JOC, was
arrested by the Gestapo and the movement's offices in the Avenue
Soeur Rosalie were seized. This measure was part of a campaign
against all forms of Catholic Action, not only against the JOC.

In the police station the following dialogue took place:
'Worship in the churches, all right. But no Catholic Action!'
'We do not agree. For religion is not only worship, it is life.'
'Catholic Action is forbidden by order of the German military
authorities.'
'I shall continue on the orders of my head, Cardinal Suhard,
Archbishop of Paris.'

The latter, since the chaplain's arrest, had openly backed him
up by at once offering shelter to the central body of the JOC in
his own villa at Bagneux. It was again through the repeated and
urgent applications of 'his superior' that Abbé Guérin obtained

his freedom on 23 December, after three months of imprisonment.

In this way, not too badly, and thanks to the tenacity of the Archbishop of Paris, Catholic Action in the working world was able to carry on in France and in Germany during those dark years.

4. THE MISSION DE FRANCE

During Advent 1955, Fr Vinatier, Vicar-General of the Mission de France, thus addressed the community of Saint-Séverin in Paris:

Since the Liberation, the missionary apostolate in France has shown extraordinary vitality and growth. It was not started by the Liberation; it was the result of long and laborious preparations in the background. But that period of excitement, revival and enthusiasm enabled it to spread.

There was then in France a Churchman who could listen to the deepest appeals of the world of today, who could encourage, in a positive way, the most varied missionary efforts. By a dispensation of Providence, this man was a cardinal of Holy Church, archbishop of the capital of France, and was thus placed at the heart of the most agonizing problems, at the meeting-place of the most generous ideas, the crossroads of all the missionary efforts. Cardinal Suhard was the most prudent of men, even in the heart of all the boldest enterprises. The Mission de France and the Mission de Paris owe their orgin to him, but how many other movements he was able to help and encourage!

It must be left to the Cardinal's biographer to describe the men or the currents of ideas which contributed to the foundation of the Seminary of the Mission de France by the ACA, on 24 July 1941, a foundation in which the Cardinal played a prominent part. Here I need only recall its preparatory stages.

The origin of this missionary movement was the discovery and realization of an enormous and shocking truth: that rural France was largely dechristianized. There was also the desire to find modern and appropriate solutions to this problem. Here certain names must be mentioned.

In 1937 Victor Bettencourt, pioneer of rural Catholic Action, founder of the review *Mon Village* (1932) and the journal *Foyer rural* (1936), published his book *L'Apostolat rural*. The work had a preface by Mgr Suhard, then Archbishop of Reims. In his last chapter, entitled 'Terre de mission, apostolat specialisé',[1] he looks forward to the creation of a 'seminary of home missions', designed to train specialized priests in a rural apostolate of a missionary type, and also an 'Oeuvre rurale de la propagation de la foi'[2] which would undertake the evangelization of the paganized countryside. Quoting some alarming figures and exposing humanly desperate situations, the author wrote again, in the same year, in his review: 'The immediate need for a clergy of conquest, supplementing the resident clergy, seems obvious. It is an appeal to the young to find the missionary priest who could give back religious and social life to lands which are dying without him.'

Abbé Féron, a priest of the diocese of Cambrai, who had been nominated by the 1936 ACA as national chaplain to the JAC, made a tour in the winter of 1937 in the Creuse department. There he found deserted parishes, 'solitary priests' (about whom Abbé Gellé lately had recently written a little book), parish registers blank for years past, regions where for a generation there had been not a baptism, not a church marriage, not a religious funeral, where not a soul made his Easter duties, not a man practised. It was here that he heard 'the appeal of the priestless Church', of which he so often spoke.

An article by Canon Audrain, superior of the Versailles major seminary, published in *L'Union* in 1938, a report by Fr Achard, member of the Mouvement des Foyers ruraux[3] (MFR, founded in June 1939), and many other voices, all pointed to identical conclusions. These were that the evangelization of the countryside compels a break with the accepted idea of the isolated resident rector; there must be missionary teams, and certainly a new type of priest, closer to his flock, there must also be a better distribution of the clergy and a real equalization between the 'rich' and the 'poor' dioceses. And all these questions must be dealt with on the national, not the diocesan level, so that the aim must be the opening of an interdiocesan seminary or institution capable of training these missionary priests.

---

[1] Missionary country: a specialized apostolate.
[2] Rural organization for the propagation of the faith.
[3] Rural homes movement.

THE TRAGEDY OF THE FRENCH COUNTRYSIDE[4]

Here, for example, are Fr Achard's remarks in his report on the
religious situation in the rural world.

Our traditional methods no longer suffice in the dechristianized countryside. For more than twenty years this problem has haunted me. Looking around during my vacations as
a seminarist, talking with country priests, I found some only
mediocre, doing themselves well, readily taking advantage
of the situation, others cynical and pessimistic, apparently
without faith in the action of grace, others sincerely pious
and zealous, but nearly always discouraged after some years
of effort. All these contacts left me with a feeling of despair: can we ever escape from this with our present methods?

My experience as a parish priest has only strengthened my
impressions as a seminarist and deepened my conviction that
the priestly ministry, as it exists at present in the traditional
setting of our country parishes, when they are practically
void of all Christian life and only preserve a few formal
practices, can produce only mediocre and superficial results,
never a profound return to Christianity. Moreover, this ministry is often demoralizing for the priest. The task is too
difficult and urgently calls for other methods.

The author then quotes some examples: as soon as a priest begins to 'talk seriously', people stop listening. To compensate for
this lack of success, he soon looks for a diversion in gardening,
bee-keeping, archaeology or local history. . . .

He has made for himself a 'little passion' which fills his
life—would God it were always innocent—and on the side
he carries out his ministry as an honest official: he baptises,
he marries, he buries. . . . Ten years of this life and he is
completely rusted. The more ardent, who cannot be satisfied

---

[4] Report drawn up by Fr Achard for the MFR, towards the end of 1940.
Archives of the Prelature of the Mission de France, Pontigny (Yonne).

with little passions, are sometimes victims of great ones, and then there is scandal.

Those who have kept up their standards end by being discouraged and ask to be moved. The number of these deserted parishes increases every year, and in some cantons (groups of twelve to fifteen parishes) not a single mission has been given for fifty years.

NEED FOR THE MISSIONARY METHOD

The problem is therefore how to form and maintain a really apostolic spirit in the priests. But what instruments, what method, what type of life can we offer them, to provide the maximum return for their zeal?

The life of the pioneer, the settler clearing a virgin soil, requires different qualities from those of the peasant who tills a soil that has been worked for centuries. So the missionary who enters a pagan region uses different methods from those of the parish priest who takes on a 'good parish'.

First of all we must persuade ourselves that many of our French countrysides have again become pagan lands—in spite of some external rites, the importance of which should not be underrated—and that, in consequence, they must be treated for the purpose of the apostolate, as mission fields. This is a truth which has seemed obvious to me for twenty years. It is a good thing that at last we have the courage to proclaim it officially.

The apostolate to the heathen in missionary countries is entrusted to missionaries who in practice have always adopted a certain religious discipline, whether in the canonical sense, with vows, or in a broad sense, like the Société des Missions étrangères.[5]

The apostolate of the most dechristianized regions of France seems to me to require apostles formed in a similiar discipline. All other solutions seem to me insufficient and doomed to failure.

[5] Society for Foreign Missions.

Turning to the 'other solutions', Fr Achard rejects the mere 'export of priests from the richer diocese to the poorer'. He regards it as 'illusory, lazy and an almost useless solution. The overstaffed dioceses—are there still any?—will usually send only their less capable priests to their poorer neighbours. This contribution might suffice to keep worship going, but could not revive a region.' He equally rejects groupings intended to strengthen the inner life or stimulate zeal, such as third orders or associations of priests. 'This solution is still inadequate, because it is not only a problem of spiritual worth but also a question of method. And this solution does not touch the traditional system of the parochial apostolate.' So he envisages a community life at the service of the mission: 'We must start from the idea of mission in the fullest sense, mission in a non-Christian land, and borrow from the missionary apostolate most of its characteristics, which give it its value.'

The training of the rural missionaries and the organization of their work should be entrusted either to a society of secular priests, like the Missions Etrangères, or to a religious congregation. Fr Achard continues:

The dioceses which would like to make the experiment would apply to the Society of the Mission de France, or to a missionary congregation of their choice, and would entrust them with a part of the diocese, a district of two or three cantons, an *arrondissement*—obviously the most dechristianized part. It would need to be a big enough territory, with a special regime and largely autonomous, rather than small islands scattered among the network of ordinary parishes.

The Achard report goes on to consider the training of the missionaries, to be given in a special seminary; he expressly mentions community life as a statutory element of the Mission and describes the action of a team. Round a central village where the missionaries live, the deserted parishes are taken charge of jointly by five or six priests, 'provided with small cars'. But this joint charge is not enough to constitute the presence of the Mission in a given area: new methods must be added.

The missionaries must be allowed a certain freedom as regards the organization of religious ceremonies, and likewise for those of burial, marriage and baptism. They should not be bound to the strict application of diocesan scales of payment, or the traditional uses at burials etc., if they conclude that another method would give better results. They should be allowed to abolish the differences of 'class' as to hangings, candles, etc.; to simplify certain ceremonies (with full respect for the liturgy); to speak of certain truths to those who attend a burial and whom they will not have a chance to meet again; to explain in French, at baptism and marriage, the meaning of these sacraments, etc. There is no question of allowing eccentricites or extraliturgical fancies. All this would be discussed in the missionary team and submitted through the district head to the bishop for his approval.

Subsequent paragraphs of this report concern relations with the bishop of the diocese under whose jurisdiction the missionaries are placed, questions of financial and administrative autonomy, and finally the relations between the missionaries and the other parish priests.

They must form a family, in an atmosphere of manly, frank and cordial friendship; a real team, in which each member is always ready to back up his comrades for the success of the common task, not selfishly pursuing the success of his own work. Sincere zeal for souls and an intense spiritual life must triumph over the difficulties which will inevitably arise from faults of character and divergent views.

With the diocesan clergy relations must be cordial, so as to leave no excuse for jealousy. Willing to help, the missionaries will devote themselves to helping neighbouring priests, provided that the task is one which is worth the trouble and does not interfere with a greater good elsewhere: not, for example, assisting at a pompous funeral where 'class' requires a certain number of priests, while at the same time a group of young people is deprived of its chaplain. They will not willingly go to preach a sermon for some occasion of ceremony, but they will gladly go to help organize Catholic Action in a neighbouring canton, or to preach a retreat to Jocist militants.

By its example, a district which is well on the move in a diocese will reanimate the courage and apostolic spirit of the other priests. It will preach by the witness of its example. To all the cynics who repeat that nothing can be done it will prove the possibility of movement by moving.

Abbé Féron knew and followed all these notes and plans, all this work of reflection. Convinced that they contained the elements of the true solution, he confided these ideas of Mgr Chollet, Bishop of Albi, who asked him to make a précis of them for a report which he himself presented to the ACA in February 1938.

The project of such an 'institute of the missionaries of France', very imprecise, of course, and slackly defended, did not then arouse more than moderate interest among the bishops. To some, it was chimerical, to others it seemed too fine.... Some considered it financially impracticable. Still, the idea seemed to be the answer to a problem too serious to be eluded. The Assembly decided to let it go ahead.

The Sons of Charity were the first to be considered for taking charge of the 'Seminary of the Missions'. But their superior declined this offer on the ground that the members of his institute were not sufficiently rural in origin to supply suitable key men. For a time there was thought of an interdiocesan seminary at Fontgombault, a solution encouraged by Cardinal Verdier, but it came to nothing. Finally it was Cardinal Suhard who, in March 1939, made the first approaches for this foundation to Mgr Picaud, Bishop of Bayeux and Lisieux. It was Cardinal Suhard also who, on 29 March in the same year, wrote to the Carmel at Lisieux and asked it to accommodate this 'spiritual basilica' in the shadow of the Basilica of St Thérèse, being persuaded that a work of this sort ought to be founded near an important missionary centre. In 1939 the ACA ratified these steps and confirmed this choice. But in the winter of 1939-40 the Cardinal had to take a rather firm line with Mother Agnès, the prioress of the Carmel, who wanted to alter the nature of the foundation markedly in the direction of a sort of 'Theresian seminary', too closely tied to the local pilgrimage and the cult of the 'little saint'. These differences of view delayed action for some time.

Further, the necessary men had to be found. The Cardinal approached the Sulpicians, and Fr Boisard nominated, as superior of the new foundation, Fr Augros, superior of the Autun seminary, whom his bishop agreed to 'hand over' at the Cardinal's request (26 August 1941). The 'second in command' was to be Fr Lorenzo, parish priest of Ivry, to whom the Cardinal had

proposed the scheme during a talk in May. 'Does this interest
you?' he had asked, after expounding the plan. 'If it is what I
think it is, it does, and from two points of view: we are all completely unadapted to the situation, from top to bottom, bishops
included. We need missionary bishops. And secondly, I have had
enough of the gospel of the ecclesiastics; I want the gospel of
Jesus.'

The official foundation took place on 24 July 1941 during the
meeting of the ACA, and it was with these two men, still on
their own and with little support, that the Cardinal awaited the
opening of the first session. Paragraph 24 of the minutes of the
Assembly makes this note:

Mission de France. His Eminence Cardinal Suhard gives
us hope that this project will shortly be realized. . . . The site
and considerable financial resources are now assured. The
question of personnel and publicity is being studied. It can
be assumed that the opening will not be delayed for more
than a few months.

In September all the French bishops received the following cir-
cular from the Cardinal:

For too many years the dioceses of France specially affected
by the lack of priestly vocations, and those where the apostolate is known to be more difficult, have suffered a notable
decline in the level of Christian life, and in some of their
regions appear to be almost completely dechristianized.

In order to win back to Christ and the Church so many
populations now practically separated from them, it has been
decided that, under the exalted patronage of their Eminences
and Excellencies and archbishops of France, the 'Mission de
France' should be created, and that a seminary should be
established for the training of priests who wish to devote
themselves to the apostolic work of the Mission, leading a life
in common, and of seminarists who wish one day to join
the ranks of these priests.

The seminary of the 'Mission de France' has been founded
at Lisieux, near the Carmel in which lived and died St

Thérèse of the Child Jesus, that apostolic soul who spent her life, and now spends her heaven, 'praying for priests and missionaries', and whom the Church has proclaimed 'patron saint of the missions'. . . .

These first students of the seminary of the 'Mission de France' could be sent by the archbishops and bishops who wish to avail themselves of the apostolic co-operation of the Mission for the benefit of their own dioceses, in order to be trained for missionary work in the spirit required and to be given the necessary guidance and brotherly collaboration.

Other priests and seminarists could be received in the seminary, with the permission of their respective ordinaries, to prepare themselves for working one day as 'missionaries of France' in dioceses other than those of their origin or family domicile.

In view of the interdependence of the dioceses, and the part which religious life must play in the restoration of our country, it is in our interest, my lords, that the work of the 'Mission de France' should succeed, and that its activity should be guaranteed by a sufficient number of excellent priests.

I am therefore confident that you will welcome it with joy and good will etc.

Emmanuel, Cardinal Suhard,
Archbishop of Paris

Were the bishops to whom this letter was addressed lacking in good will, or merely in pleasure, in support of this common work? The first recruits, in fact, were neither numerous nor excellent. Several diocesan bishops saw it as a chance to get rid of their 'undesirables' and refused to part with their best men. When Fr Augros arrived at Lisieux on 8 September he found himself in the unfortunate position of being a superior with neither staff nor students. Painfully surprised at what he called the 'obvious indifference of the bishops', he then turned to the Cardinal, who encouraged him with this letter of 22 November 1941, which we may regard as the real foundation-charter of the new work.

Dear Father Superior,

The problem faces us, and it must be resolved with all prudence and courage ... and confidence!

The real reason which justifies the 'Mission de France' and the seminary of this Mission is this: there are vast regions in France which, because of their loss of Christianity, are similar to mission fields. Now these disinherited regions have, in fact, no missionaries, either because in those regions there is and always will be a lack of priests to evangelize them, or because the very few priests who come from there are not prepared for a missionary life. And that is a grave danger, not only for those deserted regions, but for the whole country. Hence the need:

(1) To call to the help of these dioceses priests who come from more favoured regions and to give both to them, and to priests belonging to the said dioceses who desire it, training for the missionary life.

(2) This leads me to make clear that although they are distinct by their training, and perhaps by their manner of life, from the priests of the ordinary diocesan clergy, these missionaries will always consider themselves as belonging to that clergy, will make it their duty not to become isolated, and under the bishop's orders will try to work in close collaboration with the other priests, though sometimes in their own manner.

In these ways, we hope, they will be able to draw their colleagues on to follow them. That would be a success. In a word, we do not wish to destroy, reverse or overthrow anything, but to build, to advance and to help in construction and progress ... on new foundations and according to certain rather new methods. For a work like this, there is nothing so valuable as brotherhood in action.

(3) This is perhaps the place to reply to an objection: under this scheme, what will happen to the parishes? The answer is that we have no intention of wrecking the parishes,

THE MISSION DE FRANCE

upon which and for whose benefit we mean to build. But at present, while these parishes may exist in theory, they are in fact formally non-existent, and certainly not operative. Our aim is to make the parishes 'living and operative', then adapted to their milieu, and finally to stabilize them in that 'parochial state' which will be an 'operative and viable' state.

(4) In the formation of the missionary priests, we have to insist on a solid intellectual, and above all theological training. The reason is that the missionary must have knowledge in himself, because in his knowledge lies, in part, the secret both of his prestige and of his spiritual nourishment. He must know in order to instruct others. His hearers may be ignorant of religion, but they are not necessarily ignorant of secular knowledge, nor intellectually impoverished. Even from that point of view they have needs which must be satisfied. They listen to those whose teaching grips them. He must have the knowledge to train Catholic Action leaders who are destined to devote themselves and also to know themselves with a view to guiding others. He must know how to adapt himself by clear and well-considered teaching.

It follows, then, that while the seminary of the Mission does not aim at forming intellectuals, it must aim at forming cultivated minds, with a love for intellectual work which they carry with them into their apostolic labours. It follows that the teaching given them will aim at forming, not so much 'men learned for themselves' as men who know how to teach and possess the method of teaching, for in that spiritual pedagogy lies the apostle's secret. It follows that the teaching in the seminary must be clear, objective, positive and scholastic, without subtleties, but plotted on the axis of a sane and luminous doctrine.

May St Thérèse guide and sustain your efforts, dear Father Superior, and then success will be certain.... But it will be so, only through what it has cost, and in the measure of what it has cost.

Please believe in my entire devotion and in my faithful
attachment to you and your work, which is the work of God!

A man as active as Fr Augros could not sit down under this first
rebuff. Since he had no seminarists at Lisieux, he had to go and
find them where they were. Taking up his pilgrim's staff, he set
out, and between January and July 1942 he toured sixty dioceses,
visiting bishops, giving conferences and making the foundation
known.

He met with varied receptions. At Châlons and Coutances
the bishop refused to see him. At Verdun the bishop said he was
'constrained' to give him an audience. 'I am obliged to receive
you, am I not? You come with a little reflection of the purple.'
This remark illustrates the fact that while it was the Assembly of
24 July 1941 which gave the Mission its existence, it was the
Cardinal's persistence which effectively carried it through. His
colleagues trusted him, some, like Mgr Fillon of Bourges, wholeheartedly, others with a somewhat sceptical acquiescence.

After his tour of France, Fr Augros summed up the spirit of
the Mission in a number of the *Semaine religieuse* on 1 August
1942:

To understand the full significance of the French bishops'
decision (in the Assembly of Cardinals and Archbishops of
24 July 1941), certain facts must be borne in mind:

(1) The dechristianization of the countryside (already a
fact in vast areas, and on the increase) and of the big towns
(where the Church reaches between two and ten per cent
of the inhabitants), with this corollary: the lack of priests.
In order to have priests we must have Christian families.

(2) This dechristianization does not consist simply in the
absence of Christian practices or of faith, but in the fact that
social life (political, economic and domestic) is not influenced
by the gospel.

(3) While this state of things has well-known contemporary
causes, its real causes lie far back and very deep. We are
witnessing a crisis of growth among mankind.

To cope with this situation, the episcopate has concluded
that we need:

(1) A clergy more equally distributed territorially. Where

the main task is to preserve, we have many priests, but elsewhere there is famine.

(2) A more organized clergy, instead of an isolated clergy: communities of priests, in charge of one or several parishes: an apostolate of communities co-ordinated by the bishop.

(3) A missionary-minded clergy, animated with a spirit of service, which implies a forgetfulness of self and a self-denial perhaps greater than for one sent to a distance. In this highly-developed society which has to be won back to Christ, the priest must be one who is prepared to 'manage' nothing, to keep nothing in tutelage, but consents to accept that very humble but thrilling task: to infuse the Spirit of Christ into all human life, so that it may be spontaneously and totally lived for God.

To attain this end, it has been decided to found the Seminary of the Mission de France: to bring together and train for their missionary task those seminarists and priests whom the Holy Spirit may call, especially, we must hope, from the richer dioceses.

What stage has the Seminary reached? Only God could say. He alone sees how the sowing and the germinating proceed. A new term will begin in October.

The enterprise encountered not only sceptics but opponents. On 4 August the Cardinal's successor in the see of Reims, Mgr Marmottin, wrote him these lines:

Your Eminence,

Allow me to express to you the astonishment I felt on reading the short article on the 'Mission de France' in the last number of the *Semaine religieuse de Paris*. I have read it through two or three times, and have read it to my staff; we have not understood it very well. I do not like the phrase 'crisis of growth among mankind', which I think is a feature of all times, nor the words 'Christianity which up to now has remained in a state of infancy'; I had never suspected it.

On the other hand, I am surprised to learn that priests must 'manage nothing, keep nothing in tutelage', and this in order 'to infuse the Spirit of Christ into all human life'. I thought we were doing nothing else, even before the Mission de France.... I am disturbed. I was so already, when I saw and heard the author of this article. I beg your Eminence's pardon for thus telling you what I think.

Fr Augros' efforts, however, were successful. In October 1942 about thirty students and priests under instruction (among whom was Abbé Godin) gathered around Frs Augros, Lorenzo, Lévesque and Perrot, to form the first 'year' of this Seminary of the Mission, in which (in the words of a Lisieux slogan) 'with no compulsion but much demand' a new spirit was to be formed.

WHAT IS THE MISSION DE FRANCE?[6]

In order to make the Mission known, Fr Augros published a brochure in 1941 (republished in 1945) setting out the history, spirit and objects of the foundation. The Cardinal provided a short preface for the book in which he defined his own idea of the work.

There is a fact which must be made known: there exist in France dechristianized regions, so dechristianized that they no longer possess, and never can possess by themselves, enough priests to evangelize them. How can they emerge from this state without the help of better-provided regions?

There is a truth which must be admitted: spiritually, as from every point of view, France is bound up with the rest of the world. But, even more surely, the various regions of France are bound up with one another. While the good workmen of the gospel must always remember to carry the good news to distant continents, it is imperative that they

[6] Extracts from the preface (1945 edition) to the brochure by Fr Augros, superior of the Lisieux Seminary, *La Mission de France* (in the *Annales de sainte Thérèse de Lisieux*) and from an article by the same author in *Masses ouvrières*, no. 12 (May 1946).

should also think of those regions of France which are so near but so disinherited.

Above all, there is a conviction which must be spread abroad: faced with the chief obstacle which bars our path —the indifference or populations which can no longer react to a religious or even spiritual influence—this new apostolate requires a new adaptation and new methods. The methods of former days will not suffice to bring about the conquest of the dechristianized masses, and on the other hand we have the right to make the fullest use of the means of action now at our disposal, especially for the training of children.

Further, we must never forget that the priests who assume this task need to be sustained against discouragement and to find in more appropriate forms of apostolic life the support which makes it triumph over such difficulties. Nor can we forget that such priests must be well equipped from the double point of view of discipline and doctrine, as a necessary condition of success in a venture which some have considered daring. Well, then, the future missionaries must have a special kind of preparation! And so the Mission de France must begin with a seminary.

The vocations are satisfactory both in numbers and in quality. The spirit there is good; I have observed it during the various visits I have had the joy of paying you. An intense spiritual life and a serious intellectual formation go hand in hand with fraternal charity, which unites all persons under the leadership of a team of instructors who are themselves perfectly united. Lastly, the seminary remains closely linked with the existing missionary communities, with whom thoughts, prayers and sacrifices are exchanged.

God be praised for so many graces!

St Thérèse has protected the work entrusted to her. For the Mission de France remains more than ever under the patronage of St Thérèse of the Child Jesus.

The saint's apostolic and missionary ardour, which was the

complement to her 'little way', her purely supernatural zeal,
which is an example of inner life for our missionaries, and
the patronage she already extended to the foreign missions
of the universal Church, all invited us to put ourselves under
her protection.

The material support on which we counted at Lisieux
has not been lacking, nor the support of the Carmel, heir of
her favours, her spirit and her promises, nor the special
kindness of the Bishop of Bayeux and Lisieux. To these
outstanding benefactors of the Mission de France we take
the opportunity of publicly expressing our gratitude.

With all my heart, therefore, my dear Superior, I renew
my blessing, not only to this brochure but to all your labours.
For the results already obtained I add the expression of my
satisfaction and my gratitude, which extends beyond you to
the Society of St Sulpice and to all your assistants.

In the course of time the Superior of the seminary developed a
wider view of the Mission's aims and methods. The blunt candour of his tone and the ideas he put forward brought him some
harsh letters, including some from his brethren of St Sulpice,
and the review which published these lines lost several sub-
scribers. The text which follows reflects the spirit of the Mission
de France after five years of work; the war is over, the priests
who were prisoners of war have returned, the first communities
have been founded and the mission to the workers is about to
begin. The first battles, too, have been joined and difficulties
abound. All this must be remembered if we are to understand the
style of these pages and estimate how much they contribute
which is new, under the appearance of a 'sign of contradiction'.

The JOC was born in Belgium, one fine day, simply
because a priest realized with anguish in his heart that the
working class had apostatized so completely that an adoles-
cent, brought up as a Christian, could not keep his faith once
he started work. He was plunged into such an atmosphere that
paganism seeped into him, in spite of himself. And when
Pius XI sanctioned Canon Cardijn's work, it was because he

too realized that during the nineteenth century the Church had lost the working class.

Each had the same attitude, because they became aware of the same evil, requiring a very definite remedy: the workers' apostles must be workers. They alone can remake their brothers as Christians, because they alone enjoy their confidence, and above all, because they alone, being part of the working class, can modify its spirit, change its mentality.

And what is true of the working world has been found equally true for the other social classes and milieux: the Church is no longer present to human society. She can no longer act as leaven in it: hence all the pagan atmosphere which penetrates men's souls. Christ can resume his place and inspire the whole of life (personal, domestic, professional, etc.) only by the action of a thoroughly incarnated and profoundly Christian laity.

If the Church is no longer present to human life, it is not only because there are practically no workers, employers or peasants who radiate Christianity, but also, and perhaps more, because in her whole set-up (priesthood, liturgy, theology, etc.) she is now no longer capable of being present. She is not adapted to modern life. But why this lack of adaptation and this separation? It is because, for the last three or four centuries (but especially in the twentieth), there has been, particularly under the influence of scientific discoveries and consequent technical inventions, such a rapid and profound change of civilization that the Church, imprisoned in ancient habits of thought and action, and preoccupied with defending herself against all sorts of errors and heresies, has not kept abreast. In this twentieth century, when everything is being transformed at breakneck speed, she has remained with an equipment which is medieval, cast in the moulds of the age of the fortresses.

Therefore, what the present needs of the Church require is not simply some powerful specialized movements, but an *immense missionary effort,* organized for the conquest, not of new lands in China or Africa, but of a new civilization, one which is on the way to spread all over the world, a missionary effort which, though different from others in its direction, has the same needs for adaptation and incarnation.

What is the real difficulty in the way of planting Christianity in China? It is not simply the crossing of the ocean, it is the encounter with a new civilization, totally different from our Greco-Latin civilization. It is the problem of freeing Christianity from its wrappings in a European or French mentality and incarnating it in a completely new psychology. It is a tough job, which has not yet really been done, and will not be well done until the day when there are enough Chinese converts. It is they who will create a Christian civilization in China by a synthesis between Christianity and their own mentality.

The same task has to be performed at home with the same difficulties and the same requirements. All the more reason to undertake it and therefore to adopt its methods.

A NEW TYPE OF PRIEST?

The author next speaks of the role of Catholic Action and especially that of the laity. Then he defines the place of the priest in the missionary movement:

The priest, because he is a man, is in constant danger of formalism. He always needs to renew his awareness of what the Holy Spirit wrought in him on the day of his ordination and wills to carry out through him in the Church. If ever he ceases to do this, at once you have priestly officialism. The Church has only to remain in peace for a few years and, unless the Holy Spirit actively intervenes, the clergy as a whole will be bogged down in officialism. And it will take the shock of great events—fruits of the Spirit or of the evil spirit—to force the priest and the whole hierarchy to become clearly aware of God's demands on them.

It is certainly necessary to react against a notion of the priesthood which, on the pretext of making the priest a cleric, ends by putting him among the worthies of the middle class, or else making him a sort of monk.

The priest must be incarnated in order to incarnate Christ and all his power of life with him, and to make him the effective yeast in the heavy dough of humanity. This necessity is even more urgent and goes even further than is commonly supposed. No doubt it raises a problem of dress, speech, standard of living and dwelling-place. But there is more to it than that: it is a question of mentality. The priest has a middle-class mentality and his Christianity is usually allied to that mentality, just as in the European missionary who goes to China religion and culture are linked.

And there is a question of civilization. Christianity in its current expression (theological and liturgical) and in its apostolic action is bound up with a vanished civilization. By that very fact it is cut off from the present civilization, which is thereby condemned to be pagan. The problem is how to incarnate Christianity in another mentality, another civilization. That is a question of life or death.

We can then understand how all these priests, burning with apostolic ardour, who feel cut off from those they are charged to save, experience an urgent need to break with all that separates, and long to become one with them, to the point of becoming laymen among laymen.

They will have to learn to measure more precisely how far the breaks should go. Christ made himself a carpenter: he did not cease to be the Word of God. Fr de Foucauld became an Arab without ceasing to be a priest of Jesus Christ. St Paul was a tentmaker without ceasing to be an apostle.

One day, perhaps, our Lord will call priests in some way

... to become working men, artisans, peasants, not just for a period but permanently.

All these will still have to be able to remain priests, all the more so because they will look less like them, and all the more so in the essence of the priesthood.

The priesthood is not a matter of behaviour. It is a matter of soul, of inner life, of ontological and psychological relation with Christ, of redemptive function in the Mystical Body. That is what must be saved and made effective in the modern world. It is that essential priesthood which must be incarnated in the present civilization. That is what our age needs.

It was in order that mankind should be saved that our Lord willed to remain present to all ages, all places, all civilizations, under a perceptible form, in that sacrament which is the priest. If we refuse to be that sacrament there will no longer be in the world that spring of living water to which Christians constantly need to draw near that they may drink.

Our dream, in the seminary of the Mission de France, is to discover and construct a priesthood completely stripped of all that is not essentially itself, all clerical or ecclesiastical wrapping, all laicization (or specialization), a priesthood which, because it is very pure, is capable of being incarnated in all conditions of time or place, among country people, townsmen or the working class; one which is capable of being itself and playing its part under conditions of persecution as well as in a setting of normal life.

Will we achieve this? At all events, we are striving to work in this direction, trying to discover, by looking back into the remotest past, the great prophetic and priestly tradition which is at the origin of the Church of today: from Moses to Christ and from the apostles to the bishops and priests of our time. We do this chiefly in order to penetrate their spirit, to grasp the profound aim which animated these

men, to understand better the mission which they received
from the Father, and how they performed it.

And in so far as we make this discovery, we must live by
it, must identify ourselves with what is essential and eternal
in it: must accumulate in ourselves the dynamism of the
Spirit, the strength of God, the redeeming charity, so as to
be ready for the necessary commitments when the Father's
will demands them. And all this, unreservedly within the
hierarchy, because the Church, the Mystical Body of Christ,
is essentially hierarchical, and the simple priest is only, in the
Church, the fellow-worker of the bishop.

That is how we are trying to proceed here, seeking to
fashion priestly souls, completely free as regards all that is
not essential to the priesthood; open to the world in its
state of flux; anxious to enter into it so as to animate and
divinize it; careful not to bind ourselves by any organization
whatever to anything in it which is only the expression of a
moment; willing, at all costs, to follow its movement, until
the day when it has found its balance and is settled, at least
for a time. Only then will there be question of our doing a
work which is in any way definitive, or of thinking to build
the structures of Christendom. Until then, whatever we create
or organize must be regarded as simply experiments, temporary arrangements.

5. THE MISSION DE PARIS
AND THE WORKER-PRIESTS

Easter, 1943, 25 April. In these days of privation and suffering under foreign occupation, Paris lay under the burden of an immense lassitude. At Notre-Dame, the cathedral was packed for the High Mass of Easter. The Cardinal spoke to his people: [1]

My brethren,

On this Easter Day, the fourth of the war, we feel as never before the need for peace. Is not the Paschal feast, above all others, the feast of peace? But what a contrast between the peace which Christ promised on this day to his followers, and the strife and destruction let loose on the world! For there is the heavenly Easter and there is the earthly Easter. One exists in the eternity of a cloudless day, the other exists in strife.

Here on earth, however, we must go to him who is 'our Pasch', the Christ who is immolated for us. He alone can guide us in this earthly pilgrimage. To this Christ you are united by prayer, you are united by the sacrament you have received. I invite you to unite yourselves again to him in spirit: to bring your thoughts into agreement with his thoughts, your Christian souls into harmony with the soul of the risen Christ: 'Have this mind among yourselves, which you have in Christ Jesus' (Phil. 2:5). So let me say in a few words what Christ our Pasch is, and how we ought, in Christ, to share in the spirit of Easter.

In the first place, Christ our Pasch is the risen one, triumphing over suffering and death, bravely bearing them both. The morning of Easter marks his triumph. At that

[1] *Semaine religieuse de Paris*, no. 4648 (1 May 1943), pp. 227-9.

moment his power overcomes every obstacle. But this never-
to-be-forgotten triumph is but the consequence and, as it
were, the fruit of the suffering. The victor is the same who,
three days before, was brutally treated, insulted, flogged,
made the butt of every kind of abuse. The same, remember,
who throughout that terrible drama 'was silent' (Matt. 26:
62), who accepted and submitted. The same who, always
calm and dignified, and wholly inclined to the will of his
Father, consented to be the 'man of sorrows' (Is. 53:3). His
resurrection is inseparable from his passion. If he triumphs
today, it is because yesterday he suffered, he agreed to suffer.

Christ our Pasch is also the just one, the holy one, in whom
right and honesty triumph. That was his pride and his great-
ness in the hours of humiliation. Hated and persecuted he
certainly was, but it was for bearing witness to the truth. It
was because, against proudly paraded injustice, he went to
the defence of the weak and oppressed. It was because he
opposed the straightforwardness of simple and upright souls
to the hypocrisy and falsehood of the Pharisees. It was because he always opposed the power of right to the pretended
right of force. Thus what shines out in him is not some
particular quality, some personal privilege; it is right itself
and justice which are represented, the right and justice for
which he lived and died, the right and justice of his Father,
into whose hands he commended his spirit.

And Christ, our Pasch, is he who triumphs over hatred
by the power of love. Let us follow him through that long
martyrdom, when every human passion is unleashed against
him. From his lips we cannot hear a single complaint, murmur, or reproach. For his worst enemies he has only words
of pardon. Till the end, his only care is to deal gently with
them, to draw them to him, to save them all. And the thirst
which consumes him on the cross is but a sign of his immense
desire to welcome all souls and to give them to his Father.
Yes, my brethren, that is what Christ our Lord willed:

to save all men, because he first loved them all. And the summit of his triumph is that through this universal sacrifice he has secured the most decisive and lasting of conquests, the conquest which makes subjects of men's hearts.

This, my brethren, is what we see in the risen Christ: our Pasch! May all eyes be turned towards him! May all hearts go out to him! He is our help at all times, but especially in the hour of distress. We can count on him. He will save us. He will save us by his power. He will save us, above all, by letting us draw salvation from him, in his spirit and his grace, which are the spirit and grace of Easter.

The grace of Easter, my brethren, is first of all the grace of resurrection and hope. He who has it may be tried, he may suffer, but he is never discouraged, never in despair. The more his powers are worn out, the more they are restored. He may be, in St Paul's words, 'afflicted in every way, but not crushed; perplexed, but not driven to despair; persecuted, but not forsaken; struck down, but not destroyed' (2 Cor. 4:8-9). 'My power is made perfect in weakness' (2 Cor. 12:9). From that power he can draw renewal every day.

The grace of Easter is a grace of energy in the face of obstacles and suffering. It was with the scars of his passion that the divine Redeemer loved to show himself to his apostles and friends in the days before his ascension. As is the master, so are the disciples. No one is strong in this life, certainly no one can be sure of his strength, who does not bear in himself the testimony of suffering which has been mastered and the trace of wounds which have been healed by patient and vigorous effort.

The grace of Easter is a grace of sincerity and truth: 'with the unleavened bread of sincerity and truth' (1 Cor. 5:8), that is, a grace which guards the rights of justice, and also the courage which affirms those rights, as Christ affirmed them at the cost of his life. In this courage, as well, lies the Christian's freedom: his freedom to serve truth and justice, even if it means offending public opinion and standing up to its attacks.

Finally, the grace of Easter is a grace of universal charity. The risen Jesus hated no man; he loved all men, he died for all. When he had risen, he stayed with them to teach them to love one another. Therefore, if a man would be united to him, he must love his neighbour, all his neighbours! The risen Jesus wants to extend his family to the whole world, without distinction of caste, nation or origin. So whoever wants to be joined to his life must accept these family bonds, which are the bonds of an affection without limit. The risen Jesus wants to give peace to the world. So whoever would share in his work must develop charity in himself and around him. For between nations as between men, there is one condition of peace which is irreplaceable and dominates all others: a mutual understanding, which alone can unite men whose stock of natural egoism always tends to divide them.

On this day, my brethren, let us rally round the victorious cross, the standard of our Head: *Vexilla Regis prodeunt*.[2] Ranged behind that cross, and firmly united to Christ, let us pray for the salvation which can come only from there. Call down that salvation on a distracted world which has lost its way. Call it down on our country, always present to our minds, on our prisoners, on our dear ones who have been called to labour in a foreign land, on so many homes in distress, on all who suffer in body or in soul. Call it down especially on souls, so that among the many evils they have to endure, they may find at least, by the grace of Christ, purification, holiness and life. Amen!

---

[2] 'The royal banners forward go'; the hymn of Vespers in Pass

FRANCE, A MISSIONARY LAND?

The next day, Easter Monday, about four in the afternoon, the Archbishop's secretary, Abbé Le Sourd, came to him in his office. In his hand he carried a big file of typescript, with this title on the cover: *Mémoire sur la conquête chrétienne dans le milieu prolétaire, par l'abbé Godin, aumônier fédéral J.O.C. Paris-Nord et J.O.C.F. Vincennes, et l'abbé Daniel, vicaire à Saint-Eloi, aumônier J.O.C. Paris-Est.*[3] The Cardinal already knew these two priests, having followed their efforts and plans for three years. 'Take this, your Eminence, and read it. I think it will interest you.'

At dinner that evening Abbé Le Sourd questioned him. Yes, the Cardinal had begun to look through the script, but its first pages seemed 'diffuse'. He was not very impressed, 'he did not see where it was leading'. He was no doubt going to give up reading it.

'No, your Eminence, keep on with it! The first impression will not last, you will see!'

Back in his room, the Cardinal opened the big volume again. Page after page, it gave a detailed, unsparing description, backed by figures, facts and personal experiences, of the extent to which the diocese was paganized, such as he had never before realized. France, the authors said, is really a 'mission field'; the methods of apostolate are partly ineffective, partly inadequate. It is urgently necessary to find something else.

The hours passed; the Cardinal read on. From chapter to chapter he plunged deeper into a world of indifference, atheism, immorality, the existence and reality of which were revealed to him more intensely than ever before, by hundreds of concrete examples, some of them real tragedies.

When he had finished his reading and closed the book, night had passed. It was dawn on Easter Monday. The Cardinal had not slept.

Driving down to the country house at Bagneux where he went, very rarely, to take a day of rest, the Archbishop said to Abbé Le Sourd: 'I am shattered. I knew a lot, but I would never have believed that things had come to such a pass.'

Before leaving, he had telphoned the superior of the little seminary to join them at Bagneux. It turned out that Fr Augros actually had an appointment with him for the same day: he had to discuss the problems of the Lisieux seminary in the academic

---

[3] 'Memorandum on Christian conquest in the proletarian world. . . . '

year then ending. But in fact the whole day was given up to an impassioned discussion between the four men on the book.

'Your Eminence,' said the superior, 'I think there is much exaggeration in Abbé Godin's pages. In any case, if they were true, they should not be published. The situation they describe is so black that they would discourage many priestly vocations.'

When the Cardinal had returned to his house that evening, he was still under the spell of his emotions of the previous night. During the following days he spoke to everyone about the manuscript, which never left his table. Finally, on 1 May, he received the authors.

Abbé Daniel has preserved a record of the interview. The Cardinal began with counsels of prudence. Certainly, he said, adaptations are necessary, but the task is difficult, and one must take account of what exists and the mentality of their colleagues, of the present parish priests. The traditional parish, of course, cannot cope with all the tasks or with reaching the world which does not come to it, but still, it exists. If priests have to be present to the workers' world in a new way, that way must complement the parish, not destroy it. He understands and accepts the criticisms levelled against the *embourgeoisée* parish,[4] and the scandal given to the proletariat by certain structures of the Church. Yes, something must be done, certain priests must be set free from the parochial ministry and the customary tasks, including Catholic Action, so that they can devote themselves entirely to the Mission. At all costs we must 'fill up the ditch and level the wall' which separates the Church from the working class. We must 'launch the Mission'.

The main lines of what was to become the Mission de Paris were laid down in the course of that conversation on 1 May. In each parish a priest would be selected to be devoted to this task; a central diocesan organization would co-ordinate the work and maintain liaison with the archdeacons, and the whole work would be placed under the Archbishop's personal supervision.

The project for which Abbé Godin was asked to form a team, culminated on 1 July 1943 in the official foundation of the Mission de Paris. On that day, in the Cardinal's office, there were still only five men: Frs Augros, Lorenzo, Levesque, Godin and Daniel. And—a vital point—there was no superior. Abbé Godin insisted absolutely on remaining 'at the bottom'. Who, then, would agree to run an enterprise so far from 'classical', so full of difficulties? During that summer the Cardinal approached six priests in turn, including Mgr Chevrot, rector of St François-Xavier, and Abbé

---

[4] Adapted to the middle class; respectable.

Michonneau of Petit-Colombes, but faced with the magnitude of the enterprise, no one dared to accept.

In September, at the Cardinal's request the *Mémoire* appeared as a book, with a preface by Abbé Guérin, under the title *La France, pays de Mission?*[5] and thus this realistic, blunt report, which many persisted in regarding as 'a bad book', was brought before the public.

But in fact there was no one more profoundly priestly and supernatural than Abbé Godin. He had written: 'Not to be a priest-photographer, or a priest-radiographer, or a priest-bee-keeper, or a priest-gardener, or a priest-mechanic or a priest-speculator.... *Simply to be a priest.* You don't become a priest for your family or for your mother or your sister, but only for God.'[6] He wanted to be entirely and absolutely a priest of the gospel, ready for all the sacrifice which God wanted from him: 'How far must one go in evangelization? That depends on the graces given to each.... In fact it is impossible to make the sacrifices demanded by the life unless one also makes, in addition, extraordinary sacrifices.

Finally, he knew that 'the more pagan a milieu is, the more will the human element have to pass through the cross in order to become Christian. The path from the human to the divine goes through Calvary.'

Such was the supernatural realism of the priest who wished to be, like St Paul, 'a fool for Christ'. 'Since when,' he used to say, 'have we become Christians in order to do reasonable things?' Every kind of boldness, then, can be allowed, or rather must be risked, for the question is not 'Is this humanly, or ecclesiastically possible?' but 'Is this divinely necessary?'

It was now November. The team was formed. Abbé Hollande, rector of St Anne-de-Polangis, had at last agreed to lead it. On 4 December the Cardinal thanked him for this in these words:[7]

To carry out a work which is commanded by my conscience as an archbishop, and which seems to be so obviously timely, requires much devotion, much self-denial—and also wisdom. It is because I have observed these qualities in you that I have entrusted you with the task of starting it.

Now it is for God to do the rest, or rather for God to

---

[5] English translation, substantially, in *France Pagan?*, London, 1949.

[6] *France Pagan?*, p. 7.

[7] Quotations in the following correspondence are from private sources.

bless the effort and sacrifices demanded of those who will be its first workers. In this path which, though not the easiest, is at least the most fruitful, your archbishop will not fail you. He will work and pray and, if need be, suffer with you!

Today, he thanks you and blesses you.

BIRTH OF THE MISSION DE PARIS

Without further delay, the team met on 20 November at the diocesan house at Combs-la-Ville, in the Seine-et-Marne department, for a first day of contacts, study and reflection. Then followed the long retreat at Lisieux which marked the real start of the enterprise. A report of the following year says:

In order to help them in thinking out the problems facing them, the team called in various experts on contemporary religious and social questions: Fr Chabannaux (of the Foreign Missions), Frs Desbuquois, Villain, Daniélou, de Montcheuil and Varillon (all Jesuits); Frs Chenu and Thomas Philippe (Dominicans); Canon Tiberghien; Frs Michonneau, Guérin, Hua and Dewitte; Frs Augros and Levesque (Sulpicians); Abbé François Laporte, Mlle Paulette Gouzi, Pierre Metay, Paul Hibout and the Daumont family. Abbé Godin was really the moving spirit of those days. He revealed unsuspected theological knowledge, true psychological insight and exact knowledge about the religious needs of the world of the workers.

On 4 January the Cardinal wrote to Fr Hollande to congratulate him on this first stage:

This mission is anything but restful. It is even probable that you will sometimes find it very burdensome. But is that not the pledge of the abundant fruits reserved for it? Moreover, you will not be alone. Neither from the side of this world nor, certainly, from heaven, will you lack timely help in the days and hours when you need it.

E

On 13 January he himself went to Lisieux and gave the team his personal directives, the plan of which has been preserved:

Today a great thing is happening at Lisieux: so thanks be to God, through St Thérèse, for both the Mission de France and the Mission de Paris! Souls are on the move, there is a general stirring: it is realized that our country will rise again only when it is a Christian nation, with a missionary soul. To that end, the Mission de France and the Mission de Paris are *dynamic ideas*.

1. We must realize that the Mission de Paris is a great enterprise. The work of the Mission is the specific work of Christ. He came to save souls, he came only for that. The masses are cut off from the Christian community, so the priest must have the missionary spirit. *We do not do the whole of our duty in attending to those who come to church; that would be apathy, a defect in pastoral understanding.*

2. The bases of the Mission: first, the charity of Christ. Then piety, to show the true face of Christ (the piety must be nourished on the gospel). Devotion and total giving of self. We must be prepared for checks, trials, contradictions, misunderstandings. Prudence, which does not exclude boldness,—and a great generosity. Doctrine: we must convince, instruct catechumens by giving them as much of the totality of doctrine as they can take. Discipline: that will be the strength of the group, and the way to avoid aberrations.

3. The stand to be taken. You will have your stand once you have some success. Meanwhile:

In relation to the pagans: you must go in among them, hence boldness. But always remain priests.

In relation to existing Catholic societies: you must use them and be useful to them. In fact it is from them that you will get the first missionaries. Hence sympathetic understanding and good relations.

In relation to the parishes: they exist, and *the Mission must complement them*. Hence, play fair with the parish priests.

The direct object of the Mission de Paris is to convert the pagans. Its indirect object, *to show the Christian community that it has to take a new attitude.* A shock has to be given. Much has been done in this last fifteen years, especially with Catholic Action, but we must go further, and it is for *the Mission to show the direction*: hence, emphasis on truth, modesty, humility, and respect for all good that is being done. Charity towards fellow workers. Frankness towards the Christian community, so that it may realize its duty to make conversions. Put in the souls of Christians a salutary uneasiness.

4. How the Mission is to proceed. Think out a method: then experiments, corrections, necessary adaptations. For success, account must be taken of each man's qualities: each must form himself, re-form himself. You must have tenacity of effort: the Mission is a long-term enterprise; the missionary must be upheld by his love of Christ and his love of the Church.[8]

We too often give the impression that we are 'going round and round' with the people we have already won: the Church must be conquering.

On 15 January 1944, during the midnight mass in the chapel of the Lisieux seminary, the first seven members of the Mission de Paris took the oath drawn up by Abbé Godin.

'In the presence of the Virgin Mary, according to the judgement of the team, and so long as I belong to the Mission, I bind myself on oath to devote my whole life to the christianization of the working class of Paris.'

That night, in the train going back to Paris, Abbé Godin confided to Abbé Guérin: 'Now I can go off. The Mission is launched.'

The good Lord was to take him at his word and demand the sacrifice of the one who had been the soul of the new movement. On the morning of 17 January, in the little room at 47 Rue Ganneron (later to be the centre of the Mission de Paris), they found

[8] *France Pagan?*, pp. 196-8.

his body, asphyxiated by the poisonous fumes from his coal stove. Humanly speaking, his death was pointless, an incomprehensible setback, at the very moment when the work was beginning. 'Unless a grain of wheat falls into the earth and dies. . . . ! That was something Abbé Godin had understood for a long time, ever since he had written:

Yes, I know it is the fate of the corn to be mown down,
And of the grain to be ground under the millstone,
And of the good white bread to be eaten in the end. . .
And no doubt that is the reason . . . ,
Since your Law is a law of redemption,
that everything must be paid for,
that there must be some to pay for the others and for me.

So the Mission de Paris began, in January 1944, with only six priests and a few laymen. We must note that in these first days, while all were agreed on entering as fully as possible into the life of the workers, the question of the priest being a worker was not yet raised, as such. The situation of the worker-priests had certainly been considered for practical reasons in connection with the chaplains to the STO—joining the 'volunteers' for the working-parties had been the only way to get into Germany—but the Mission had not yet expressly chosen this type of 'presence' in the workers' world. It was some months after the foundation of the Mission that Fr Hollande went to the Cardinal (with whom he was in constant touch) to tell him: 'Your Eminence, several of our Mission priests have come to see me lately, without consulting one another, but all with the same idea. They say: "We are getting nowhere. It has occurred to me, if the Cardinal will allow me, to sign on as a workman." ' To which the Cardinal is said to have answered:

'Three or four, you say, and independently? But if this was the Holy Spirit. . . . We must not grieve the Holy Spirit. . . '

After the first experiences of the STO, the Cardinal had had no further hesitation about the principle and usefulness of thus engaging in the world of labour. Besides the theological 'consultation' of Fr Le Blond, he also had in his hands a 'prophetic' document, written fifteen years earlier by Cardinal Laurenti, formerly Prefect of the Congregation of Religious.

It was in 1929, during the Jocist pilgrimage to Rome, that Abbé C. Boland, on the advice of Fr Lebbe, had requested an audience of Cardinal Laurenti. When Abbé Boland had expressed his mind for three-quarters of an hour, the cardinal had given him every encouragement for the projects of which he spoke, and later sent him a letter, dated 9 July 1929, to provide him with sanction in the eyes of all his ecclesiastical superiors. I quote this document here, for it concerns the history of the Mission, and doubtless played some part in Cardinal Suhard's decisions.

Monsieur l'Abbé

Some time ago you told me orally of your plans for the evangelization of the poor factory workers by living their life, in a certain manner and for some time, in order to get near them. I must first of all pay tribute to your zeal and devotion for such a noble cause. As to the means you propose to use, I will tell you quite simply what I think, in systematic form:

1. In some regions socialism is robbing us of a great mass of the workers, plunging them into the abyss of the grossest atheism and materialism. It is a sinking world of men.

2. In this very critical and exceptional situation, the ordinary means seem insufficient. To save souls and bring them back to Christ, an exceptional, extraordinary effort is necessary.

3. First of all, we need thoroughly to know this world, which is so largely unknown to us, to know its needs, material and moral, all its dangers, its sufferings. *It is also necessary for it to know us and begin to love us.*

4. What you propose is in itself extraordinary and exceptional, but it seems to meet the situation, which itself is very exceptional.

5. The application of your plan, however, should be limited to a few carefully selected men, well prepared and supported by mutual aid, with a properly drawn-up rule of life, and under the supervision of the bishop.

6. On these conditions, I think that with the consent of the bishop (if he is pleased to give it) the scheme could be tried. The experience you yourself may gain (always with the bishop's assent) could give us more positive evidence by which to judge it.

7. I must add that this is my purely personal point of view, and it is only as a private person that I express it.

I send you my best wishes for the success of your apostolic desires, and pray God to bless them.

With my most respectful homage,

Your very devoted

Cardinal Laurenti

EUCHARISTIC LIFE AMONG THE WORKERS

There were times, certainly, when the worker-priests felt that the Church's juridical structures were greatly impeding their freedom of action. Their complaints did not yet concern essential matters: the crucial problems of the workers' mission, especially trade union membership, arose mostly after 1949. The questions raised at this initial stage chiefly concerned the necessary adaptations of the priest's life to his working milieu: giving up the cassock, easing the obligation of the breviary and, especially, modifying the celebration of Mass.

On this last point it would be tedious to list in detail all the requests, letters, entreaties and interventions which the Cardinal and the leaders of the Mission de Paris had to produce in 1946 and 1947 in order to obtain certain exceptions from the common law for the worker-priests and their new communities. One example will suffice: on 14 April 1946 the Cardinal wrote to a very high authority in the Roman Curia and asked for 'permission for four priests of the Mission de Paris, who work all day in a factory, to celebrate holy Mass in the evening'. He received his answer by return of post (16 April 1946):

'In view of the fact that the priests engaged in work cannot celebrate holy Mass in the evening with the necessary devotion, although several are recommended by your Eminence,' it was decided that 'this permission should not be granted you; thus these priests will be able to go to bed earlier, and so have sufficient sleep'.

Firmly resolved not to let himself be tyrannized by officials, and also being anxious about a certain climate of ill-will and slander against his first missionaries, the Cardinal thought it necessary to send Frs Augros, Hollande and Laporte to Rome in November 1946 to discuss certain questions face to face. Their report of 3 December plainly reveals the situation at that time:

1. The picture we gave at Rome (to the Pope, the Secretariat of State, Cardinal Pizzardo, etc.) of the missionary problem as it exists in France, and the missionary solutions we are trying to apply (including the presence of the Church through the worker-priests), has, we think, been perfectly understood and even encouraged particularly by the Pope and Mgr. Montini. The request we made for the evening Mass (even in the week) caused no surprise, and even met with agreement in principle, at least for the Mission de Paris.

2. This reception is due to the fact that the authorities of the Church are *worried*, because of what is happening in Italy and in the whole world, which they know more about, now that the frontiers are re-opened. And they are *open-minded* towards anything that can make the Church's mission effective in the post-war world, especially *open* to what comes from France, which they believe to be in the vanguard, for good or evil.

3. If they do not themselves take practical initiatives about the apostolate in the dioceses, it is because, as they see it, this is the business of the bishops, who are the men on the spot, really responsible for this field, and also because, being themselves out of touch with the realities of life, and feeling that situations are so varied, they are afraid of taking sides.

4. Struck by the importance ascribed at Rome to the bishops, we are convinced that a great step forward could quickly be taken if the bishops, seeing the situation clearly, had the courage to inform Rome of the exact state of their dioceses, and to demand, with the authority of those who feel their responsibility, the measures and reforms required by the situation.

5. Having so often observed the prestige enjoyed by Cardinal Suhard, we return convinced that he could do more than anyone else to make the needs of the present situation felt at Rome and to obtain the necessary measures for France (and indirectly for the world), especially if he spoke in the

name of the ACA (which carries weight there), and addressed
the Holy Father directly, nor letting himself be discouraged
by delays or even refusals.

In order to reach and influence the Pope more effectively, the
Cardinal asked one of the chief promoters of the Mission to draw
up a plan of his personal letter to Puis XII. On the margin of
the document which follows, Abbé Lalande added this ironical
note: 'His Eminence would be very grateful to M.M. ... if he
would kindly turn this petition into chancery style, if possible
without weakening the force of the facts as experienced.'

The missionaries, priests and laymen of the Mission de
Paris live an apostolic life, right amongst the pagan mass of
the workers. The only Christians they usually deal with are
converts. They wish to have the hierarchy's commission to
plant the Church inside these paganized communities, in
which, moreover, their priesthood is being exercised in a
very evangelical manner.

But, surrounded by paganism, they cannot lead a life as
hard as that of the first Christians without an intensely
eucharistic life. *Without the eucharist no Christian community
is possible.*

In the Paris region men begin their work at seven or half
past seven in the morning. They often have an hour's journey
or more to their place of work. They must therefore leave
home between six and seven. On the other hand, it is in the
evening that they have their family life, their leisure, their
apparently free life, after working for eight and a half or ten
hours. Even on Sunday, full life only begins in the afternoon. In the morning, they absolutely must rest, to make up
for the short nights during the week and to preserve their
physical strength, undermined by five years of food restrictions. Secular meetings never take place on Sunday morning,
nor do cultural or electoral meetings, nor sporting events or
amusements (cinemas, etc.). For the workers of the Paris

region, it nearly always needs heroism to be present at Sunday Mass.

Now, our Christian militants absolutely must be frequently nourished on Christ if they are to live fully by him and to give him to others; this need arises from their apostolic responsibilities in their milieu, and the moral risks they run in their work. We can prove by countless examples that young men and girls who communicated frequently before their marriage but can now no longer do so, hindered as they are by children, by the weekly shopping (which has to be done on Sunday morning), by fatigue, and the impossibility of getting to a morning Mass in the week. The conditions of social life and of work deprive the greater part of our Christian militants of the eucharistic life.

Our communities of newly-baptized, too, need to be given a eucharistic formation, but this is impossible, for the reasons adduced above. Besides, these new believers need to be initiated gradually into the sacred mysteries. The existing parochial life can neither welcome them usefully nor train them seriously. That training would be valuable during Masses in which they all really take part, Masses said in the evening after work, among their natural community, so that they should not feel out of their element.

Several priests of the Mission de Paris work, with my permission, in factories. They have to say their Mass at half past five in the morning, before going to work. Now they only get to bed at half past eleven or midnight, for their apostolate takes them at night into the families of their workmates. They cannot go to bed earlier, so as to be better prepared in the morning, for then their manual work would lose much of its proper purpose, which is to spend their evenings with the families of the non-Christian workers.

Further, it must be admitted that few physical constitutions can stand that rhythm of life: going to bed around midnight, rising at five and putting in eight or ten hours' work. Finally, a Mass said on jumping out of bed is scarcely prepared as it should be. The mind is then completely drowsy, whereas on return from work, mind and soul have been prepared by the gift of self at every hour of the day.

In view of such a source of devotion, which would be multiplied tenfold by a eucharistic life, I ask, for our priests of the Mission de Paris (for their sake, and to enable their militants and new Christians to share in the eucharistic banquet), authorization to celebrate Mass in the evening—after three hours of fasting from solid food and one hour from liquid—on Sundays and weekdays, when they judge it necessary. They would have to report to me on their use of this favour.

I am perfectly aware that this favour would be exceptional. But I do not hesitate to ask your Holiness for it, for while I give my trust to this team of priests, I know that if they are to accomplish a pioneering ministry in the pagan milieu, these missionaries to Paris need particular liberties and special aids.

In addition, this privilege which your Holiness may deign to grant them would rightly be regarded by the people they evangelize as a maternal gesture on the part of the Church, showing that she can stoop to the disinherited and place within their reach the divine treasures which it is her mission to bestow.

Whether this document actually reached the eyes of Pius XII, I do not know. But we do know that the Cardinal sent him the following letter, dated 6 January 1947:

Most Holy Father,

Knowing how kindly you received and blessed Fr Augros, Superior of the Mission de France, Fr Hollande, Superior of the Mission de Paris, and Fr Laporte, member of the same Mission, during the private audience you deigned to give them, I venture once more to have recourse to your paternal benevolence, to ask your Holiness to be pleased to grant authorization to the priests of the Mission de Paris to celebrate the holy Sacrifice in the evening.

It is, in fact, practically impossible, at least for any length of time, for these priests, so heavily engaged in the life of labour, to say holy Mass in the morning, at dawn. And on the other hand, at that early hour no one is present, while in the evening the whole group of neophytes, whom they have been able to gather round them, throngs the altar in a fervent and united community.

I dare to think that this echo of the primitive Church in our paganized society will once again touch your kind and understanding heart.

In the most filial spirit I entrust this request to your Holiness, and assure you, from this moment, of my profound gratitude for whatever you may judge right to do in this direction.

May your Holiness deign to accept the homage of my very respectful and profound attachment in Christ, and to give your fatherly blessing to the whole diocese of Paris.

DO NOT MAKE TWO CHURCHES

These questions of Mass and the eucharistic fast were solved during that year. But already other problems were arising, and on 15 February 1947 the Cardinal had to sign the last detailed report, demanded by the Holy Office, on the activity and type of life of the first worker-priests. Moreover, some of the anxieties felt at Rome at this time were shared by the Archbishop. One day he confided in the Rector of a big Parisian college:

Monsignor, I am afraid, I really am! I asked them to recite, if not the whole breviary, at least the little hours, or Lauds and Prime, or else Vespers and Compline at night, or else, if they cannot say the breviary, to pray, for one can pray without one's breviary. But I fear that they are not doing so. They don't tell me all they are doing. How can they carry on, poor fellows, if they don't pray?

There was also the question of wearing the cassock. Mgr Suhard, no doubt, did not see what an anachronism this was in the new conditions of life, but fairly soon he gave up requiring it.

More serious was the charge brought against those priests that they were founding a new Church, separate from the others, and not preparing these new Christians to enter the 'normal' parishes.

To all this, Fr Depierre replied, from his community at Montreuil, in this letter of 7 June 1947, some months after the appearance of the pastoral letter *Rise or Decline of the Church*?

Your Eminence,

Although you know how profoundly the priests of the Mission de Paris are united in light and faith, I want to write to you today only in my own name, as I feel I am far too unworthy to represent the corporate opinion of the organization.

Several times Fr Hollande has reminded us that you were worried about us, doubting our loyalty to the Church in the matter of wearing the cassock and faithfully reciting the breviary. God is witness that I understand and bless your fatherly care for your priests. I even think that you can never be too demanding about our priesthood and our 'Catholicism', although your pastoral letter has set us very high standards to follow. Here, very simply expressed, is my opinion on this subject.

1. If you order us to wear the cassock always, I shall obey you at once, without any hesitation, seeing it as the will of the Lord. If you ask us only to leave it off in case of necessity, I believe I am speaking the truth in saying that when, as bearers of the gospel and men of the Church, we penetrate to a certain point in the working world, it becomes necessary to live among them and be like them, sharing everything with them, except sin. Otherwise they will never acknowledge us as *their shepherds*, they will not follow us

or call us by our name of 'Father' and, since we are not living in the *sheepfold*, we shall never be able to call them by their names.

If you think we are separating ourselves from the Church, ask the three curates and the Dean of St Peter and St Paul at Montreuil how 250 of the real working class *all* took part in all the prayers of the Mass, at a recent wedding in *their parish*. Of these 250, at least twenty-five were communists, including the reader of the epistle and the gospel, the choir-master and the Mass server. Ask them how, ten or twelve times this year, at double or triple baptisms of infants *in this same church*, a dozen or two of adult workers came each time to recite with us all the prayers of the Ritual and (as I always require) to promise to bring up these little baptized children to live in the Catholic faith and Catholic love. At this moment a long preparation is going on for five adult baptisms in our Montreuil communities—a mother aged forty-eight, a mother aged twenty-four with her two children, a man of thirty, head clerk at the Ford factory, a young man of twenty, just starting business, and a communist girl of eighteen. Four times in the year (twice in the convent of the Sisters of Charity!) we have got together 20, 24, 32 and 12 men, workers, for a *two days'* retreat (a Saturday and Sunday), on the Trinity, on the mission of the Word made flesh, on the Catholic Church and on vocation. Once there were nine communist couples at this silent retreat of prayer for two days. Once, as Fr Hollande can tell you, there were two national directors of the CGT,[9] three or four wardens of youth hostels and two or three communist 'fellow-travellers'. So that they may really know the *Church* and not just my priesthood, I have also arranged for them regularly to meet other priests, Dominicans, Jesuits, curates, or people

---

[9] Confédération Générale de Travail; it is comparable in scope to the Trades Union Congress, but definitely Communist.

from other movements like Jeunesse d'Eglise or Economie et Humanisme.

I beg your Eminence to excuse me for all these reports, which tell you sufficiently about our prayer, our cares, our daily Masses, our continual suffering for the kingdom of God, our daily crosses, all in order that faith, hope and charity may increase. Tomorrow, 8 June, the whole quarter (where lately only one family went to Mass) is giving at least the fruit of a family self-denial, or a sacrifice out of wages, so that the first Mass of our new priest may be *their sacrifice*. And this effort includes the members of the communist cell.

2. To me, the breviary is my daily happiness in the *Opere divino* of all priests. Although I am not always literally faithful to the whole of it, it is my joy. That is the truth, I assure you. How could we baptize the world without sacrifice, without prayer, without love?

That is why, your Eminence, while I fully understand your anxiety about your humble fellow-workers, I beg you to understand also the supernatural demands which the very mission entrusted to us lays on our shoulders. Do you believe we can 'baptize these peoples in the Holy Spirit' without faith in that Spirit, or convert adults without giving them the evidence of a life which tries to be holy, or build churches without losing ourselves in the unity of Catholic love? Do you believe it?

Ask Fr Hollande how we test all the vocations which are put before us.

Asking your pardon and your fatherly blessing, I invite you again, in the name of these new Christians, to *come here* to see for yourself the depth and breadth of their Catholic faith.

Your son in the priesthood...

This invitation of Fr Depierre, and many others like it, were gladly accepted by the Cardinal. He went several times to dine in the Rue Ganneron and with the Capuchin Friars of Nanterre,

and with one or other of the Mission's communities. He also
went to share a meal with several workers in their homes. Fr
Hollande writes:

Twice, in fact, true communists came in after the meal
for a courteous discussion with the Cardinal. Also, nearly
every month some of our new Christians, and sometimes
communists, went to talk at Archbishop's House with the
Cardinal, who reserved an hour or two for them. 'Come and
see me again', he used to say, and he could recognize them
several months later.

During this stage of the Mission's life, moreover, the Cardinal
was in constant touch with Fr Hollande, who, between 1943 and
1949, was received ninety-six times at Archbishop's House. From
these audiences the superior carried away reflections, encourage-
ments, sometimes sallies of wit, and carefully recorded them. In
1945 he quotes:

Go ahead; never mind what people say about you, even
ecclesiastics. So long as you keep me informed about what
you are doing, and are faithful to the doctrine of the Church,
you have nothing to fear.

The next year:

You will have your troubles. With generous priests like yours,
there are bound to be some blots, some exaggerations. So
much the worse: I must be informed, but I shall not make
a tragedy of it. We must keep our eyes on the essentials. I
have pledged my responsibility as archbishop of your Mission.
I know that your work will be made easier when certain
parishes are more welcoming; there are some things which
must be left to my successor; I launch the idea, that's all.

On the first members of the movement and the spirit which
must animate priests and laity in it, he writes:

You see, we are only beginning. What we must aim at is
a revival of the Church. Since the foundation of Catholic
Action the laity have their well-defined place in the Church,

but priests must be able to inspire these layfolk, who are no longer willing to be sheep. We need priests with a lively faith which inspires respect; detachment is not everything: there must be a faith which astounds, which attracts.

You have got to find priests who are ardent but also *well-balanced,* loving the Church above all, and also obedient. With them you can go forward. It is absolutely essential to destroy these walls which separate the Church from the masses.

There are obstacles which annoy us. Some are not serious; they are the growth of centuries and will fall by themselves if we do not suppress them, but for the moment they annoy us. It is the truth of the gospel that we have to inculcate.

He again confided in the superior of the missionary team his fear at seeing that Pius XII did not understand this work:

During a conversation I said to him three times: 'Well, most Holy Father, do you approve of what I am doing?' He never answered 'Yes'. The third time he only said: 'Supervision, assiduous and personal supervision. . . .' Then I told him that I was responsible for those five million inhabitants of Paris and that God would call me to account for them. I cannot agree to this wall of separation: you must help me to know these masses and to bring them to know God.

Finally, these words, confided one night to Fr Hollande, showing how the Cardinal expected the Mission de Paris not only to carry Christianity into the working world, but also to give a 'shock of missionary spirit,' to the whole diocese:

There are priests who feel no uneasiness. All I have been able to do is to sow uneasiness wherever I went.

THE CHOICE OF MEANS

The misunderstandings from which the Mission suffered in 1946 were easy to foresee. It was to the Cardinal's credit that he accepted the risk and would always come to the defence of his missionary teams. From this period comes the following reflection:

What you are doing is not classic. Being a good priest is not a matter of being classic, but of taking account of the Holy Spirit, of the needs of the Church and the needs of the times in which we live. Don't be afraid of taking initiatives. In the Church we are too often satisfied with routine. All I ask of your priests is that they should not go against the positive law of the Church. If there are people who are not pleased, they have only to come to me: I shall see them.

And they came. There were ecclesiastics, Christian employers, unofficial emissaries of the Government. There were also well-meaning souls, wanting simply to learn about the aims and spirit of an enterprise which shocked them by its novelty. This is how the Cardinal answered one of them, on 25 November 1947:

Mademoiselle,

In reply to your letter of 20 November, I should first like to say that I was very touched by it. It expressed thoughts which are very dear to me, since they concern the extension of the kingdom of God and the sanctification of souls.

However, I am not surprised at the divergent tendencies you have noticed in certain methods of evangelization. You need to know the aims pursued by this apostolate, which people call modern, but is really the oldest of all, since it comes down from the very origins of Christianity.

We know from the revelation of the gospel itself that it must be preached to every creature. Now, it is a fact of which we must be aware that in the present movement of events and the present situation there is a whole class of people which in fact is not reached by the preaching of the gospel. I do not for a moment deny that the classic methods have had, and still have, all their value, still less that they are employed with great devotion by those in charge of them. But souls must be reached, and we must admit that there is a whole series of souls, a whole multitude, which is not

only outside the fold, but is walled in, so to speak, in a sort
of enclosed field where the Church's influence does not penetrate.

That is why certain priests and laymen, moved by the
revelation of the gospel, have searched for a way to gain
entry to this hitherto impenetrable domain. Naturally, in this
process of approach or, we might say, of groping, there may
be some hesitations, perhaps also some false steps, here and
there, which are still excusable. But the primary intention
remains, and that is undoubtedly in the line of the gospel
and of Christ.

What, then, should be our attitude to this movement?
Surely, one of respect, esteem and sympathy. I should even
venture to say that the movement ought to be encouraged by
Catholics.

As to possible aberrations they too cannot leave us indifferent, for every aberration, in this sphere, might injure
the movement as a whole, which is beyond dispute. It is the
hierarchy's duty to put things right where the need is felt.
We may even expect that in the course of time, and after a
fair trial, there will be tactical modifications, as may be
thought useful or necessary.

For the moment, Mademoiselle, it is the duty of all Christians to be at least concerned about this state of affairs,
since it touches the honour of Christ and the extension of
his kingdom, something which cannot but haunt all Christian
hearts. It is our duty to pray for that intention, since that
prayer is directly joined to the prayer of Christ, who wills
that all should be one in the unity of the fold. Lastly, it is
our duty to sanctify ourselves, so that by repercussion our
personal holiness may flow back on to the state of the world.
'If ten righteous men are found in the city, I will not destroy it.'

These, Mademoiselle, are the reflections promoted by reading your letter. I hope I have given you satisfaction, but

also, what is still better, the great desire to take part yourself, in your position and according to your means, in this
crusade of Christian charity which, at the same time, is and
must be the crusade of salvation.

Accept, Mademoiselle, the expression of my faithful devotion in Christ.

'A WORK OF THE CHURCH'S LABOURERS'

In conclusion, here are some pages from his diary, solitary medi-
tations in the presence of the Lord, showing us how the Cardinal bore in his heart the efforts, hopes and future of 'his
Mission.'[10]

1 May. Being ill, I cannot leave my room, to my great
regret. It is the time for reflection.

I think especially about the Mission de Paris, which I
have so much at heart. It has a good reputation in civic,
and even in parliamentary circles. It is regarded as a precious
leaven. But it is also a spectacle to the world. It must not,
by neglect or ill-will, compromise 'an achievement of the
first rank, which goes beyond it'. Above all, its members,
who are obliged to approach certain secular positions, must
not become secularized in spirit. They must remain more
and more attached to what is essential to the priesthood ...,
especially attachment to the breviary. Attached in mind, heart
and will. So every day they must stick to reciting Prime in
the morning and Compline at night. I have just expressed
my mind to Fr Hollande. It would be a good thing to express it to each of them.

More and more, we see that human means are useless for
rebuilding the City. Decidedly, it is only the divine element,
applied at the right time, that can be of any use.... On this
twofold condition, that it loses none of its divine sap, and

---

[10] Cardinal Suhard's unpublished diary, for 1, 5, 6, 7, and 8 May 1947.

that it is applied to the temporal sphere.... Our aim is, by redemption, to heal a sick world.

5, 6, 7, 8 May. During all these days I have thought much about the diocese. The reception given to my pastoral *Rise or Decline of the Church*? convinces me that what I wrote in it was ardently awaited and inspires people's minds. All the same, that letter will not be effective unless it is lived, that is, unless the directives I gave find an echo in men's hearts and are put into practice by effective action....

In this connection I think specially about the Mission de Paris. Following up my reflections, I reach these conclusions:

1. That it is a great undertaking, not only in the effect it has already produced or may produce in the immediate future, but more in the principle it lays down for an apostolate of conquest in the circles cut off from the Church.

2. That this mission must succeed; otherwise there would be a delay, damaging in itself, in the present and in the future which depends on this mission, at a time which is especially serious in the world's history.

3. That this mission must succeed in the present at first, because a delay or a setback in the beginning would postpone the problem till some undetermined time in which the opportunities of the present might not recur; and also, I admit, so that in my unworthy person, and the help I can offer it, it may find a means of development which may not occur again.

4. That in order to succeed, its labourers must produce a work and an activity 'without flaw', which means that the work done must really be that of the 'Church's labourers', on the basis of devotion, disinterestedness, sacrifice, but also of the genuine 'ecclesiastical spirit', which dwells in souls and shines out externally (I am here thinking of the ecclesiastical obligations of the breviary and wearing the cassock...). These labourers must know that men's eyes are on them.... While carrying out a *new* work, ... they must in all things

remain faithful to the Church. By this means they will disarm the criticisms which are bound to be levelled against them.

5. Finally, the labourers in such a work must be persuaded of all these things and live by them and be attached to them. My duty is to convince them of this.

THE YOUNGER CLERGY

To conclude this chapter we may well ask what influence the Mission de Paris and, more generally, the missionary movement of the years 1944-6, had on diocesan life and the state of mind of the clergy. A man well qualified to answer our question would be M. Levassor-Berrus, Superior of the Deacons' Seminary in the Rue du Regard, for his post brought him into constant touch with the young priests of Paris.

At a day of priestly vocations, he presented to the Cardinal, the auxiliary bishops and a group of Parisian parish priests, a report on 'the mentality of the younger clergy', in which we can see that, while he was careful not to alarm unduly the susceptibilities of his audience, he showed a very real esteem for the spiritual and apostolic aspirations of the ecclesiastical 'new wave'.[11]

Let me describe them. They are moved by a twofold impulse: the missionary impulse and the community impulse.

Missionary effectiveness

Ever since Pentecost the missionary spirit has never ceased to breathe on the Church, showing to souls, and especially to the souls of priests, the sad plight of those whom St Paul calls the 'Godless' and the 'Christless'. From time to time this powerful wind has blown the missionaries to distant lands, but today it seems to be imperiously directing the zeal of priests and lay people towards that paganized or completely pagan mass which fills the poorer quarters and suburbs of our cities, and even our countryside. That holy anxiety

[11] From *Semaine religieuse de Paris*, no. 4833 (21 December, 1964) pp. 895-900.

for the salvation of the masses is not the monopoly of the younger clergy: you too, gentlemen, feel it gnawing you.

But among the younger clergy it has, perhaps, some particular psychological features. First, a rather impatient feeling for *effectiveness*. They have a certain craze for new methods, they consider that the classic methods do not bite deep enough to break into that block of mankind which they long to unite to Christ and the Church. And if they are somewhat given to excess, to a too human desire for tangible results, are not others in danger of an opposite fault, comforting ourselves with a sort of mystique of failure?

Granted that supernatural effectiveness escapes our methods of proof, and that even the apparent barrenness of our efforts sometimes stamps our works with the genuine mark of the cross, still, we cannot at the outset interpret failure in this mystical sense. We must see if there are not more immediate and more tangible causes, and our first duty is to put them right by continually re-thinking and adapting our methods.

A quest for effectiveness, I said. This leads our young priests to separate the *essential* from the *accessory*, in their apostolic ideas. The intention is good, though its application is often unjustified, clumsy or premature. The alleged accessory may appear at first sight as an obstacle, a barrier which holds the apostle up or bars him from access to the kingdom of God. Examined more closely, it is seen to respond to some inescapable necessity and to embody a tradition rich in spiritual values, or to be still an effective means of apostolic action. Such things as liturgical adaptation, the problem of Catholic activities, or even of finance, cannot be treated with such youthful nonchalance.

And yet our juniors do us a service by forcing us to a candid criticism of our customs and by inviting us to ask ourselves whether some of them are not really outdated, and should be ranked among those 'traditions of men' which our Lord declared to be obstacles to the work of God.

Finally, our young priests are haunted by the longing for missionary *penetration*. An unfair but significant word is sometimes heard on their lips: the 'ghetto'. Don't our Christian communities tend to turn inwards, to be shut in on themselves, with an instinct for security and protection, instead of opening out in an attitude of sympathy and conquest? The word, I repeat, is unfair, because under the terrible pressure of a pagan society, Christians certainly have to stand shoulder to shoulder, but that should be to breach the wall, not to take shelter.

In their desire for the parish to be more and more filled with the missionary spirit, better equpped with missionary institutions, our young priests are surely faithful to the spirit always approved and stimulated by their archbishop.

The team spirit

Our younger clergy, or at least a great many of them, are also animated by a strong community spirit; it is expressed in a word: the team.

Thank God, the community spirit exists in this diocese and has produced very fruitful results. There are many lively and active priestly societies, providing our young priests who join them both with the friendly atmosphere in which their priesthood can develop, and with the conditions of methodically co-ordinated apostolic work, not to mention their influence and attraction on the faithful themselves. The remedy for the scourge of isolation lies here.

But here, too, I think, the aspirations of our younger priests contribute or require something new. In the first place, where the priestly community exists, it can develop into the team. That means that work should be more fully pooled, personal views should be more decidedly subordinated to an idea arrived at by mutual agreement, under the responsibility of the head. This also means that without rash interference, but also without false timidity, the group takes charge of each of its members and takes an interest in his development as a man and a priest.

On the other hand, the team, thus defined, can be formed even where the community, in the strict sense, cannot exist. With goodwill, unselfishness and charity on the part of all concerned, this type of priestly collaboration, in which activities and souls are united, can be tried and more or less completely practised, in any parish whatever.

The missionary spirit, then, and the community spirit: these are the keys to the deepest aspirations of our younger clergy. These two motives are so obviously traditional that they need no justification. If such were needed, one could point out that they have been largely aroused in these days by the development of Catholic Action, the Church's own institution: their origin is therefore as genuinely Christian as it could be.

A metal in the melting-pot

I have devoted some time to this analysis, and must hasten to trace some more features in the portrait of our young priests, which comprises, as I said, both light and shade.

First the light. Our young men feel the pull of poverty. Is it only because they can guess its apostolic bearing in this age of riches and penury, of black market and restrictions? Is it only because they see in it the means to disarm that most widespread, tenacious and harmful of the complaints against the Church? Is it only because they wish to appear before the working class as their brothers in lack of property? It is more than that. They love poverty as St Francis of Assisi loved it, as the universally neglected spouse of the crucified. In it they love their Master, Jesus.

Another ray of gospel and Catholic light: they want a Marian spirituality. They share in that growing devotion—I almost said 'invading', in the best sense of the word—which is drawing the Catholic world to our Lady, mediatrix of all graces, and hence the ally, queen and mother of all apostles.

And now the shade. They need to develop in themselves the spirit of obedience. The appeal of novelty, impatience for effectiveness, and, above all, the contagion of this world in revolution in which they live, rather blind their eyes, I must admit, to that great redemptive virtue, that fundamental disposition of the Church's man.

Their feeling for the interior life is as keen in them as in their elders. They believe in it, many are hungry for it; they ask themselves, in return and often anxiously, how they can maintain and strengthen it in the framework of life prescribed by their apostolic activities.

Rather exaggerating two sound ideas—the distinction between monastic and apostolic life, and the need to be a man of prayer in the midst of action, *in actione contemplativus* —they may sometimes be tempted imprudently to abandon the traditional exercises, as if in practice these were not indispensable for the *exercise* of the interior life.

Yes, the state of mind of our young clerical and priestly seminarists is certainly very complex. This generation is putting out to sea, and some gusts of the world mingle with the wind of the Holy Spirit to fill its sails. A proud humanism, even some unconscious naturalism, slips into these conquering souls, who combine the love of their age with love for the Church.

It is metal in the melting-pot; it contains dross, which must be eliminated. But the metal is of good quality.

Do not moralize ...
You know as well as I do that while the educator must have his eyes open to the faults of his pupils, he must, still more, believe in their resources and trust them boldly. And that is

precisely the attitude I would suggest to you, in relation to our young men.

They will often annoy you by their audacities, but in their fire you will recognize the enthusiasms of your own youth. They come along with ideas, with an often correct instinct for the tendencies of the modern world, with that liveliness and vitality which give them a quite natural influence over their own generation. These are apostolic endowments, and if they have much to learn from you, you also can be enriched by contact with them.

How can we influence these young curates, remembering the aspirations which move them, and which I have tried to analyse? Not, certainly, by an exclusive appeal to the past. You will influence them by helping them to realize their legitimate aspirations and to restore or strengthen threatened spiritual values.

Help these young priests to thrill with love for the Church. Thus you will obtain or, if need be, restore all the essential values. Do not moralize to them. But bring them face to face with their priesthood, their Mass, and that Church which is Christ's spouse and their mother. Show them that she is essentially hierarchical, as the condition of her unity, and you will help them to understand and practise respect for authority, and obedience.

Show them the spiritual tradition of the Church and its roots in the gospel, and you will help them to understand and practise the renunciation proclaimed by Christ and lived by the saints, which is the antidote to those germs of naturalism they may have contracted.

Show them the example of the poverty to which the Holy Spirit is already guiding them, for that, too, is the true ornament of the Church.

6. A DIOCESE IN A STATE OF MISSION

THE DUTY OF THE APOSTOLATE

We have seen how the Mission de Paris was founded, not only with the idea of freeing the priests from parochial work so as to put them entirely at the service of the workers' mission, but also in the hope of giving the whole diocese a vigorous 'missionary shock'. And in fact we find that in the months after the Cardinal had read the manuscript by Abbé Godin and Abbé Daniel, his writings and words were full or urgent exhortations to the parishes to face 'the missionary problem'.

On 6 June, presiding at the festival of our Lady of the Missions at Cygne d'Enghien, he remarked at the end of the ceremony:

The Catholics of France need to have, more and more, the spirit of conquest, the missionary spirit. There are the foreign missions, and many apostles are needed to go far away to preach the gospel and win souls to Christ. But in France too there are many heathen to be evangelized and converted; that work is absolutely necessary, and all must understand how urgent it is.

At Beaune, on 21 July, for the fifth centenary of the famous hospices, he remarked, on the subject of the Christian ideal:

It can be said of that ideal that it is the guarantee of a civilization and that it consecrates the moral health of a nation. For if a country lives by the respect if shows for what is great and strong, it also lives by the respect it professes for what is weak, frail and suffering. The care of the poor, the care of the suffering, these are the basis of all the values which contribute to individual and collective recovery,

and notably of the sense of order, social understanding and
the apostolate of conquest.

Haunted by this problem of 'the moat to be filled in, the wall
to be razed' between the unbelieving world and the Church, the
Cardinal naturally took as the theme of his 1944 Lenten pastoral
'the duty of the apostolate'.[1] In the first part of the letter he
drew a picture of the religious state of the country, giving his
main reasons for hope, in the realms of religious practice, intellectual life and 'apostolic enthusiasm'. He also described the 'indifferent crowd' and the 'mass of prejudice, ignorance and mis-
understanding' which kept it estranged from the Church. The
conclusion of the first part consisted precisely in an appeal to
hope:

The task is certainly difficult! It is a whole world of men
that we have to raise up. What matter, if it has to be done?
Remember the famous words which express the courage of
the apostles and the first Christians, sent out to conquer the
world: 'The state of faith does not allow us to speak of impossibility.'[2] What is necessary must be done. That is why
we issue our appeal. We want to stir up in all minds, not
only of believers but of all patriots, the healthy uneasiness
which will prepare for the resurrection. We want people to
speak often, and in all circles, about this religious distress
of the masses. We ask pastors of souls, whose mission it is
to teach and warn, to be the first to obey this instruction.
We also ask our farsighted Catholics to bear witness by their
talents, their situation, the integration of their lives, before
the body of the faithful, so as to echo our words.
  For my part, I shall endeavour not to fail in the duty
which lies upon me. 'For Zion's sake I will not keep silent'
(Is. 62:1), says the prophet! 'Zion' is the whole company of
souls who constitute our heavenly country; 'Zion' is the

---

[1] *Semaine religieuse de Paris*, no. 4690 (26 Feb. 1944), p. 61, and no. 4691
(4 March, 1944), pp. 65-7.

[2] Tertullian, *De Corona*, c.11, quoted by Bossuet, second sermon for
Pentecost.

Church of Christ which gives shelter on earth to us pilgrims, and guides us to the goal of our journey; 'Zion' is France, our country, with its heritage of nobility and moral values which are the strength and the pledge of its temporal and spiritual future. To despair is disaster. It is an equally grave disaster to build one's hopes on illusion. A shock must be administered to Catholic opinion! Our faithful, now on the alert, must decide to do everything in their power to give to Christ the souls for whom he waits!

MISSIONARIES IN SPIRIT

In the second part he goes on to find 'the means to remedy the present situation', and presents the diocesan community with a whole missionary programme.

We mean to require the Christian community to be missionary: missionary in spirit and missionary in fact!

Now, those Catholics are missionary in spirit who are convinced that they are God's ambassadors, by the grace of their baptism and the mandate of their confirmation. They are missionaries in spirit who remember that the whole gospel is a missionary story, because it tells the story of a Saviour-God, who came to earth to rescue men from ignorance and spiritual death: a God who devoted his life to calling the human race to penitence, that is, to conversion: a God who has united human fellow-workers to himself, to continue his work till the end of time; a God who healed bodies in order to save souls; a God who rejoices more over the conversion of one sinner than over the perseverance of ninety-nine just men; a God who will not be satisfied till all men have returned to the Father in the unity of life and the embrace of beatifying love.

They are missionaries in spirit who, seeing the unbelieving masses and reflecting on the consequences of their unbelief, experience the same grief and distress as St Paul when he

entered Athens and saw the whole city given over to idolatry:
'His spirit was provoked within him as he saw that the city
was full of idols' (Acts 17:16). They are missionaries in
spirit who have learned in the Master's school to esteem and
love those men, who lack only the light to make them true
sons of God. They are missionaries in spirit who give the
first place in their programme as Christians to the conversion of souls, and especially of those nearest to them. Finally
and especially, they are missionaries in spirit who are not
content with desires, regrets and intentions, but go on to
deeds and have decided to be missionaries in fact, in the practice of their lives. The Christian community must not stop
short of that. Only so will it once again be its true self and
conform to the Gospel.

The wind of the Spirit

Yet our words on the apostolate would be worth nothing if
we did not insist on the need for the Christian community
to be moved by a powerful wind of love and an ardent
thirst for justice: in short, with that evangelizing spirit
which causes the true face of Christ to shine forth outside it.

The most fertile ages in the life of the Church have been
those when the whole body of believers was animated with
this spirit. The whole community of the Church was then in
movement. We think of the earliest days of our era, when
young and old, slaves and patricians, soldiers and merchants,
Romans and Jews, Greeks and barbarians, exposed to the
same perils of persecution and martyrdom, emulated one
another in zeal for the propagation of the faith. Burning
with zeal for the risen Christ and longing for his spiritual
victory, they were all conquerors. It was their testimony,
sealed in their blood, which changed the face of the world
and conquered paganism. Or think of the origins of our
Church of Paris, where people such as Denys, Marcellus,
Geneviève or Clothilde, living in times as troubled as our

own, but helped by loyal souls, built the 'holy city', which it
is our mission to defend and restore. Think of the periods
we call the 'ages of faith', in which the Church is often supposed to have been at rest, enjoying a sort of calm supremacy
over the world, though in fact she was threatened, battered
and attacked, and owed her strength only to the very fierce
struggle she had to wage against a world of enemies. Think
of the age of St Louis, which was an age of crusades, and
still more an age of missions, for Louis of Poissy, Francis of
Assisi, Dominic Guzman and Thomas Aquinas were con-
verters even more than fighters; and in spite of their rough
ways, the crusaders, lords or serfs, rich or poor, priests or
laymen, were inspired by the same love for Christ and the
same desire to enthrone his kingship on their common effort.

In this age of upheaval, our minds too are called to be
shaken by the wind of the Spirit. If it is to survive, the
whole Christian community must start to move. It must be
given a new impetus. Our very trials, in which God warns us
to have recourse to his mercy, can enable us to become
artisans of a magnificent religious revival.

And in fact, if everything bids us have recourse to God,
there is in that need a profound reason to direct our path
to an apostolate of conquest. For to have recourse to God
means not only to pray to God but also to take in hand the
divine cause and strive to defend it; it is to bring about, as
far as in us lies, what we know to be the will of God. Now
we cannot doubt that in the present state of affairs the will
of God is that the world should be freed from the materialism in which it is bogged down, and that the moral ruins,
infinitely more dangerous than the material, should be made
good. It is God's will that a strong effort should be made
in concert, to give back to Christ a world which is his heritage but, whether by neglect, forgetfulness or malice, has
been withdrawn from his influence. It is God's will that
Christians should give themselves to accomplish this revival,

so as to take their minds off their own sorrows and profit from the supernatural benefits of their trials. It is God's will that the Church should be defended by Christians and that at no time and in no place should she suffer an eclipse which might imperil her vitality. It is God's will, above all, that Christians, should follow Christ's example and fully give themselves in the apostolate to their neighbours, for 'greater love has no man than this, that a man lay down his life for his friends' (John 15:16).

Faced, therefore, with the evils which threaten us, and conscious of the resources of generosity and devotion to be found in our faithful people, I confidently launch my appeal to the apostolate. I call on all Christians to work to bring the world back to Jesus Christ!

THE 'GREAT RETURN'[3]

One of the most important religious events of the year after the war was the *Grand Retour* or 'Great Return' of our Lady of Boulogne. This devotion had two aspects. First, it was a popular movement of Marian piety. Around the four replicas of the statue of our Lady which traversed France from Lourdes to Boulogne, a vast stream of prayer and conversion passed through eighty French dioceses, which welcomed the Virgin on her journey in some twelve thousand parishes. From 1945 to 1946, between ten and fifteen million persons lined the route of the statue.

But it was also a time of strength in the life of the diocese. During winter, all the parishes of Paris received the Marian pilgrimage and the entire diocese, perhaps for the first time, joined in one and the same devotion. The Catholic Action movements joined with the parishes; groups and societies worked together for the success of this vast current. When, therefore the capital bade farewell in June to the effigy of Mary, standing in her symbolic boat, the Cardinal transformed this ceremony, at the Colombes stadium, into a great manifestation of diocesan life. A crowd of 120,000 is said to have packed the steps of the stadium, on the night of 29 June, to join in the vigil of prayer, the spoken choruses, the litanies and finally the Midnight Mass.

At a time in the national life when the need for union and

<hr>

[3] *Semaine religieuse de Paris*, no. 4809 (6 July 1946), pp. 449-51.

reconciliation was most acutely felt, the Cardinal chose to speak of the unity of the diocese around the eucharist, and of the role of Christians as reconcilers between the world and the Church of Christ.

My Brethren,

In this night which enfolds us, an image has arisen which catches our eyes and unites our hearts: Our Lady of the Great Return prepares to leave us. She came to us with full hands, but she does not leave us empty-handed. In exchange for her graces we have given her our hearts. And her boat, already weighed down with the treasure of the provinces, sinks deeper in the sea of our humanity under the overflowing weight of the souls of Paris.

I recognize myself in these divine 'catches', and I wished, in order to show her our love, to offer our Queen one last picture for her to take away, to remind her of us.

THE UNITY OF THE DIOCESE

That picture is the diocese of Paris, For it is here, all complete, tonight. It lives, it thinks, it thrills, it prays, in this vast crowd overflowing the steps of this giant arena.

Here it is in all its richness and diversity; here are the centre and the suburbs, the factory and the faculty, the artisan, the lawyer, the working man, here is the ancient basilica and the little church of the work-yards. Seen from high heaven, what a lovely tapestry for our Lady!

But above all, the diocese is here in its unity. This is the first time in its long history that it has been thus assembled, and shows, by the mere visual representation, the idea of its totality. You can surely feel it, my brethren: around your rector and your priests you form a distinct family, a group with its traditions, its habits, its own style. In their turn, these little communities, recognizable by the banners of their patron saints, are ranked closely together, rubbing shoulders

F

as brothers in the family of the diocese. All together, in a fervent, reverent circle, they surround the high altar where your archbishop is about to offer the sacrifice of Christ, who unites Christians in his Blood, in one immense mystical Body.

In order to signify this unity better, all the parishes are about to offer, at the same time, to the same rhythm as their pastor and father, the single sacrifice of the Church of Paris.

This living community, this profound sense of belonging —this is the great joy we give to our Lady, this is the great lesson we must draw from this unprecedented gathering. The hour has struck when Christians are beginning to understand that they are and must be *catholic*, that is, corporate and universal.

Corporate! Yes, because man belongs, in fact, to natural groups, and it is through them and with them that he works out his salvation. May this night's gathering help you to understand it. May it decide you to come out of your individualism, so as to enliven and restore, from within, the groups in which you live: the family, the place of work, the quarter, the town, the country.

CHRISTIANS IN THE WORLD

And not only them, but all mankind, for so will you be universal. Beyond your parishes, there is your diocese, this diocese of Paris, whose glorious history and prodigious influence were but now recalled to you. But, beyond this diocese and all the dioceses of the world, there is the Church, which unites them all, in her desire to save them, Do you ever think of it? Tonight, at least, you feel it. This stadium, overflowing with your numbers, all mingled together, is the image of Christendom.

But here I must give you a warning. In a little while, those benches will be deserted, the lights extinguished, and you will find yourselves alone again, as you walk the sleeping streets. How much will then be left of your present emotion, your ardour, your *élan*? What will be the value of your 'return in the night' to a world which ignores, misunderstands or opposes your joy?

It must be a 'great return', your own this time. You will go back more confident, more prepared for the conquest of your brethren.

Conquest? Yes, but a peaceful conquest, for it is concerned only with winning souls for Christ. The Church wants no other gains. She seeks neither temporal influence nor political powers. The Church is not a party, nor a clan, nor a faction. She is simply the true, the only family of mankind. She would be stifled in anything that confined her to a territory, a country, an epoch or a culture. She is at ease only in the bounds of the wide world.

Therefore, my dear brethren, for you to be apostles does not mean to isolate yourselves, to be stiff, to preserve in order to avoid loss, but to mix, to give yourselves, in order to increase and to live. For the time has come for the Church when the missionary apostolate is no longer a luxury or an exotic vocation, but a question of life or death: she must penetrate, or disappear.

THE PATHS OF SALVATION

But do not delude yourselves! Souls do not sell themselves, they give themselves. They give themselves to those who have learned to understand them, to love them, and for their sakes to pray, to offer, to sacrifice, in secret. We shall win souls only by our tears, our sweat, or our blood. We shall save them only by prayer and penitence.

But these will by no means dispense us from action. On the contrary, they lead us to it, and they prevent us from sinking into hypocritical verbalism, or crusades without foundation. The inner life will give power to your action. Nothing else will make it realistic. 'When a man is hungry,' says St Thomas, 'one gives him bread, not a speech.' Let these words, which simply repeat the gospel, be also your programme: you will only transform souls, and society, by social justice and charity.

You will not manage this alone. In the days in which we live, everything is done in common. In the apostolate the unit is not the individual but the team. That alone provides its members with spiritual sustenance and conquering boldness. That has been proved true, especially in the last twenty years, since the first Jocist section showed the way to all the specialized movements.

But Catholic Action does not stop there: it aims to unite in an immense fraternal stream all those cells at work, all the differentiated groupings. But has that full unity, that mystique of sincere union between all the movements, been accomplished? In all honesty we must admit it: not yet.

So my last and urgent advice to you is this: continue to act in your natural milieu. But at the same time, build bridges between your movements. They must be neither watertight nor parallel: they must meet, not only in love, not only in congresses, but in life. Then and only then will you show to the mass of our pagan or indifferent brethren (who constantly reproach us with having betrayed the gospel) the true face of the Church. Only then will you plant in them the desire to come into her, there to find in their turn the brotherly love for which they long.

To be united among yourselves: to be united, beyond your own ranks, with all men of good will, indeed we may say, with all men: that is the resolution you must carry away tonight from Colombes. That is what we are going to ask, all together, of Christ and his mother!

May our Lady hear us! May she bless all those, without exception, who are making sometimes superhuman efforts to create a spirit of concord and mutual aid between all French-

men! May her love grant that through our fraternal coh-
esion and enthusiastic co-operation we may be the builders
of French unity and of the peace of the world!

THE PARISH, A MISSIONARY COMMUNITY

The parish, as the basic cell of diocesan life and apostolate, with
all the complexity of its problems, was often the Cardinal's main
preoccupation. The republication in 1946 of Abbé Michonneau's
book[4] on the problems of the parochial apostolate gave him an
opportunity to define and explain publicly his own reflections as
priest and pastor on the various aspects of the parochial mission,
in the preface he contributed to it.[5]

It is always a great pleasure for the shepherd of a diocese
to learn about a priestly effort for the conversion of souls,
and to see a priest proposing a method of apostolic life
which is adapted to the needs of a world in which the
planting of the Christian faith is an increasingly vital
problem.

For some years now zealous priests have been meditating
on the solemn statement of Pius XI that the scandal of the
nineteenth century had been the loss by the Church of the
working class. And in these last years, too, this meditation
has borne fruit in many new ventures, to which the whole
Christian community owes much of the renewal of its vitality.
The very success of these ventures calls for a new exploration of the work of Christian conquest in the world of the
common man. The religious work of the last twenty years
in France has given rise to demands which are directly met
by Fr Michonneau's activities.

While the Catholic Action movement has been a privileged
instrument of this rechristianizing work, it is also important

---

[4] *La Paroisse, communauté missionaire*, Eng. trans. *Revolution in a City
Parish*, Blackfriars, London, 1949.

[5] The translator has been helped by the freer and more summarized
translation of this Preface in the English version cited above.

to realize that only the parish, the local and all-inclusive seat of the redemption, can be the really adequate element, the primary cell, of that work.

The task of the parishes devoted to the work of re-christianizing is therefore to make full use of all the lessons of the effort of apostolic conquest in the past decades, and to take part in all the methods of action thus brought to light. But above all it is necessary to recreate a complete setting of religious life, capable of spreading the message of Christ at all levels of the life of those who live in the parish. Only so can the mass of the people be won back.

THE APOSTOLATE AND CRITICISM

The description of such a missionary apostolate and of a pastoral life wholly dedicated to these fundamental Christian problems of our age, cannot fail to appeal to the heart of many a priest, anxious for the spiritual progress of his own parish. It will also raise many problems for those who are trying to form themselves for the sacred ministry. In particular, it will help them to reappraise the role of the diocesan clergy; its usefulness, or rather urgent necessity, will appear still more evident, through this special work of conversion in the parish. In this connection a few simple remarks may be useful.

In the first place, we must all realize that no real progress is likely from an attitude of mere criticism; charity is constructive. It is true that all through the different ages the Church has had to make known the redemption and the graces of the Spirit in conformity with the needs of the time. But those who work in the Lord's field must remember that the developments of Christian life ought to aim, not at suppressing, but at making perfect. The younger generation, in particular, should remember that if it now enjoys such a wealth of faith and religious life and so many opportunities to spread the Christian spirit, they owe them to their elders, who often ploughed and sowed in difficult soil, where others, with rather hasty zeal, think they have only to change all the methods in order to reap an immediate harvest.

But the real apostle is no critic. He is the servant of the work of Christ, and knows well that he is only a humble link in a long chain of generations and so can never doubt that his first duty is joyfully and obediently to accept the fruits of time-proven wisdom. It may be that certain customs and plans must gradually disappear, to be replaced by others more suitable to our own times, but, at the same time, we must recognize that there was a day when these were useful. We must avoid the childish error of thinking that our generation is destined to settle every problem, to reconstruct everything. Even our methods and the results of our work, good for today, may prove inadequate and be judged tomorrow. Those preparing to become apostles of Christ will save time and gain in efficiency if they remember these fundamental truths and refrain from criticism which is often misinformed and based on inexperience.

PRIESTLY SPIRITUALITY

Thus there are some who too hastily ask whether the demands of a missionary apostolate do not demand a revision of priestly piety, even speaking of modifying the traditional forms of priestly prayer: mental prayer and the breviary. Such was never the aim of this book. Rather, it proposes to revivify these basic practices of prayer-life by means of a constant solicitude for the work of Christ and the sanctification of the parish. It would be really short-sighted to think that there is any incompatability between the missionary ideal of a priest who is in contact with the dechristianized masses and the demands of the interior life, without which the priest would soon find himself stripped of the spirituality he thought he had. The interior life has its inexorable demands: it must be sustained and deepened by intimate converse between the soul and God; it must take part in the common prayer-life of the Church, and the natural expression for this is the breviary. The effort of preserving that intimate spiritual life and of harmonizing it with the conditions in which they can effectively spread the influence of Christ, will sometimes seem hard to those who take them both seriously. But they cannot solve the problem by avoiding it. And it is simply avoiding it, to suppose that a priest can accomplish his apostolic task without using, today as formerly, these same basic elements of apostolic spirituality, mental prayer and the Divine Office.

THE PRIEST AND HIS CULTURE

The demands of this apostolate do not require the priest to abandon all care for true culture, as some might think from reading the chapter in this book which is devoted to that problem. What is demanded is that the priest should know how to be accessible to his flock, and so he must somehow share in the popular cultural world of his parish. It may be that Fr Michonneau does not sufficiently distinguish between that illusory familiarity with the popular mind which would result if a priest were to jettison the traditional elements of the culture proper to a man as a minister of God, and the true adaptation by which a priest can be both understanding and understood, without thereby ceasing to elevate and spiritualize the souls entrusted to his care. The first attitude would be a deplorable levelling-down, and would seriously compromise the apostle's usefulness. Only the second is worthy of an apostle who is bringing Christ back into the world.

But we must not deceive ourselves. That adaptation demands constant effort from all of us. The acquisition and the free intellectual use of the traditional heritage of the sacred sciences are still necessary to the priestly life, but we must not let this general training be acquired in too abstract a manner, thus losing its power to influence.

As for the secular sciences, which the Church has never ceased to hold in high esteem, it is precisely through them that the priest can gain an entrance into the interests of our world and make Christ known in it.

In any case, we may be sure that if working people are sometimes offended by seeing priests who find it hard to come down to their level they will be even more hurt to find in us, even on the human level, the same common and vulgar limitations they see in themselves.

THE ROLE OF OBEDIENCE

And finally it should be clear that apostolic endeavour can never succeed without constant obedience to the hierarchy, whose function is precisely to organize the whole Christian life in the area entrusted to it. There are priests who too readily conceive of their priestly ministry as a series of daring experiments undertaken on their own responsibility. These rash undertakings seldom produce any lasting good. Obedience to the hierarchy is not, of course, a condition intended to stifle all boldness in the cause of Christ, to curb every impulse of generosity. But every isolated effort can gain real benefit from the supervision and support which the heads of the hierarchy can furnish, because of their greater vision, and because through them we practise submission to the over-all work of Christ. Preoccupied with some urgent problem, we think of some particular solution; but have we taken a sufficiently wide view? Is our zeal in step with the whole Christian community, which is guided by the Holy Spirit? These questions can only be solved by constant reference to the judgement of the hierarchy and in constant submission to its decisions.

This does not mean that we should always wait for the initiative to come from above: that would be a lazy solution. None the less, it is always a duty, in all circumstances, to submit our projects to the approval of superiors, and to ask for the advice and judgement necessary to maintain the apostolate in obedience to the Church.

It goes without saying that no apostolic work can prove its worth or attain its object unless the dignity of the priesthood is upheld, and the priestly bearing, always and everywhere necessary, is maintained. In other words, wherever he exercises his ministry, the priest must always grow in the esteem of men and be not only innocent but ever more pleasing in the sight of God.

AUTUMN OR SPRINGTIME OF THE CHURCH?

On 22 February 1947 the *Semaine religieuse*, as in other years, published the Cardinal's Lenten pastoral letter to his people. But on the cover of this little bulletin, under the title, was printed: 'Abridged edition to be read from the pulpit.' 'What is the complete edition like, then?' grumbled many a Paris rector, on seeing these thirteen closely printed pages.

The full edition appeared in due course, in two numbers of the *Semaine religieuse,* on 15 and 22 March. When the letter appeared in book form, it formed a brochure of seventy pages— almost a small book.

'We have never seen the like!' groaned the critics. It was the custom or rather the tradition for a Lenten pastoral to be a short, pious address, its lofty sentiments clothed in soothing expressions. But in this unprecedented letter everything was new: its size, its title, its style.

How could an archbishop dare to talk about the 'rise or decline of the Church'? Does not the Church possess the promises of eternal life? Could she ever sink into decline? The Cardinal had personally chosen this title in preference to one proposed by his collaborators, 'Autumn or Springtime of the Church' which was more expressive, but too poetical for his taste.

The tone of the letter, too, seemed novel. It was modern, solid, energetic. There were none of those formulas, clichés or padding one had come to expect; no 'My very dear brethren' in every paragraph. Yet it was more than a father speaking to his children, it was a man speaking to other men, his brothers, in the language of their day.

From the end of February abundant notices appeared in the press. Apart from a few discordant voices, the praise was unanimous. The appearance of *Rise or Decline* was hailed as a great event in the Church's life. Mauriac wrote a report on it in *Le Figaro*. Claudel, in his letter of congratulation, asked for a complimentary copy with a dedication. On 1 August Fr Merklen, chief editor of *La Croix,* proposing the Cardinal's health at a reception given by *Bonne Presse* at the Palais d'Orsay, praised the letter in these terms: 'A document full of candour and doctrinal precision, which will be a landmark in the religious history of our land. Even the enemies of our faith have recognised it as a decisive act, and their usual line of attack on the Christian religion has been upset by it.'

Several French bishops, on the other hand, refused to admit that a cardinal could so much as consider the decline of the Church. (The Cardinal knew this, and a year later took his revenge wittily, during a ceremony in Notre-Dame. Seeing some particularly hoary heads passing in front of him he leaned over to his neighbour and asked in an audible whisper: 'Decline or rise of the Church?'

In carrying out this work, Mgr Suhard had made use of the advice and documentation of some collaborators whom he had instructed his secretary to consult before and after it was drawn up. This in no way lessened the credit due to the Cardinal, who had constantly followed and supervised the labours of the team, had inspired certain passages and finally signed the text, thus taking on himself the entire responsibility for it.

'It was a libel,' wrote his secretary, 'to say that he simply signed other people's ideas. That is absolutely false. I kept him continually in touch. He was not always the first to hold these views, but they became his own, and he was perfectly capable of refusing an idea, just as well as he could clearly bring out, in a speech next morning, some view maintained before him the previous night.'

The Cardinal had begun to think about his next pastoral during December 1946. He entrusted this work to his secretary, Fr Lalande, who had already collaborated on his Lenten letter on the family. Like Fr Le Sourd during the German occupation, Fr Lalande was in daily touch with a great number of people. In the course of his duties he was visited by many persons, with whom he spoke about the state of the Church in France.

'To me,' he said, 'who had just spent four years as a prisoner, the climate of French Catholicism was something new and strange, and certainly complex. The intellectual atmosphere of Paris was so different from what I had known in the Sorbonne before the war. There was a strange, bubbling effervescence. Everything was questioned. New authors appeared. Sartre had replaced Bergson as the fashionable philosopher. From the point of view of the apostolate, new formulas were now approved. The Church was confronted with a new world, and Mounier had been able to write a book like '*L'Affrontement chrétien*. It seemed to me, and to many others whom I saw at Archbishop's House, that there ought to be a document, that the Cardinal of Paris should intervene, because men's minds were disturbed and divided. There were denunciations to Rome. There was integrism, with a new *'Sapinière'*. There was also the danger of *Jeunesse de l'Eglise,* which was already inclined towards perilous positions, and was distrusted by the Cardinal. There had also been the abrupt departure of General de Gaulle, and a climate of civil war which we tend today to forget. That letter must be seen again in its proper setting, for it was by no means an academic essay, but something essential and living, called forth by events.

The choice of subject had been roughed out in a talk between the Cardinal and his secretary as they drove along the canal bank at Aubervilliers. Fr Lalande then set to work and began to get his documents together. Fr d'Ouince and the Jesuits of the journal *Etudes* were enlisted and their colleagues of *L'Action populaire,* chiefly Fr de Lestapis (another close collaborator on the letter on the family), Fr Bigo and Fr Villain, the superior, who said: 'For Cardinal Suhard, our house is open to you; we promise you all our help.' Other priests too were consulted, and provided documents or shared in the preparation of certain passages: Frs Hollande and Depierre, Fr Hua, Fr Guérin of the JOC, Fr Berrar, chaplain to the Paris students.

While he often praised team-work and the team-spirit, the Cardinal had his own peculiar way of practising them! In his impatience for results, he dogged his secretary's footsteps, harried and queried him, at every meal, on the stairs, in the car, to know how far he had got, how the work was progressing, when it would be finished. He would put calls through to one or other of the team, several times, to verify a note or some information, he would demand a complete report on half a page of text, insert unexpected developments in the plan, cut out this, lengthen that. His wretched secretary, on the verge of a nervous breakdown, was forced to flee to the mountains to reach the end of his task. The Cardinal, who never took holidays himself and could never understand why anyone else should, made as if to stop him. 'If I go,' pleaded Fr Lalande, 'you will have the document much sooner!' 'In that case, off you go!' Thus it was in a little hotel in the Contamines (in Savoy), on the corner of his bedside table, in an icy room where he worked till two in the morning that Fr Lalande succeeded in finishing his work. As soon as the manuscript had been read through by Fr Lavasor-Berrus and Fr de Lestapis, it was sent straight to the printers.

It was necessary, as I have said, to compose an abridged version for public reading, before the appearance of the full text in the following month.

Rise or Decline was not very well received in Roman circles. Fr Merklen, finding that nobody there alluded to it, asked Mgr Montini what Pius XII, who never mentioned it, had thought about it. The then Secretary of State replied with a smile: 'When the Holy Father likes a text, he at once tells his entourage all about it.'

Besides the title, the subject and the manner of its treatment, Pius XII did not greatly appreciate the dimensions of the work, which looked like an encyclical. Even in Paris, it became common to refer in conversation to 'the Cardinal's encyclical'. In the spring of 1949, Fr Bellanger, chaplain to the lightermen, when at Archbishop's House, let fall the word in his presence:

'You too!' said the Cardinal, 'you speak of my encyclicals! All right, I'll tell you. When I was received this winter by the pope, I put the question to him: "Holy Father, it is being widely said that I write encyclicals. Your Holiness knows well that I have no sort of intention of playing the part of a pope. If in these last years I have treated at some length of important subjects of the day, that is because I thought

I was fulfilling the primary duty of my office as father and shepherd of my diocese. But now I hesitate. Shall I continue?" The pope replied, with the greatest kindness and a humility which put me to shame: "Continue: your letters instruct and edify me. Besides, the Gregorian University never awarded me its gold medal, as it did to you!"

It is difficult to quote extracts from *Rise or Decline of the Church* without upsetting the general balance of the letter, which always recalls the transcendental aspect of the Church before dealing with its temporal aspects. The pages reproduced here are taken from passages devoted to the Church's action, mission and incarnation in the world. The reader is advised to remember that these are always balanced by other pages in which the Church's mystical aspect is more specially emphasized.

THE CHURCH LIVES IN TIME

After a long statement of the problem of peace and the unity of the world, the Cardinal answers it with an analysis of the mystery of the Church. He first develops her transcendental aspect and, following Pius XII, represents her as the 'Mystical Body of Christ' He affirms her aspect of finality and perfection, her qualities of 'rock' and 'norm', which no change can alter, 'no attack impair, no solicitation corrupt'.[6]

But this sublime reality must not blind us to another, namely, that the Church is also in time, in history, *inter mundanas varietates*.[7] For the Church is a body: 'It is because the Church is a body that she is visible to us,' says Leo XIII,[8] and Pius XII affirms 'It is therefore an aberration from divine truth to represent the Church as something intangible and invisible, as a mere "pneumatic" entity.'[9] Invisibly governed by her founder and indwelt by his Holy Spirit, the Church is also a visible and hierarchical society

[6] Translation from Cardinal Suhard's *Pastoral Letters*, pp. 12ff.

[7] Prayer for the Fourth Sunday after Easter.

[8] Leo XIII, *Satis Cognitum* (*Acta Sanctae Sedis*, vol. XXVIII, p. 710).

[9] *Mystici Corporis*, Eng. trans. *The Mystical Body of Jesus Christ*, C.T.S., p. 12.

in which the pope and the bishops wield an authority without which there can be no orthodoxy in faith and no discipline among the faithful.

CONTINGENT

Because she is the Body of Christ, his incarnation in the history and geography of the earth, the Church is first of all contingent. She belongs to a special time and place. Why here rather than there? Why was she born in Palestine rather than in China? And why during the reign of Tiberius? The Church is as she is, but she might have been very different. The battle of Poiters for long settled her extension and her destiny, and in all such events we can only accept the mysterious outcome of men's actions and the workings of Providence. If such and such a saint had not lived, if such and such a religious order had not been founded or a particular continent had remained unexplored, the Church would have neither the same forms nor the same extension: she would not be what she is today. As a community inside history, the descendant of the chosen people who prefigured her, she must submit to the vicissitudes of the centuries and the laws of human society. She takes to herself men as they are, with their customs and their heredity.

HER GROWTH . . .

Because she is also a body, the Church does not remain stationary; she develops, changes and grows. To her is applied the parable of the mustard seed: 'Of all seeds, none is so little, but when it grows up . . . all the birds of the air come and settle in its branches' (Matt. 13:31-32). She is also 'the whole fabric bound together, as it grows into a temple, dedicated to the Lord' (Eph. 2:21-22). That growth, however, has certain clearly marked features.

She is first of all *Catholic*, that is, she extends everywhere. The geographical and ethnological aspect of the Church's extension is frequently commented on, and rightly; for the way she has made her way into the heart of countries and the diverse sociological entities making up the world is an event without precedent. 'While the City of God is in exile on earth,' says St Augustine, 'it enrols its citizens from men of all nations and tongues. It does not worry about differences in culture, laws and way of life.'[10] But the Church has proved equally well what we may call her *vertical catholicity*: she has embodied herself in the continuing existence of the world, just as much as in its geography. She has passed through, and put on, all the civilizations of history. She has suited herself to time as she has suited herself to space. Each age has lent her its 'stature' and its features.

... IS AN ORGANIC GROWTH

These successive incarnations do not destroy the Church's continuity; they are merely the various 'moments' of her growth among men. That development on earth is not principally, or uniquely, quantitative, through the enrolment of new members, but an organic development; and it therefore has a direction. The direction it will take cannot be deduced in advance from her existence as it is at this moment, and we cannot lay down beforehand the 'temporal' line in which the path of the Church will run.[11] Life always contains an element of the unseen. But we do know the Church's ultimate goal, to which that growth is directed and which defines her: the Church is meant to 'complete' Christ. And at the end she will be his 'pleroma'.

[10] *De civitate Dei*, bk XIX, ch. 17.

[11] 'As Christ is a living being, the Church is a living organism which develops under the thrust of her vital principle: nor, before living, does she wait for theorists to define her and lay down the conditions in which they will allow her to live' (J. Leclercq, *La Vie du Christ dans son Eglise*, p. 77).

When we consider her from that aspect, we see, first of all, that the successive 'actualizations' of the Church, far from impoverishing her, make for her growth. The civilizations of history, as they succeed each other, no more exhaust the Church than individuals, by their increase, exhaust the species. On the contrary, each of the societies as well as the social forms in which the Church becomes incarnate, all help to 'complete' Christ. The body has need of the Head (John 15:5; Eph. 4:16), but the Head also has need of the body. 'And yet it is also certain, surprising though it may seem, that Christ requires his members. . . . He wants to be helped by the members of his Mystical Body in carrying out the work of the redemption.'[12] This conclusion is of the highest importance if we are to understand the relations the Church has with the world, and therefore if we are to see the action to which the Christian is pledged. The world, for its own life, needs the Church; and the Church needs the world for her own development and completion.[13]

UNTIL THE SECOND COMING

Since the Church is the 'pleroma' of Christ, it is understandable that she wishes, uninterruptedly, to enlarge her boundaries and become more perfect. She feels the duty laid upon her to grow, right down the centuries, to the dimensions of humanity and in the whole diverse and concrete range which its individuals reach in their ideas and their forms of culture.

---

[12] *Mystici Corporis*, E.T., p. 27.

[13] 'Nebuchadnezzar saw a small stone—Christ—which, split off from the mountain by a human hand, grew until it became a large mountain and filled the whole earth [Dan. 2:34-35]. Detached from the mountain the stone grew and became a mountain, because this body, which has taken only a microscopic part of the mass of the human race, expands to vast proportions because of the numbers coming to it from every side, and does not stop growing until the end of time and until it has filled the whole earth' (Adelmann of Brescia, ed. R. Heurtevent, p. 300).

The Church is not Catholic only in fact, but also in intention. Her 'end' is Christ's second coming, that is, the eschatological triumph of Christ, 'the alpha and omega'. She has to make for him, and be to him, a finished body: 'perfect manhood, the maturity which is proportionate to the completed growth of Christ' (Eph. 4:13), intent on penetrating and assuming everything the world has, 'except sin' (Heb. 4:15). 'During the whole period between the first coming of Christ and the second, the Church is being built up, under the influence of the sevenfold grace of the Holy Spirit, until she becomes complete at the end of time.[14] She can know no rest until she has carried out her unique mission, which is to 'make God ruler of the world' and re-establish in his Son the whole of creation redeemed by his blood. The doctrine of the Mystical Body is completed by the doctrine of the kingship of Christ.[15]

CHRISTIANS IN THE CITY[16]

Is the mission of the Church confined to the apostolate? There are some who think that it is; and we have seen the objections they raise to her being 'embodied in the tem-

---

[14] Raoul of St Germer, *In Levit.*, I, 17.

[15] 'The foundation of this power and dignity of our Lord', writes Pius XI, 'is rightly indicated in Cyril of Alexandria. Christ, he says, has dominion over all creatures, a dominion not seized by violence nor usurped, but by his essence and nature (*In Luc.* 10). His kingship is founded upon the ineffable hypostatic union . . . and by reason of the hypostatic union Christ has power over all creatures'. And Pius XI quotes Leo XIII: 'His empire includes not only Catholic nations . . . but also those who are outside the Christian faith; so that truly the whole of mankind is subject to the power of Jesus Christ' (Leo XIII, *Annum Sacrum*, 25 May 1899) and continues: 'Nor is there any difference in this matter between the individual and the family or the State; for all men, whether individually or collectively, are under the dominion of Christ' (Pius XI, *Quas Primas*, Eng. trans. *The Kingship of Christ*, C.T.S., pp. 9, 11-12).

[16] See *Pastoral Letters*, pp. 48-54.

poral'. According to these theories, embodying the Church would constitute a betrayal of the kingdom of God, which is not of this world, and a compounding with the present-day self-worship of society. We have already dealt with the false ideas such arguments involve.

WORK IN THE WORLD LEGITIMATE

Let it be enough to recall briefly here that without 'incarnation' the Church ceases to exist, and that an attempt to deny man's life 'according to the flesh' ends in destroying the supernatural itself and becomes Protestantism. For if it be true that the Church is the kingdom of souls, that her end is absolutely supernatural, and that thereby she does not directly pursue the happiness and civilization of man in this world, she is none the less concerned with them from another point of view. Because man is body and soul, mortal and immortal, she is concerned with whatever in him serves as a natural ground for the supernatural; for 'grace does not destroy nature but elevates and perfects it'. Further, as the messenger and an instrument which is 'one with the redeeming Christ' of whom she is the living incarnation,[17] she owes it to herself to extend the benefits of the redemption to the whole created world. Christ did not come to excommunicate the world but to baptize it in his blood. From that moment the Christian has not only the right but the duty to 'complete' creation, and to work at the city of his world. 'The

[17] 'Our Saviour acts as God, but also as man . . . . Remaining man, he continues to act in the way men act and not solely as God acts. In our world, he uses not only his divine omnipotence, or purely spiritual forces, but also all the resources . . . of nature . . . which he created. The whole of humanity, that is, all the human, can be and ought to be employed by Christ. Every noble human activity should become 'sacramental', that is, become supernaturally efficacious' (L. de Coninck, 'Les problèmes de l'adaptation en apostolat' in *Nouvelle Revue Théologique*, October 1936, p. 686).

temporal is a wounded reality, and it must be loved with a redeeming love.[18]

CHRISTIAN OPTIMISM

It will be seen how far we are from the false picture men choose to make of Christians: mistrustful of the present, unarmed against it, useless, to society.[19] Yet it is precisely by our works, effective and real, that we shall be judged. 'I was hungry ... and you gave me food ... a prisoner and you came to me ...' (Matt. 25:31-46). The path the Church invites us to follow is no other: it is an authentic 'engagement', to 'increase and possess the earth' (Gen. 1:28) by our work and our discoveries, and then make of that an offering to the Creator—what could be more religious than this? 'The Creator of all things himself placed in the heart of man those irresistible aspirations towards finding a happiness on earth which is consonant with them; and Catholicism approves all the just efforts made by our civilization and progress properly understood for the perfection and development of humanity.[20] And Pius XII writes in the same vein: 'It would be a wrong interpretation of our words to take from them a condemnation of technical progress. No, we do not condemn what is a gift of God who at the time the world was created hid in the inner recesses of the earth

[18] 'To love the creatures of God, human joys, human effort, is not only allowed but ordered; it is necessary if we are to be like Christ and perform our duty .... The Christian loves the temporal as something which is meant to help him to reach God .... What Christianity therefore energetically condemns is not love of the temporal but idolatry of the temporal' (J. Mouroux, *L esens chrétien de l'homme*, p. 16).

[19] 'The Christian is not a coward afraid of facing life, or a weakling who shrinks from joy, or is frustrated. He is lucid and decided and knows that everything has to be purified—nature, love, even the person; and that with Christ he is capable of so doing' (J. Mouroux, *op. cit.*, p. 21).

[20] Pius XI, *Caritate Compulsi*, 3 May 1932.

treasures which the hand of man had to draw from it for his needs and his progress.'[21] Do not therefore be afraid that you will be less of a Christian the more you are a man; and each fresh conquest of the earth is a new province you bring within the universal domain of Christ the King.

The words of Pius XII are categorical: 'The Church cannot shut herself up and remain inert within the secrecy of her temples and by so doing desert the mission laid upon her by divine Providence, to form the whole man.'[22]

'Set yourselves therefore to the task, ... do not stand idly by in all this destruction. Step forward and rebuild a new social order for Christ. ...'[23] The question has been settled: not only must we be 'present in the world' but we must embrace progress. 'For a Christian who weighs history with the Spirit of Christ there can be no question of a return to the past, but only of the right to advance upon the future and to go from strength to strength.'[24] These last words we here make our own, and in the most categorical fashion we say to you: Go forward, work at the building of the new world. It depends on you whether it will be Christian or not. The world will belong to those who conquer it first. Upon you therefore depends the task of securing the second Spring of the Church.

In the real life around you, what are you going to do? It is the question St Paul asked on the road to Damascus: *Domine, quid me vis facere?* He received the prompt answer: *Surge, ingredere civitatem* (Acts 9:6). Entering society, becoming an active citizen within it, calls for a two-sided programme.

---

[21] Pius XII, Christmas broadcast, 1941.
[22] Pius XII, speaking to the new cardinals, 20 February 1946.
[23] Pius XII, Christmas broadcast, 1943.
[24] Pius XII, 13 May 1942.

THE TASK OF INTELLECTUALS

We have explained the general part to be played by intellectuals in drawing up the 'Catholic synthesis' which will reconcile tradition with progress, transcendence with incarnation. It remains for us to set out here the particular tasks their important mission lays upon them.

Their rightful autonomy

We remind you first of all that their work is to be done in independence. 'The Church has no intention of taking sides against any of the individual and practical forms by which peoples and states are trying to solve the gigantic problems facing their domestic organization and international collaboration, as long as these solutions respect the laws of God.'[25] It is not her mission to resolve directly problems which belong to the technical sphere. She leaves to the specialists their rightful autonomy; she is not held in fief by any system, in science, social questions or politics; and she gives her children freedom to follow their choice and pursue their researches. The latter have their own methods and their own object. It is necessary to make this distinction so as to avoid any confusion of 'spheres'. Let no one therefore expect from the Church what it is not in her power or duty to give; she will inspire everything, but she does not herself fashion civilization.[26] It is not for her to lay down what the struc-

[25] Pius XII, Christmas 1942.

[26] 'Within the limits of the divine law, which is the same for all and whose authority binds not only individuals but nations, there is a wide field and liberty of movement for the most varied forms. . . . The sole desire of the Church . . . the guardian and mistress of the principles of faith and morals, is, with the educational and religious means she possesses, to transmit to all peoples without exception the clear stream of their inheritance and the values of the Christian life so that each nation, in the measure suited to its particular needs, may use the doctrines and the ethical and religious principles of Christianity to establish a society worthy of man . . . the source of true well-being' (Pius XII, Christmas 1940).

tures of tomorrow shall be; she respects too highly the rights
men have and their freedom to initiate.

Thinkers and the initiative that belongs to them

But what she cannot herself do Christians can do and must
bring to pass; because, being also of this world, they have
an equal right with others to share in the search for truth
and to take part in all the debates and transformations
of a city to which they belong. The 'children of light' are
only too often less clever than the 'children of darkness';
and that fact, when it was voiced by our divine Master, was
not given as a precept. That Christians have been behindhand
in ideas may be a fact, but it is no virtue.

We therefore tell you, Christian thinkers, that your duty is
not to follow but to lead. It is not enough for you to be disciples; you must become masters. It does not suffice to initiate; it is necessary to invent.

Disinterested research

Your researches will deal first of all with truth simply and
solely, and with disinterested knowledge. You will pursue
truth for its own sake and without anticipating its applications. You will penetrate the secrets of nature more and
more deeply; and the unique mystery they constitute is a
constant appeal to climb higher in your search, even to God
himself. You will put together the conclusions you arrive at
in your specialist sciences and will endeavour to build up a
cosmic vision of the universe. In doing all this, you will
allow no consideration of interest, not even of apologetics, to
enter in: you will seek only for what is. Your loyalty will be
equalled only by your openness of mind and the effective
co-operation you show with all those, believers and non-
believers, who pursue truth 'with all their mind'. You will
have no hesitation in devoting yourselves, with all your powers

and in the 'delight of knowing', to your 'vocation of scholar-
ship'.[27]

In building the future city

Along with this, you will not hesitate to apply your researches
in another sphere also, that of civilization. What in fact is
the question at issue? It is a question of building the new
world, of specifying and preparing the structures which will
enable man to be fully man, in a city worthy of him, of transforming all things to make of them a Christian world.[28]
This is a vast programme, far beyond the capacities of one
generation, and one which demands two things. First, a process of analysis: you have to pronounce upon our present
civilization to judge it for its condemnation or its correction.
As I said recently,[29] you must draw up an objective balance-
sheet of our urban civilization today with its huge concen-
trations of human beings and its continual growth; the black
spots of its inhuman production, unjust distribution and dis-
sipating leisure. Then, secondly, by a process of synthesis,
beginning with the weaknesses of the present order, but
above all starting from its aspirations and the promise it
contains, you will draw up a plan of urban civilization and
of humanism on a vast scale, seen in relation to the nature
of man, his capacities and his needs. The whole sum of your
accumulated labours is to be directed towards that gigantic

[27] P. Termier. On this subject, see the words of Pius XII to a group of
French professors and students, 24 April 1946, on 'The Joy of Knowing'.
'That happiness is offered to you: do not despise it. . . . You will be more
eminent, even in your own line of study, the more you know how to enlarge
your outlook.'

[28] 'You must use all your natural gifts in the service of Christianity. And
so I hope you will not hesitate to have recourse to those parts of Greek
philosophy which may help; for this branch of knowledge is part of one's
general education, a preparation for higher studies'. Origen, *Ep. ad Greg.
Thaum.*, 3. (Bibliotheca Veterum Patrum, Venice, 1788, vol. III, p. 436).

[29] To the doctors and students of the Laënnec Conference, 15 November
1946.

synthesis of the future world. Do not show yourselves timid
in this task; but in the name of a science in which none
should be your equal, defend, exact and impose your masterly
vision, which will liberate man and the world.

Beginning with man

In the researches you make and the reforms you propose,
you alone will be the best humanists, for you alone have it
in you to provide the emerging civilization with a standard
which will be complete, namely, the right conception of man.
It is the Christian conception of human nature, and it alone,
which will save man from being dehumanized. Instead of
leaving him to be crushed by technical developments under
the pretext of liberating him,[30] and instead of beginning
with technical progress as a good in itself which justifies all
the sacrifices individuals and our society now make, you will
invariably begin with man himself and recognize him as an
independent 'person'. It is for him that the city is being
built. It is the city which is made for him; *it* will some day
end, but *he* will continue to live by his soul, which is immortal; and even at the resurrection of the dead, his body
will continue the body he knew on earth. It is perhaps not
necessary, in undertaking to elaborate social life, to be a
Christian; but it is necessary to be a Christian to succeed
completely in making man and his society; for only the
divine view of men can bring God's creatures to the supreme
development he intended them to reach. For it is this view
which reminds them that their 'aspirations are infinite' and
ever unsatisfied until they have been transcended; and that
to stop short at a point of development and name it the
'golden age' is imprisonment and death. From that aspect,

[30] The 'Catholic Centre of French Intellectuals'—CCIF—took man and
the questions which the development of technical progress raise for him as
the subject to be studied in 1947. Individual groups are already at work on
this very real problem.

it is part of the Church's mission to remind the world—as she has repeatedly done in the past and continues to do today —of the needs which temporal organizations must meet if the image of God in man is not to be disfigured.

It is for this reason that in social questions today the Church equally rejects a liberal economy which converts struggle into a law of progress as well as theories of the State which would swallow up the freedom of the individual in favour of an anonymous power, and instead puts forward solutions in which the organizing of the city comes from the united efforts which all together contribute freely and willingly, with respect for natural societies: the family, contracts, the various professions, and others.

Reforming structures

Your mission at this present time, therefore, carries with it the duty of research into, and a profound reform of, the structures of society, and that in every sphere. The most urgent need is in social and economic life. We are aware that courageous leaders of industry, in close contact with the working classes, have listened to the pressing appeal the Church in France addressed to them only recently, when we reminded them 'simply but firmly' that the principles governing the relations between capital and labour should be 'directed more and more plainly towards partnership'.[31] They are working boldly, as can be seen by their ideas and by what they have already accomplished to find a new outlook and to organize their factories along these lines, by associating the workers in them with administration, ownership and profits. We are also aware that large numbers of the laity are anxious to promote a genuine professional organization which, in due proportion, will unite accepted members of the profession who are representative of its interests with adequate control by public authority. In their application

[31] Statement by the ACA of France, February 1945.

such reforms involve technical questions of many kinds upon which it is not for me to pronounce. But they are in line with the ideas already put forward by the encyclical *Quadragesimo Anno*. They are necessary if the problems of economic and social life are to be solved, and they lay down the conditions without which there can be no transformation of the proletariat. We therefore warmly encourage those of the laity whose responsibilities allow them to act in this matter to take part in this development, and to persevere in it without being discouraged by the difficulties of all kinds which they encounter.

What we have said here of industry we apply to all the other sectors of public life: civic life, economic life, 'Political' life in its wider sense, international exchange, culture, education, leisure, the arts, and others. Christians must be present everywhere; that is the watchword we continue to give you and in the clearest forms we can. Let Christians become the 'leaven' and the mass will be transformed.

A CALL TO ALL[32]

Do not think, however, that the building of the future city belongs to the intellectuals alone. It is not necessary to be a scholar before you can share in this great work; and every Christian is called to it. Each one in his sphere of action can bring his influence to bear. 'The duty of this present hour is not to wring our hands but to act. Let there be no repining for what is or was, but reconstruct what is emerging and what must emerge, for the good of society.'[33]

Who—unless he shuts his eyes—cannot see the sorrows which surround him and the evils to be relieved? 'What priest, what Christian, can remain deaf to the cry coming from the depths of the masses who, in the world of a just

[32] See *Pastoral Letters*, pp. 55-8.
[33] Pius XII, Christmas message, 1942.

God, cry for justice and brotherhood? The Church would be denying her own self, she would cease to be a mother, if she remained deaf to the cry of anguish which reaches her from every class of humanity.... For us, *misereor super turbam* is a sacred watchword.'[34] Before he began to teach the people, Jesus Christ used first to tend the sick ... and he even gave a similar power to the apostles, with the command to use it.[35]

Thus, let each one set to work and drive his roots ever more deeply into the surroundings in which his life is cast. For one it means work in a welfare organization, or one which aims at securing better conditions of housing or of work; for another, action in a trade union or a profession, or accepting his responsibilities in a family association. Some will enter town planning, others youth movements or rehabilitation schemes. And by the living experience we have of them, we are certain that those of the faithful, who are active in Catholic Action or who have been trained in it, are particularly fitted for these many tasks. Day by day each can contribute his stone to the edifice all are raising together. It is enough to do this without heeding criticism or obstacles, with the 'faith that moves mountains'. 'You say,' exclaims Tertullian, 'that we are not men of the world. What do you mean? Do we not eat like you, dress like you? Do we not share the same way of life, the same human needs? Do you take us for aboriginals and savages, roaming the woods and exiled from civilization?'[36] Do not have any doubts about the results which will come from action which is thus bound up with life. At the time, you will not see the results of your groping and perseverance, but a day will dawn when your children and your grandchildren will thank you for the earthly dwelling you prepared for them.

[34] *Ibid.*
[35] Pius XII, quoting Matt. 8: 16; Luke 10: 8-9; 9: 6.
[36] Tertullian, *Apol.*, XLII, I (*PL*, I, 490-1).

CONCLUSION

Do you now see the lines of opportunity opening before you? Are you going to remain timid and despairing when such a splendid field of construction awaits you?

BEYOND OUTWARD APPEARANCES

We know that some are tempted to consider the task impossible. Never, perhaps, has the world lain so heavily upon our hearts, and there are undoubtedly days when everything seems dark. A world without God, the rising tide of sin everywhere, the repeated threat of collective suicide, the cries of distress assailing us wherever we turn, these are indeed enough to unnerve us. The anxiety which each feels in his own heart, how can he not extend it to the Church? What can she do, what is to become of her, in a world which has moved far from her and is bent on striking her name from the list of the living? Yes, it is indeed true that the task can appear beyond the power of men and impossible even for the Church, seemingly outflanked everywhere, and submerged by the deluge of the age.

And yet, look beyond the appearances: we know, even now, that in the struggle which has been joined, the Church is victorious already. Without illusion, and having calculated the price she will be called upon to pay, she repeats the words with which Christ inspires gave her: 'Have courage, I have overcome the world' (John 16:33).

BEYOND FALSE SYSTEMS

Our faith in the Church is grounded first of all in the insufficiency inherent in all that is not herself. The new messianic systems now being put forward as the answer to our hopes and our ills always fall short in one respect or another.

At the very time when the attraction they exercise is the
strongest, they provide obvious signs of decline to those who
have eyes to see. It has been said that the body takes its
revenge; today we ought to speak of the spirit taking its
revenge. The world cannot expel God with impunity, and the
hour of his return has sounded at last. The body of man can
be broken and ground to powder, but no one has the power
to stifle and kill his soul; and today his soul has begun to
speak. That can be seen in the disillusioned masses and felt
in the eager searchings of the intellect. Never, perhaps, have
the systems of men felt the craving for God to the extent
that they do today. So that when we look upon the Church
it is not doubt which assails us, still less fear or a feeling of
shame, but joy and pride. For these are systems and promises which pass, whilst the Church outstrips them all. She
would be stifled in such messianic theories, closed and muti-
lated as they are. Her youth withstands their power to grow
old.

THE IMMORTAL YOUTHFULNESS OF THE CHURCH

Ever youthful and undying, such is the lesson of the past
as well as of the present. What age before our own has
known such hopes as these? If there is no effect without a
cause, it is equally true that there are no causes without
their effect, and how can what is being sown today not
flower and bear fruit tomorrow? Whatever may come about,
we know now that in every class of society there are Christians who, in spite of error, opinions and perhaps persecution
and death, will witness to Christ and his undying Church.
We know that whatever may be done or said against God
will be answered in the hearts of others whom love of him
inspires. Anything may happen, persecution, heresy, war; but
we believe, more than ever, in the undying youthfulness of
the Church. At this point we cannot do better than to use

those words of Newman about the Church's second springs. 'Yes, my Fathers and Brothers, and if it be God's holy will, not Saints only, not Doctors only, shall be ours—but Martyrs too, shall reconsecrate the soil to God. We know not what is before us ere we win our own. . . .' But the call to joy follows the call to courage: 'We are engaged in a great, a joyful work'; and if we are to escape our present ills it must be by going forward. 'The world grows old, but the Church is every young.'[37]

Of the youth which is the ground of our hope we now know the secret: it is the mystery of the Church. 'One of the qualities of the Church which scripture praises most,' says Bossuet, 'is her perpetual youthfulness and her ever-enduring newness. And if you are perhaps astonished that instead of the novelty which is receding at this moment, I speak of a newness which does not end, it is easy for me to satisfy you. *The Church of Christ is always new, because the Spirit who is her soul is always new.*'[38]

---

[37] Newman, 'The Second Spring' in *Sermons Preached on Various Occasions*, Longmans, London, 1898, pp. 178, 176.

[38] Bossuet, *Sermons pour le Temps de Jubilé*, Metz, 1656. It should be noted how the Fathers always go back to the mystery of the Church when they forecast her permanent youthfulness: 'What makes you say "The Church has vanished from the world"? She will vanish only when her foundations fail. But how can Christ fail? And while Christ stands firm, the Church will never waver till the end of time.' St Augustine, *Enarr. in Psalm. CIII, Sermo II, no.* 5 (*PL*, 37, VI, 1353).

'The world', he says in another place, 'believes that Christianity will be short-lived and soon forgotten, On the contrary, in the words of the Psalmist, "it will endure as long as the sun endures." As long, that is, as time lasts, whose measure is the rising and setting sun, the Church, Christ's body on earth, will never fail.' *In Psalm. LXXI* (*PL*, 36, V, 906).

'Never leave the Church, for she is the strongest force on earth. She is your hope, your refuge, your salvation. The Church is higher than the heavens, broader than the earth; never growing old, but always in full vigour.' St John Chrysostom, *Hom. de Capto Eutropio*, no. 6 (*Opera Omnia*, Paris, 1721, p. 391).

... AND HER SECOND SPRING

With such a vision before us, and hopes such as these, we are now in a position to conclude.

What is to be thought of the Church which was called dead? The storms which men and ages have known have been unleashed upon her to engulf her; and like the ark she has weathered the flood and each time has found new shores for wider growth. Today as in the past the world will not be saved from the deluge with the ark.[39] Today as then, 'the Spirit hovering over the waters' sends out to it the dove, his living symbol, which bears his olive branch; and that witness to an unexplored continent in no way resembles a handful of withered leaves. It has the grace and damp freshness of Spring.

[39] *Haec est arca quae nos a mundi ereptos diluvio, in portum salutis inducit* ('This is the ark which rescues us from the flood of this world and brings us into the harbour of salvation'): Preface of the Mass for the Dedication of a church, Paris proper.

7. THE WORLD OF LABOUR AND ITS LIFE

STRUCTURAL REFORMS

Cardinal Suhard was neither an economist nor a sociologist. But he cared too much for the evangelization of the working class not to be concerned about its conditions of life, and consequently about economic and social structures. This concern was particularly in evidence after the Liberation, when amid doubts and difficulties a new economic order was coming into existence.

In November 1944, in reply to some anxious questions from his people, he wrote as follows: [1]

We hear much nowadays, in many circles, about 'structural reforms'. By that is meant—mainly in economic affairs, in the organization of industry, but also in the organization of society—radical reforms, not confined to rearranging the existing system, but aimed at establishing on new foundations the relations between the various elements which contribute to production: capital, management and labour. They would involve a real integration of the working classes in society by entrusting them with new responsibilities.

The Church is not afraid of either the name or the substance of reform. She has always favoured anything which enabled the poor, the workers, to achieve a fully human existence. She was the first to open schools for the children of the common people; she fought slavery in all its forms. She denounces the state of proletarianism as an evil. The fact that the workers are deprived of personal ownership

[1] Extracts from the 'Mot du Cardinal' of 27 November 1944, in *Semaine religieuse de Paris*, no. 4726 (2 December 1944), p. 345.

G

either over their homes or in their work, the fact that they lack the security and initiative they need in order to be fully men, constitutes in the Church's eyes the great disease of the modern world. This has been strongly maintained by Leo XIII, Pius XI and lately by our Holy Father Pius XII.

It follows, then, that the Church is bound to favour anything that helps to abolish proletarianism, and since this seems to be a direct product of the liberal capitalist system, she is bound to desire structural reforms to be applied to that system.

I realize that these reforms pose delicate technical problems. I know too that the search for technical solutions must take account not only of the present state and potentialities of industry but also of the legitimate aspirations of the workers, and must therefore be guided by a right view of the nature, destiny and dignity of the human person. This indicates the important part which Christians must play in the working out of these solutions.

I have no hesitation in declaring that to discover and apply the structural reforms necessary to free the masses from their proletarian condition is a *grave duty* of the present moment, to which I earnestly encourage all those Catholics who have some competence in these matters, especially our dear sons trained by the Catholic Action movements (of workers or the middle class), and those who are active in the Christian syndicates of workers and employers. Let them not hesitate to take a wide view! In case of need let them seek the advice of competent theologians. But they must know that on them lies the responsibility for discovering and promoting these necessary reforms. Their reward will be that they are thus working effectively for the good of France, for the union of her sons and, what is more, for the good of souls.

RENEWING THE WORLD OF LABOUR

In 1945 the Cardinal called his Lenten pastoral 'On structural reforms: the Church's teaching on property.' His chief collaborators this time were his secretary, Fr Le Sourd, with Fr Hua and Fr Villain of *Action Populaire*.[2] In the first part he recalls the Church's traditional doctrine on the nature, limits and meaning of the law of property. He condemns individualism and explains the demands of the common good and of charity in economic matters.

The second part sets forth the reasons for which the Church condemns the abuses of capitalism and their consequences, as much as those of Marxist socialism. The following extract is from the third part, entitled 'What the Church requires of her children'.

If anyone compares—as I, dear brethren, have compared—the Church's doctrine on property, either with the abuses of modern capitalism or with Marxism, which claims to take its place, he will be forced to conclude that *a change is necessary*. Not just the change of some details or even of some part of the building! It is not a question of consolidating or correcting or of better arrangement: it is a question of *rebuilding*. Many pieces of the organism will no doubt be put back in place, but it is a question of changing the whole basis of an organization, and of changing what governs all the rest: its direction, its end, that for which it is made.

In short, we have to aim at *structural reforms*. A structure corresponds to an aim. Now we have to change the aim: instead of aiming first at producing, we must aim first at giving all men a truly human life. In place of capitalism, a mere 'technique of production', in which, in the absence of a higher rule, production puts man at its service, we must put an economy which will be at the service of men—and not just of *some* men but of *all* men. Material goods, whether natural or manufactured, are all made for that end.

[2] From *Supplement* to *Semaine religieuse de Paris*, 17 February 1945, pp. 57-62.

Something is needed quite different from a more or less extensive modification of our institutions. More is needed, even, than a revolution, for 'revolution' means turning round, and a situation which is turned round is not necessarily improved or really changed. There must be a total *renewal*. Nothing less is demanded by the Church's doctrine, in comparison with which Marxism, we must be allowed to say, is a timid doctrine. The Marxist revolution simply transfers the privileged position of the capitalists to the proletariat. It leaves men enslaved to production and their hearts to the servitude of greed. Being materialist, it can do no other. But the Church claims to rescue human life from these slaveries. The revolution she brings about penetrates to men's souls, to remove their hatred and cure their selfishness. It is the revolution of love.

WELL-BEING AND HAPPINESS

'Whoever possesses, possesses for himself,' says liberal capitalism. Marxist socialism agrees, and concludes: 'Henceforth let everything be possessed by the socialist State! No more owners, all wage-earners!' which means: 'all proletarians'. No, says Christianity, *'No more proletarians, all owners! Whoever possesses, possesses for all'—must* possess for all, *can* possess for all, by the grace of our Saviour.

'Material well-being first! Production first!' says liberal capitalism again, and obtains it for the benefit of a few. Marxism repeats the cry, and seeks it for the benefit of the proletariat. But the social teaching of the gospel says: *'The spiritual first! The person first! Human life first!'* and demands it for all; for the proletariat, that they may cease to be such, and for the capitalists, for they too need to be liberated.

Now it is a fact that in their search for *well-being* neither capitalism (which obtains it for a few) nor Marxism (which hopes to obtain it for all) are able to find *happiness*. How should man find happiness against his true nature and against his spiritual vocation? Only the truth of Christ is really liberating, and it is so for *all* men, saying to all: 'Love one another'.

One can understand the recent remark of a communist to a Christian, whose life he had seen to be one of complete brotherly charity: 'You are more communist than we are.' The 'communism' of Christian love is indeed the only one which is really brotherly and 'communitarian'. In a world aged by the harshness of individualism, the coming of Christian charity will always be the great, the only, new thing.

This is the renewal for which Christ orders us to work, giving us at the same time the strength to effect it. For he sends his Holy Spirit to 'renew the face of the earth', to prepare for those new heavens and that new earth which he will usher in at the last day, when, in the words of Pius XI in his encyclical on communism, 'the promises of the false prophets will be extinguished in blood and tears on this earth', and there will sound forth 'the great apocalyptic prophecy of the Saviour of the world: "Behold, I make all things new" (Rev. 21:5)'.

MAN AND ECONOMIC LAWS

The hour is ripe for this renewal. The rigours of the war-economy, which delivered us from the techniques of liberal capitalism, if not from its spirit, summon all to reflection. The duty of carrying on the war does not prevent us from forseeing the period after the war. Shall we then have to fall back into the disorders of the pre-war economic 'crises'? That is unthinkable. The sufferings endured by the world during the frightful upheaval through which we are passing deserve a better conclusion. We repeat: there must be a change, a Christian renewal.

And let no one, in order to exclude discussion of structural reforms, plead the preservation of social peace. Peace is 'the tranquility of order'. Disorder, the existence of proletarianism, the internationalizing of money, the quest for nothing but material well-being—do you call that *order*? And, granted that capitalism preserves some good—as when it recognizes the right to private property, though it conceives it wrongly —does *tranquillity* mean *fixity*? The Holy Father does not think so, for in his Christmas message in 1942 he warned Christians against 'that hard and obstinate fixity of ideas, childishly attached to itself', and against 'a certain unwillingness, born of ignorance and egoism, to apply the mind to the problems raised by the rise of new generations, with their advances and their new needs', against 'slothful tranquillity' and against 'inertia' in that 'great spiritual battle, the aim of which is to build society, or rather, to give it a soul . . .'.[3]

And let no one plead the necessities of *technology*, as if technical progress necessarily entailed gigantic organizations, requiring vast capitalism, perhaps even socialism. Pius XII again gives the answer: 'No! technical progress does not determine economic life as if by a fatal and necessary law. It is indeed true that too often it has been bent to serve the selfish calculations of those who are greedy for an indefinite increase of capital. Why should it not be bent to serve the need of assuring private property for all, which is the cornerstone of the social order?' Moreover, technology should not rule men; men should rule technology. 'Technical progress itself' must be 'ordered and subordinated to the general good'.[4]

Further, before a revolution can take place in institutions, it must take place in men's minds. Now, in men's minds the

[3] Pius XII, Christmas message, 1942, ed. *Renouvaux*, nos 25 and 26.
[4] Pius XII, broadcast, 1 September 1944. *Documentation catholique*, 12 November 1944, p. 2.

revolution no longer has to happen: it has happened. All observers agree in recognizing that neither the workers nor, fortunately, many of the employers (especially Christians), will agree to return to the old state of things. The only question still open is: what will be put in its place? And it is here that Christians have their part to play, a necessary part which must be clearly understood.

THE VALUE OF THE TEMPORAL

It is not the aim of Christianity to establish a just social order. Its aim is to cause us to share in the divine life, to be in communion with God; that is its ultimate aim and at the same time its supreme value; that has value in itself, independently of its human repercussions. The communion with God which the Church inaugurates here on earth cannot be regarded as a means to procure some kind of human progress. 'Not to desire God for himself is to despise the divine gift.'

While man's destiny, however, is spiritual and even supernatural, it has natural conditions which involve matter, so that the Christian cannot be unconcerned with the temporal order or its economic foundations. It is the Christian's duty to create favourable conditions in this world for the Christian life. The existence of these conditions is ensured by a real Christian civilization. Pius XII accordingly invites us to restore economic life, as well as all social and international life, 'on a plan consistent with the religious and moral content of Christian civilization'. It is necessary to create a healthier juridical order and especially, in economic and social matters, to establish an order more in accordance with the divine law and with human dignity. The 'raising of the proletariat,' adds the pope, will be 'an essential element' of this new order. 'Every true disciple of Christ' must work for it with energy and generosity; for him it is more than a

question of earthly progress: it is 'the performance of a
moral duty'.[5]

Here the pope has made it a 'moral duty' for his sons, the
true disciples of Christ, to work for the raising of the pro-
letarit. What the Church asks of her children will vary in
different cases. She calls some to devise and apply the necessary structural reforms. She asks all to contribute by their
personal lives, particularly by the use they make of their
property rights, to that Christian renewal of the economic
order.

The Church requires those who are qualified by their competence, their functions in society or their professional activities, to shoulder their responsibilities in order to discover
and bring about the new structures. The Church does not
tell them the technical solutions, but urges them to find them
among those various solutions which are consistent with her
great moral principles. As I have said, the Church has no
economic doctrine in the modern sense of the word. It is the
same throughout the temporal order. *She does not wish to
legislate in the temporal order: that would be clericalism.
She does not wish to contract out of the temporal order:
that would be spiritual evasion. She provides the laity with
the doctrine which will enable them to give life to the whole
temporal order.*[6]

As the Church does not deprive her lay sons of their initiative, so she does not think of denying in any way the rights
of the State. Provided that the State is faithful to its function of high policy and does not stoop to subordinate itself
to economics, the Church claims that its intervention is indispensable. It is for the State to guide industries for the
general good of the country and to see that all its elements
have a part in the industry worthy of their dignity as rational
beings. Again, it is necessary for the State to leave indivi-

[5] *Ibid.*, p. 2.
[6] A. Ancel, *Catholiques et Communistes*, p. 16.

duals, families and corporate bodies of lower rank (particularly professional bodies) to carry out for themselves what they are capable of doing. For 'the natural object of all intervention in social matters is to help the members of the body of society, not to destroy or absorb them'.[7]

Here I wish to congratulate the members of our professional groups and Catholic Action movements for their researches and initiatives. For instance, some Christian employers have set themselves to study, and in conjunction with the members of our workers' Catholic Action have produced, a 'common plan for the reform of industry'. I need not pronounce on the technical considerations or conclusions which emerge from their work. I only wish to point to the example of an initiative which I know is not alone in this field, and to underline the importance of the problem it deals with.

MONEY WHICH CRUSHES MAN

When Pius XII denounces the exaggerated accumulations of wealth which succeed in evading their social role, he states that this happens 'under the guise of anonymity',[8] and a warning here is necessary. The system of limited companies (*sociétés anonymes*), as it has actually developed in France, seems to have effaced man behind capital. The *sociétés de capitaux* are not by themselves societies of persons: despite the efforts of the best employers, who are the first victims of the system, financial considerations are uppermost in them; capital monopolizes management and profit; finally the responsibilities are 'limited' or even diluted between a great number of stocks, the bearers of which are made incapable

[7] Encyclical *Quadragesimo Anno*, Catholic Truth Society translation, *he Social Order*, p. 37.
[8] Broadcast, 1 September 1944.

of assuming the responsibilities which are theirs by natural law.

If these statements are accurate, and if the long-awaited reforms have not yet restored, in our *sociétés de capitaux,* the primacy of responsible management and of labour over capital, this is an abuse to be forcibly denounced. Money in itself cannot possibly be regarded as an owner, for ownership is the privilege of a person. Money must remain a servant and must never command. As for man, he cannot abdicate, for the pursuit of profit alone, the social responsibilities which belong to ownership. If he insists on limiting his responsibilities or if he finds it morally impossible to meet them, he must also sacrifice a part of his revenue and give up playing the decisive role in industry usually held by anonymous capital. By refusing a part of his duties he has forfeited a part of his rights.

An illicit preponderance of anonymous capital in industry is all the more intolerable in that it goes hand in hand with a depreciation of management and the labour-force; the encylicals teach that these are the main causes of the value of manufactured articles. Whereas capital can increas in snowball fashion, without great personal effort on the part of the owner, labour is in danger of being treated as mere merchandise, its human character forgotten. 'The worker knows that in all the decisions touching his life (dismissals, wage systems, rationalization, etc.) it will be a consideration, expressed or unexpressed, of profit or revenue that will prevail over concern for his most pressing human needs. Here can be seen the vice of capitalist industry: the primacy of money over men, of capital over labour.... The whole problem is how to reverse the order of the factors by putting *capital at the service of human values,* and subordinating its profits to the payment of a just wage.'[9]

[9] Cf. *Plan commun,* no. 44, *Contribution à une reforme de l'entreprise,* Equipes patronales, 18 Rue de Varenne, Paris 7.

THE WORKER IN INDUSTRY

It is well known, too, that the worker suffers chiefly, in the last resort, from his moral situation. Too often in industry, it has been said, he is merely an interchangeable cipher, an 'anonymous accessory of his machine', 'with no material or moral independence in relation to capital', which retains all the economic power. The worker is not treated as a *person*, and that is the main thing that makes him a proletarian.

The larger the business, the more marked is this disadvantage. This is why Pius XII adopts and stresses a suggestion of Pius XI, advising that where it is not possible to obtain the same advantages with small or medium-sized concerns which are united in co-operatives as it is with large concerns, 'the wage-contract should, when possible, be modified somewhat by a contract of *partnership*'.[10] The worker must be allowed to contribute something personal to the common good of the business and to the general welfare, and to be aware of his contribution. This can mean arranging, in some way, for labour to have a share in the profits and even in the management and ownership of the business. The 'common plan', which I have quoted, claims to show that this is possible without compromising either the principle of the private ownership of the business (which is simply expanded into common ownership), or the authority of the managing director, which is indispensable to the good management of affairs.

I am not unaware of the technical and the even greater psychological difficulties of these reforms. But these reforms are legitimate and the prize is worth the trouble. Up to now the workers have been able, by the wage-contract pure and simple, to forego a part of their rights in exchange for a tacit assurance against the risks. But now, in France, they

[10] Broadcast, 1 September 1944, Cf. *Quadragesimo Anno*, C.T.S. translation, p. 31.

wish to recover those rights in order to escape from their state of dependence—a demand which is perfectly natural. The pure wage-contract was just, but it was optional. No one has the right to impose it on those who no longer desire it. New solutions must therefore be found, with generous and prudent boldness.

I also wish to encourage all attempts to restore *human dimensions* to industries, or at least to their basic units. There is a limit beyond which an industry ceases to be within a man's grasp; management, and capital even more so, can no longer be aware of the human repercussions of their actions. Man finds that he is almost inevitably enslaved to technical requirements and is himself treated as a machine.

Finally I must praise whatever can be done to bring it about that in normal conditions the worker's *wage* will enable him not only to feed himself and his family but to acquire, in the first place, the private ownership of his furniture, his house and domestic garden, and eventually to share in the ownership of the means of production themselves.

I call you, and all men of good will with you, to a real crusade against the rule of money, and for the full personal development of *all* men, not only of a few. For this end the Church needs not only those competent laymen whom I have just addressed, but all her children.

THE MEANING OF WORK

Labour Day, suppressed during the Occupation, was officially revived in 1946. The Cardinal used the occasion to remind the faithful of the Christian meaning of work. He had already done so more briefly in the previous year, without waiting for the official restoration of the day. These form the two short extracts which now follow.

BUILDING THE WORLD[11]

Pagan antiquity despised manual work as unworthy of a free man, and made the worker a slave. The modern world increasingly honours work and the workers. The Church cannot but rejoice at this, for she has long demanded it in recalling that the Son of God, when he came into the world to save all men, willed to be a working man and a member of a family of working men.

Work enables man to build the world in his image, thus in a way extending the creative work of God. Work turns a hostile material universe into a world friendly to man, a world which can be subject to him, a world which he can inhabit and in which he can begin to live as a child of God. As soon as man appeared on this earth, it was his task to work in this way for the construction of the world. The evil of sin had the effect of making this work laborious, its results uncertain and always precarious; unhappily, the malice of men sometimes works not to build but to destroy. The ambition to build a better world by work is still right and good, a Christian ambition agreeable to the will of God for man.

Work not only helps to build the world; it should help to perfect man himself and enable him to complete himself. The very effort demanded by work, the discomfort it involves, should enable man to conquer himself and excel himself, according to his earthly and eternal vocation. Work should ennoble man. It is a scandal, unhappily too frequent, as Pius XI noted, that 'whereas matter emerges from the factory ennobled, the worker emerges lowered and degraded'. The scandal is all the worse when the inhuman conditions of labour injure young girls, wives and mothers of families.

Work and production at the service of men, of all men,

[11] 'Mot du Cardinal' of 18 April 1945, in *Semaine religieuse de Paris*, no. 4747 (28 April 1945), p. 143.

of the workers themselves in the first place—not men as
slaves of a production without rule or curb for the benefit
of a few—is the principle which must guide us in building
a new world of work.

WORK AND SOCIAL ACTION[12]

This year the First of May will again be officially celebrated
in France as Labour Day. We shall take part in it, in our
various ways. Thus we shall show our wish to honour the
true Christian idea of work.

Following the example of Christ, the divine carpenter of
Nazareth, and of the Holy Family, the Church has always
shown particular care for those who toil to support their
families. All forms of work have their own dignity: manual
work, intellectual work, but also the work, so deserving but
often too little considered, of the mother of the family, who
keeps her home and brings up her children.

I wish that all honour were given to the faithful, conscientious and persevering work of those who earn their living honestly, without recourse to those unlawful methods un-
fortunately encouraged by the circumstances of war, but
condemned by conscience. Nor can I remain indifferent to
the failures, the destitution and the countless difficulties
which assail the great mass of those who live in constant
anxiety about their daily bread. I call on all men to do their
utmost to soften the rigours of this situation by generous
acts of mutual aid and charity.

But I take occasion from the present situation to draw
your attention more particularly to the grave problems arising in what is commonly called 'the world of labour.' Alongside just and legitimate aspirations which ought to be satisfied, I cannot help observing with alarm and ever increasing

[12] Appeal for Labour Day, 24 April 1946, in *Semaine religieuse de Paris*,
no. 4799 (27 April 1946), pp. 281-2.

hold of materialist doctrines which imperil both the foundations of our society and the Christian faith of the mass of the people.

Our disorganized uneasy world is trying to construct a new economic and social regime. What will it be? If profound transformations are inspired by pernicious doctrines, will they not be a remedy worse than the disease?

I am, of course, resolutely in favour of a renewal in our institutions, and of constant social progress, but always on condition that the demands of justice and charity are respected. There is no true salvation for our society except in the path of Christian civilization, whose essential principles are luminously indicated in the papal encyclicals and messages. It is therefore my duty to remind all men that it is urgently necessary to study Christian social doctrine, to be steeped in it and to do all in our power to make it the guide of men's minds and the foundation of our institutions.

Social action must therefore be intensified to respond to the pressing needs of the day. Let each take his share of responsibility and influence, so that bold yet prudent solutions may be applied in all fields. I appeal to all your devotedness, to help those already active in social organizations which are inspired by Christian principles.

To mark my desire to give the utmost possible help to Christian social action, I earnestly recommend to your generosity the collection which will be taken today in all churches of the diocese for the Social Secretariat of Paris and the Union of Social Secretariats, which undertake this difficult task. Those who are involved in this immense work are often held up by lack of funds. In comparison with other campaigns they dispose of all too limited means. I count on you to contribute, according to your means, to the development of this activity. All of us wish it well. It must speedily be provided with means commensurate with its importance

and necessity. I commit this request to your intelligence
and your charity.

THE 1947 'SEMAINE SOCIALE'[13]

Among 'social organizations inspired by Christian principles' an
important place is held by the 'Semaines Sociales de France'
(Social Weeks). Founded in 1904 by Marius Gonin and Adéodat
Boissard, and then presided over by Henri Lorin and Eugène
Duthoit, these conferences have played an important part, during the first half of the century, in disseminating and applying
the Church's social doctrine. In their annual sessions the lec-
turers—economists, philosophers, theologians, industrialists, trades
unionists and journalists—confront the social facts of the day
with the Church's thought.

After the Semaine at Bordeaux in 1939 these meetings for
study and popularization were interrupted for six years by the
war, and under the Occupation the leaders of the movement had
to confine themselves to restricted, secret activity. In 1945 the
annual session was resumed at Toulouse, on the theme 'Social
transformations and the liberation of the person'. A team of professors and technicians examined, in the light of Christian social
doctrine, the chief structural reforms necessary for the recon-
struction of the country and for the peace of the world, and the
conditions required to safeguard the dignity of the human person.

At Strasburg in 1946 the theme was 'The national community'.
The members studied the relations between the nation or the
State and the citizens, between the unity of France and individual liberties, between the human community in its totality
and the various spiritual communities. They set out to find principles and solutions capable of reconciling the existence and unity
of the French community with respect for the other national or
international communities.

In 1947 the 34th session was held in Paris. It opened on 28
July at St Sulpice, with a Mass celebrated by the Apostolic Nuncio,
Mgr Roncalli, and an address by Mgr Blanchet, Rector of the
Institut Catholique, who offered its premises to the organizers
of the conferences. The theme chosen was closely linked with the
situation of those post-war years: in studying 'Social Catholicism and the main contemporary currents' the object was to define the relations between Christian social thought and the posi-

[13] *Documentation catholique*, no. 997 (17 August 1947), col. 1069-80.

tions maintained by socialism, Marxism, fascism and neo-liberalism.

Pius XII personally attached great importance to these studies and wrote to that effect to Charles Flory, president of the Semaines. One passage from this letter is particularly noteworthy:

Besides the distinction between employers and employees, which threatens to become increasingly one of inexorable separation, there is work itself, the task of everyone's personal life, aimed at producing for society the goods and services necessary or useful to it. Thus understood, work is able of its very nature to unite men really and intimately; it can restore form and structure to a society lacking shape and consistence, and thereby heal anew the relations of society with the State. On the other hand, when men try to make the State a mere mass of workers, they misunderstand the essence of both, they deprive work of its real meaning and its intimate power to unite. In the last resort they organize, not men—workers considered as such—but a gigantic sum of revenues in wages or salaries. The danger of the State being dominated by economic forces, to the great detriment of the general welfare, is just as serious in this case as when the government of the State is subject to the pressure of capital.

Commenting on these words in *Le Monde* of 31 July, Etienne Gilson noted that Pius XII 'invited contemporary societies to present their problems, no longer from the point of view of the workers, but rather from that of work', that is, in a dimension of synthesis rising above the separate and apparently irreconcilable interests of employer and employee. He wrote:

For one thing at least is really common to the employer and the employee, and that is the industry, which is the bond, the means and the result of their common effort. Neither of them should work for the other, but both for industry. If it is supreme, then its wholly objective demands, inevitable as the laws of reality itself, will assign to employers and employees their respective places, with invincible authority. Perhaps there will have to be rather more intellectual realism than is found in the individualist idealism which afflicts too many modern minds. In particular we need to recover the meaning of that truth, once well known but now too often forgotten, that the sole judge capable of uniting divided minds is the nature of things. The only way to transcend the conflict of employers and employees, and by transcending it to resolve it, is to give back to work and its efficacy the primacy which belongs to them by right of nature.

These short quotations suffice to recall the economic climate of that period, characterized by the theories of Burnham and Keynes, intent on the search for a new basis for industry.

Charles Flory, who gave the inaugural address entitled 'The crisis of civilization and the confrontation of doctrines', alluded in his opening words to 'the penetrating vigour and breadth of views' of *Rise or Decline*. 'Masterly lectures' were then delivered by Frs Bigo, de Lubac and Chenu and by Joseph Folliet, André Piettre, Hubert Beuve-Méry, Jean Lacroix, Maurice Blondel and Marcel Prélot.

The Semaines Sociales were no novelty to the Cardinal. As Archbishop of Reims he had welcomed that of 1933 and given an address, from which a passage on the rights of the person deserves a brief mention:

The human person! The human person: that is what counts. That is what we must keep in view. To that we must always return. And for you, who are leaders of the people, this creates the duty to be kind and charitable to your subordinates, as well as just, the duty to enlarge and enrich their personalities as well as to respect them, the duty to dispose everything so that the weak may be succoured, the poor may be helped, the small and humble may be protected, the defenceless may be guaranteed, and he who is abandoned without mercy to pitiless and unscrupulous powers may not be condemned. The human person—we must always come back to that. Such is the Christian order of things: subordination of everything to the human person and, in

the human person, subordination of everything to the glory
of God, and finally peace in the city.

In this year, 1947, the Cardinal was unable to give the address
of welcome, traditionally reserved to the bishop of the diocese
in which the session was held, for he was in Rome, reporting to
Pius XII on his recent pastoral efforts in the diocese. He returned,
however, in time to give the closing sermon in Notre-Dame on
the evening of 2 August.

THERE IS ONLY ONE CATHOLICISM:
IT IS SOCIAL OR NOTHING

After greeting those attending the Semaine, the Cardinal briefly
traced the history of the movement. The Semaines Sociales, he
said, had been a ferment: they had produced 'men, ideas, successes'. They had created a climate

in which, at the beginning, one could breathe the very frag-
rance of the primitive Church. Then the inner circle grew,
and the Semaine became a rallying-point for all who were
only waiting for this signal and this impulse to emerge
from their timid solitude. From these assembled wills a
great current came into being; social Catholicism became a
reality.

'Social Catholicism'! I purposely use this term, at once so
true and so false. There is no such thing as social Catholicism if by that we mean one face of Christianity, whose
other face is not turned to the love of our neighbour. There
is only one Catholicism: it is social or nothing. But alas!
there are baptized Christians who are not 'social', and are
therefore Catholics only in name. It is for them, because of
them, that it is necessary to accept the pleonasm and to
couple with a supremely altruistic noun an adjective which
can only weaken it.

But names matter little. What really counts is that in
France there are now many Catholics, prepared, open to the
common weal, passionately devoted to the Church, who can

rightly be regarded as the products of the Semaines Sociales. Not everything, of course, in these new advances and concerted labours has sprung from the Semaines, but they have played an important part, and it will be their glory to have raised up, for God and country, such devoted efforts and such sons.

Confrontation with social currents

It is not by chance, gentlemen, nor for the symmetry of an argument that you have chosen for your subject 'Social Catholicism in face of the great contemporary trends'. On the contrary, the intention which has guided the choice of this subject is shown by all that has gone before. It is no part of my plan this evening to resume, even by naming them, those major systems with which Christians now have to reckon whether they like it or not. One fact, simply, is self-evident: these systems have a common feature. They are no longer mere ideologies, they are currents, lines of force. They no longer offer themselves as a free and purely intellectual choice they demand the adherence of a man's life, where they do not force themselves on it. Each of them constitutes a sufficient and necessary 'whole', like a sphere which calls out to be completed. In this way, knowingly or not, they are totalitarian. They admit of no alternatives, no delay, no reservations. They promise everything to all, but demand everything from each.

To this ultimatum, what will be the response of the man, of the Christian? Both the man and the Christian, if they are isolated, will yield to force or be dazzled by the mirage. In either case, it will be a human defeat. But is it enough, is it fair, to blame them for this? Will the fault not lie, on the contrary, with the doctrine or the leaders who could neither arm nor satisfy them?

All this you have understood. You have felt that a *whole* cannot be parried with a fraction; that to a fact one cannot oppose an abstract idea; that a community cannot be matched by an individual. You have grasped that Christianity is not a disembodied speculation, nor a collection of composite aspects, but a living and vital unity, a reality, the only fully human reality, because it is genuinely divine. And so, instead of concentrating this year on some particular element of our faith—however undoubtedly useful such an enquiry might have been—you have gone for the essential, which is also the most relevant. Without shirking the difficulty of such a vast canvas, nor the dangers of apparent repetitions, you have grappled with the problem in all its breadth. And, faced with contemporary centres of attraction, you have taken it to be your first duty, the most truly brave, the most intelligently effective course, to draw up Catholic social doctrine boldly, calmly and completely, on that ground which it was the first to conquer, for a confrontation without weakness and an urgent appeal to all men of good will.

Faith and works
This task is doubly beneficial. To Catholics, this parallel presentation is a reminder and perhaps a discovery. To some —too many—who have not learned to free themselves from a factitious superiority-complex, it shows the culpable error and the dangers of a certain inexcusable self-sufficiency, which entrenches them in the privilege of their baptism so as to dispense them from acting and seeking. It shows them that if they do not want to be outstripped by others they must wake from sleep and set to work, without rest or delay. For it is of little avail to possess the truth if we do not live by it and spread it. It is useless and wrong to have faith without works. To others, on the contrary, who might be seduced by the deceptive baits of the new 'gospels', this confrontation gives courage and justification. They doubted because they had never 'seen'. They had never seen the beauty and splendour of the Christian edifice. Now it is being

shown to them; they are discovering and admiring it; they are offering themselves. The case has been heard: Christ and his Church will have no keener militants.

And this has been brought about, not by propaganda nor by speeches but simply by a vision of the whole, radiating harmony, and by order, which sets every value in its place. There is now no danger of confusing the gospel with its imitations, still less of preferring the inferior copy to the original. But at the same time the opposite danger is avoided, that of denying and denouncing everything which is not peculiar to ourselves. Excellent for avoiding confusion, this 'comparative method', at once irenic and firm, is no less excellent for keeping us from separating and excluding without reason. The Word of God is spread abroad everywhere. By the way of negation it explains the error itself, which could not gain its adherents without this 'soul of truth'.

THE FUTURE OF THE CHRISTIAN SOCIAL MOVEMENT

The Cardinal then defines the role of the Semaines Sociales in this new world now being built. They must, he says, continue the work they have begun, and 'remain, if they would not be cut off and brought to an end, a centre of social thought'. They must

prepare the future development of doctrine, by being open to the new currents and the experiments constantly being started on the levels of doctrine and practice. They will therefore have to analyse the economic complexes which the Church has not yet been able to study, to discern the tendencies of the various social milieux, to weigh the human worth of foreseeable evolutions and to give loyal and filial information to the hierarchy, so that it may be able to guide mankind towards its goal with full knowledge of the subject.

Noting that this means being 'precursors', the Cardinal encourages the members of the session to set out on the road of research and action.

A system of thought on the march
Seen from this angle, the Semaines Sociales certainly deserve, in a second sense, the title of a 'walking university':
they are a *system of thought on the march*. It falls to them,
therefore, with the necessary precautions, to place at the head
of their programme the study of those structural reforms,
about which I said lately that the Church feared neither their
name nor their substance, and which the cardinals and archbishops of France, at their meeting in February 1945, described as 'necessary', saying that they were 'ready to welcome
them'.

But here, gentlemen, you must be honest and ask yourselves a question, which I do not hesitate to share with you.
Is it sufficient to stop short on the level of study? Have these
speculative researches proved to be effective?

Yes, without doubt, through all the initiatives and devoted
action they have inspired, which far exceed measurable
spheres of influence. But can this influence, certain as it is,
satisfy us? Let us be bold to admit that it cannot. That advance, valuable in less trouble times, is no longer in step
with our all-devouring evolution. We are at the heart of
action, in the heat of battle. The time has come when we
have not a minute to lose, not a force to spare. It is no
longer a question of obtaining advantages but of fighting for
life. Faced with the massive ideologies which are working to
possess the earth, pure reasoning is no longer current coin.
Not that ideas have ceased to lead the world, far from it:
they decide more of it than ever before. They decide so
much that without them the most fervent attempts, the most
generous conquests, would be exhausted or lose all shape.
And, from this point of view alone, we must not ignore or
minimize the danger to which too many youthful ardours
succumb. Because they want to succeed too quickly or penetrate too widely, they exhaust themselves and disappoint the

very people they had first won over. Soon they have no more
principles with which to convince them, no more food on
which to nourish them, no more basis for a building.

In emphasizing this danger and addressing you, my dear
young friends who listen to me, it is not my purpose, as you
know, to dampen your enthusiasm or to blame your hopes.
On the contrary, it is because I count on you that I say to
you clearly and frankly: 'Study, work, meditate.' Do not
leave to others the love of truth for truth's sake nor the disinterested pursuit of the real. Think before you express
yourselves; understand before you explain; search before you
undertake. Make no mistake: without that patient effort,
often thankless but always deserving, no lasting fruit can be
obtained. The application is worth only what the doctrine
is worth, the end is worth only what was promised by the
beginning. The conclusion follows the premises. My dear
young people, never think yourselves dispensed, even by your
sacrifices, from that serious labour, that attentive knowledge,
which it is one of your chief merits to deepen. May action
never make you give up ideas!

Pure ideas or dynamic ideas?

But those ideas themselves—and here you are right—must
never be cut off from concrete fact. *In place of pure ideas
they must become dynamic ideas.* Facts must be answered
by facts, currents of thought by a stronger current. When
invasion has breached the line and is fanning out, it is not
to be met by strategic theories. The army is mobilized,
equipped, assembled, and at one blow the total massed
strength is hurled into the desperate struggle, to halt the
enemy advance and check encirclement, until it can take the
offensive in its turn.

Gentlemen, I should not make this appeal to you if its
urgency were not justified by the approaching struggle, if
I did not already know, from your whole past, that you were

ready to hear and follow it. Was it not one of your founders, Marius Gonin, who summed up your programme in those terse words: 'Knowledge for action'? You have been entrusted with a great mission: to make a place for yourselves, in ideas and among Christians. That mission you have fulfilled. Now another lies before you, which would have been impossible without the first, but without which the first would not be complete: it is to grow in numbers and to lead! The very life of our Christianity depends on this. Like everything else it is subject to the hard law of this age of iron: penetrate or disappear!

THE SOCIAL PROBLEM WILL NOT BE SOLVED WITH CHRISTMAS TREES

Soon after the Semaine Sociale at Paris came the great strikes of November and December 1947. These movements were markedly political in character; the Communist party, having had to leave the government in May, used them to the utmost to strengthen the opposition, from whose ranks it was rejected. But these strikes were also the symptoms of a very real social sickness. Two years after the end of the war, France had not yet recovered her economic balance, and the shortage of her production caused the weight of distress to fall on the poorest classes.

In his Christmas message the Cardinal ignored the political questions involved in the conflict and dealt with its social aspect, reasserting not only charity but the primordial rights of justice.[14]

On this sacred night which enjoins a truce among men, I come to make an appeal to you. Open your eyes and look about you. You have not far to look for misery. It is everywhere. It is everywhere you look: dark slums, emaciated children, old people found dead from cold in the morning. It is also where you least suspect it: hidden distress, fathers and mothers at their wits' end over the next day. Almost all classes of society are affected. Millions of workers, low-

[14] *Semaine religieuse de Paris*, no. 4886 (5 February 1947), pp. 1603-4.

paid employees, retired people and widows, lack bread and coal.

Faced with such distress, what are we to do? Renounce luxury and ostentation? Provide a portion for the poor at the Christmas dinner? Certainly. But we must be careful. You cannot quiet your conscience with a parcel. The social question is not to be solved with Christmas trees. Charity is a good thing when it bears witness to love; when it tries to dispense with justice it is an evil. What so many unfortunates want is not some partial help with no future. It is a total and lasting solution. It is a matter of humanity.

This has been clearly seen in these last weeks. Led astray, no doubt, but borne along by a wave of remoter origin, the people of France has put the problem to itself. After some critical days it has resumed work. Public order has been restored. But the question is not closed. Nothing in the condition of the working classes has changed. The workers are sad and discouraged. The Church knows this and is moved by it. Whatever touches her sons affects her inmost being. She is not resigned to the proletarian condition, which she holds to be the disgrace of this age.

What does the world of the workers demand? Simply its rightful place in the nation. It does not wish to be treated as a minor. It wants account to be taken of its continual rise. In this field, responsibilities fall largely on the public authorities: efforts have been made and results obtained. But basic reforms must be undertaken. We must not fear to tackle them boldly.

I know that this programme meets with obstacles. The war is over, the country is poor. It is only natural that all Frenchmen should accept sacrifices, but it must not always be the same people who have to bear them. We realize the economic necessities. We know how heavily they weigh on those who are in charge of industries and the country. But on this Christmas night, when everyone feels somehow responsible for his brothers, we put this question frankly: are we sure that we have searched enough? Are we sure we have tried everything? We raise the objection of technology: could we not rather invoke its aid? Have all means been used? A determined effort cannot fail to restore the balance in the end.

But there is one condition, which is not an easy one: we must be united in order to live. Without aiming at an impossible equality, we must throw down the barriers and form one community. This is the price of social peace. Nothing can be done in hate; everything can be done in love.

Such a programme may make the sceptics smile. It will not discourage a man of good will. It is indeed Utopian, if we see nothing in man but appetites and the desire for gain. But that is not how Christians see him. Because they have faith, they also have hope. They do not believe in the golden age, but they know what can be done by grace. They know what a revolution the gospel has come to bring about on the earth. So what do the obstacles matter? One thing is certain: Christ has redeemed the world.

It is my wish, my prayer, that this feast of Christmas may remind us that there is only one road for mankind: the road which leads to the star, to the cradle of the infant God!

'PROGRESSIST CHRISTIANS'

It was the same anxiety to safeguard the spiritual character of the Church and not to let Christians engage indiscriminately in any action they liked, whether political, economic or social, that moved the Cardinal to issue his warning of 31 January 1949.[15]

We should remember that Cardinal Mindszenty, primate of Hungary, had been arrested on 27 December and that his trial took place between 3 and 8 February.

Moved by anxiety for the spiritual good of souls, I believe it to be my duty to draw the attention of the clergy and the

---

[15] *Semaine religieuse de Paris*, no. 4943 (9 April 1949), pp. 347-50.

laity to the following points, which concern both doctrine and practice.

1. I wish to affirm once more that the major problem of our time is the suppression of social injustice. I sympathize profoundly with the just claims and lawful aspirations of the working class. I know and deplore the painful conditions in which many workers live. I encourage Catholics to play their part, with all their human energies and all their Christian faith, in the establishment of a more just and fraternal human order. Make no mistake: the Church refuses to be the vessel of money. Her love and care extend first to those who have to struggle to improve their material lot and to defend their human dignity. She makes it a duty for her people to work bravely to abolish the disorders caused by the present capitalist system. They will find their inspiration in the social teaching developed in these last fifty years by the popes. But, against the injustices peculiar to the capitalist system as it is actually practised, the Church holds that there is something better to do than to favour the coming of a totalitarian and atheistic collectivism.

2. Some Catholics, anxious to shoulder their secular responsibilities effectively on the level of political action, maintain that their conscience alone is a sufficient guide to the demands of Christian morality in this field. Without rejecting the common teaching of the Church on the subordination of politics to morality, without even denying the Church's power to determine the general principles which should inspire them in their political action, they claim that in the concrete commitments of that action the Church can in no case give them light and fix their line of conduct.

This is not the first time that such opinions have appeared among French Catholics. Though developed in circles of diametrically opposite tendencies, they are wholly derived from the same fundamental error.

It is certainly true that in the political field the Christian enjoys a very wide initiative on his own responsibility. In most cases the Church allows him to fix his attitude for himself in the light of the demands of justice and love, which he can never ignore. She is then content to illuminate his case of conscience without defining it, by reminding him of the general principles which the Christian himself has to apply.

But when the Church considers that in the existing circumstances her principles impose a definite attitude, she has the right and even the duty to dictate the side to be taken. She does this only rarely and when spiritual interests are directly and seriously involved, but then she does it in full awareness that she is fulfilling her mission, and she holds that she is the supreme judge of the timeliness of her intervention.

If the opposite opinion were admitted, it would give the Christian conscience such autonomy with regard to the Church that it would reject the Church's mediating role in the order of human acts and would in practice deny the supreme dominion of God over the whole of social life. This means that no catholic can profess it without going gravely astray.

3. Certain Catholics think they can carry on their political action as Christians, some inside the Communist party, others in close and habitual collaboration with it. The movement known as the 'progressist Christians' has adopted this latter attitude. It claims to be able to dissociate the atheism professed by Communism (which for its part it rejects) from the political and social action of the party, whose practical objectives it adopts.

I must warn the faithful against the dangers involved in such an attitude, particularly those whose training leads them to figure as directors, whether on the ideological or the practical level. By thus habitually associating his action with that of the Communist party, the Catholic runs the risk of being captured, often without knowing it, by the principles of a doctrine condemned by the Church, and contributes in part to the party's success. The triumph of the Communist party will inevitably mark a retreat from faith in God, an unjust limitation upon the liberties of the Church, and recourse to totalitarian political methods, for which Marxism itself provides the theory. There are too many recent examples which the communists do not attempt to deny, for us to have any doubt about this. No Catholic should expose himself to reproach for having given his support to the establishment of a regime which involves such injustices.

No doubt it may happen that Catholics are led by circumstances to conduct their action on a parallel course with that of Communists in the pursuit of limited and precise objectives required by the general interest, but without essential links with the particular aims of the party; but the Church could never allow a habitual and close collaboration. She knows that Communism involves so grave a mutilation of man that it can never procure his effective liberation, and she calls on her faithful to work out their thought and guide their action without subjecting themselves to a theory and an action whose fundamental principles are on so many points in contradiction to our own, even in social and political matters.

In order to implement this policy, I count more than ever on the priests and lay militants who, as they live among the workers, share their anxieties, their cares and also their hopes. They have my confidence: all the faithful should know it, and I am happy to assure them of it once more.

8. THE CHRISTIAN AND HIS ACTIVE PRESENCE IN THE WORLD

At first sight the bulk of the speeches, sermons or messages addressed to the diocese between the end of the war and the Cardinal's death may give an impression of extreme diversity. At demonstrations, it might be, or pilgrimages or congresses, the Cardinal addressed students, doctors, intellectuals or officials. He spoke to them in very different words, carefully adapted to each situation, so that each of these pronouncements has an originality and a style of its own. Yet these very diverse utterances seem to be basically united by one dominant concern: that in every social or professional milieu 'the mission' should be carried on by the members of that milieu and according to the laws of its life, faithfully respecting all the human values rooted in it, which through grace can grow into Christian virtues.

The Christian actively present in the world, acting in the world as it exists, with hope and realism: that is the teaching common to all these pages.

MESSAGES TO STUDENTS

The ceremonies at the beginning of the university year at the Sorbonne or the Institute Catholique, the students' Easter Mass and the Chartres pilgrimage were the special occasions when the Cardinal could make contact with the student world, as he loved to do. Each time he used the occasion to urge the young intellectuals to realize their responsibilities as Christians in the world now being built. But the relevance of these passages extends far beyond his youthful audience and equally concerns the active presence in the world of every adult Christian.

COMMUNICATING CHRIST THROUGH THOUGHT[1]

My dear friends,

I rejoice to see you gathered around this altar. It is a good time to address you: in the freshness of the Easter Mass, the early morning quiet of Notre-Dame; a long term behind you, and before you the thrill of going down for the vacation. All this makes you receptive, as I can feel. But you don't want me to give a sentimental exhortation—that would not satisfy your hunger; you want bread.

In a few moments I shall break and distribute to you the bread which is the body of Christ. But before that I want to share with you the bread of his doctrine, by giving you the guidance you expect from the shepherd of your souls.

To choose this guidance I have only to look at you: this gathering of yours is a homogeneous assembly. Your levels of education, I know, are unequal, your courses very different. But one common feature unites you, dear sons and daughters, in the fraternal fervour of your faith: you are all students. That fact both inspires my message and dictates your duty, which is *to communicate Christ through thought.*

To communicate Christ? Yes, that is what you want, and you believe in it, often already by experience. But by thought. Here something checks you; among the stronger of you it is reticence, among many it is discouragement. You may have been led to lose faith, now, before the conquering power of words, since you have heard, suffered and known too many propagandist campaigns which have all succeeded and then collapsed merely because each is followed by another. You might be tempted to lose faith in the power of thought and the diffusion of ideas, because every day you see, with indignant sorrow, a month of truth destroyed by a day of falsehood. You wonder if it is still ideas which lead the

---

[1] Sermon at the Easter Mass for students at Notre-Dame, 7 April 1946, in *Semaine religieuse de Paris*, no. 4797 (13 April 1946), pp. 249-53.

world, since the crowd only demands pictures, sounds and advertisements. You doubt the value of ideas because men have assured you, repeated and proved to you, that everything now results inexorably from number, money, strength; in short, from the 'primacy of economics'. You might finally lose faith in ideas because you are oppressed by the present and by your circumstances; you lose heart. And there is also the temptation to evasion, a real evasion on the part of those who go abroad in order to escape further struggle or suffering.

You, my friends, will have nothing to do with that fear of life, that selfishness! But you might perhaps accept more easily that 'evasion on the spot' by dreaming or by living in the ivory tower of the sceptic, the dilettante or the disillusioned. Reject that tempting solution with all your might; it would mean death to our country.... It would mean your death too, and the weakening of the Church!

For if you as students give up belief in thought, who will believe in it? And what will *you* believe in? If the salt loses its savour, who can replace it? It is precisely in the ages of iron that doctrine and truth are needed. It is because the world has lost its way that it needs a guide. And besides, to recover faith in yourselves you have only to cross our frontiers; then you would see what is expected of France, of her culture and her Christian values. Then you would understand how great is your task and how noble your destiny. You would grasp the role of Paris!

Freedom and obedience

But here a problem arises. In your frankness you have spoken to me about it; we meet it constantly in daily life: the problem of obedience.

Many will ask: how can we communicate Christ unless we are free? And how can we be free, when thought is subject to the Church's control, and apostolic action to her authority? To act, to convince, to win souls and minds to Christ—those

H

are your whole ambition. You believe in the Church, the Mystical Body, and you give yourselves to our Lord, with all the passionate and wonderful logic of your twenty years. And then in your fervour you are astonished or indignant when you find that you are sometimes contradicted, often moderated, by the Church's authority. You feel this conflict of freedom and obedience in yourselves, and it distresses you.

What should we think, my friends, of this state of mind? That it exists is a fact, though it is still nascent and limited. That you should *feel* it is only natural at your age, for you have habits of free criticism in these disturbed times when every value is called in question. But for you to *consent* to it would be wrong or, rather would be an error, a display of ignorance. For as I want to show you with all affection and all clarity, authority and freedom in the Church, far from being opposed, are reconcilable and their agreement makes for progress.

In the first place, the opposition is not between the authority of the hierarchy and the obedience of the faithful; it is between the caricatures of each, between despotic rule on the one hand and anarchic freedom on the other. In that case, of course, there is conflict. But that is neither the Church nor true freedom. It is agreed that the Church holds from Christ the unconditional right to teach the faith and to decide in matters of morals, worship and discipline. Christians must never forget this. But in fact we know, from present examples and from past ages, that she uses this right only with wisdom and moderation. It is a feature of her history which we can never too greatly admire, that she has always adapted herself to all Christians, taking account of their different races, languages and varied social classes. She has never imposed on them a single, rigid method of conquest. Always realistic, she knows how to respect the peculiar genius of her people. Is not this attitude, in the past as in the present, a reasonable guarantee for the future?

If, then, in view of this discretion the freedom of the faithful were seen as 'the right of Catholics to act as they please' without limit, everywhere and always and in all directions of thought, piety and the apostolate, then indeed there could be no agreement. There can be no understanding between anarchy and despotism. But would not such a claim be as frankly unreasonable as it would be disastrous?

Is this the case in the Church? Of course not! In principle as well as in fact, the Church is the 'Mystical Body', but it is a body of 'thinking members'. They are attached to the Head, but the Head cannot be imagined without them. Everything admittedly comes from the Head, but everything also meets in it. Apart from the deposit of revelation, which cannot be touched, the hierarchy's directives are rarely an absolute command; they are often a response, a reflex movement to a local stimulus which comes from the members. This movement is sometimes a refusal or a prohibition, but it is more often consent and support.

History shows this. For example, it was the desire to see the host, repeatedly expressed by the common people in the Middle Ages, that led to the universal use of processions of the blessed sacrament, benediction and exposition. It was the devotion of the faithful to our Lady which led to the rosary being approved and propagated. The same is true of the cult of the Sacred Heart. Nor was it the hierarchy which created the religious orders from above: it merely approved the constitutions presented to it by their founders. In the intellectual field the Church has allowed different schools of theology and spirituality. When Rome speaks, then, it is only after first listening and watching. Authority permits more often than it invents. Its commands are no less divine for that, no less inspired, no less firm. But they are all the more human!

Freedom of thought

So you see, my dear students, you have an immense role to play. So far from being passive or hindered in your movements, you have the whole wide world open before you. On the morrow of the resurrection, St Paul's words sounded forth: *Omnia vestra sunt!*' All things are yours!' (1 Cor. 3:23). Who then can number your free opportunities? They are almost infinite.

As for freedom of thought, do you think that even in the field of revealed truth, or in its relations with the rest of knowledge, you can ever exhaust all the reality offered to you? Your whole life would not suffice to list it, classify it, explore it, adapt it. And there you must preserve the principles of analysis and free research, of logic and intuition, required by each of these disciplines. Get to work, then, and go to the sources. Do work that endures. Found laboratories and study centres. Carry out research. Make use of all that has been acquired by true science. Be the thinkers of your time. If you can, and if you must, be the precursors and the artisans of the future. 'All things are yours.'

On the level of life, have you not an immense freedom of choice, of expression, of methods? Are you not more baffled by the vastness of the problems than by their narrowness? And is the field of souls so limited that you cannot spend your lives in tilling or cultivating it? Is not the diversity of movements and methods of conquest a sign of the Church's intelligent and liberal tolerance? She knows that you are indispensable in this pioneer work of direct and continuous contact with the masses. She listens to your observations, your judgments and suggestions. Can you be sure that under certain other banners you will find such a hearing and such generous autonomy?

Initiative and progress

Thus, my dear friends, your freedom is in no way hampered,

and your enterprises are a factor of progress for the Church, provided always that you are closely united to her through the hierarchy. You will be thus united by obedience—which will not be constrained but joyful and filial—to the commands and directives of religious authority. Without this super-natural, willing acceptance of the instructions of the pope and the bishops, your actions will be deprived of life. They could even be heretical, if they proceeded from a dangerous illuminism, each one thinking himself the guardian of the truth, on the pretext that the Holy Spirit is 'poured out on all flesh' (Acts 2:17). The Holy Spirit has indeed been poured out on each one of you since your baptism, but he is so in necessary union with the Church, which is the Body of Christ. In individualism there is no security! In matters of dogma and morals it leads straight to disaster. Have you ever thought what an immense service the Church performs for you in preventing you from straying from the path? Obedience to the infallible teaching authority, which is the pledge of security, then becomes the very condition of free-dom. *Veritas liberabit vos*! 'The truth will make you free' (John 8:32).

'All things are yours,' says St Paul, 'but you are Christ's!' And where is Christ, if not in his representatives on earth? Where is he more certainly found than with those who suc-ceed his apostles and hold from him the power and order of government?

'Where the Church is,' says St Irenaeus, 'there is the Spirit of God.' St Ignatius of Antioch says: 'You must have but one and the same mind with your bishop ..., your priests are united to the bishop as strings to a harp.... Thus Jesus Christ is hymned.'[2]

In two months, my friends, you will be on the road to Chartres. I am told that you have chosen 'The mystical Body' for the theme of your students' pilgrimage. I con-

[2] Epistle to the Ephesians.

gratulate you. I very much hope that these few reflections may lead you to emphasize the special grace for discovering and spreading the truth which is conferred by this loving submission of the faithful to their pastors.

But count even more, for that end, on the communion which you are going to make in a few moments. You are going to receive Christ. When you have received him, your hands joined on your breast, your heart's converse with him will be enriched by a great certitude: that you are equally one with all Christians. Total communion is union with Jesus, but also union, in him and through him, with all our brethren in heaven and on earth: it is the communion of saints.

Then you will no longer be alone. All the sweetness, all the holiness of the world will flow into you, give you peace and exalt you. Open your hearts to the Lord. Offer him your faults, your victories, your desires, your sacrifices. Give yourselves to him as he gives himself to you. And promise him without reserve to know him, to love him, and through him to save your brethren. Amen!

THINK RIGHTLY, THINK EFFECTIVELY[3]

First of all, think! Think, because so many men never think, and have neither time nor taste nor ability for thinking. Think, for around us and perhaps within us there are so many things to be made or remade which can only be made or remade wisely and solidly if they have been maturely pondered and thought out. Think, for it is still true that the world is led by ideas. The experience of the ages proves it. But ideas cannot really guide men and events unless they have been worked out, put together and brought into agree-

[3] Extracts from a sermon to the students of the Institut Catholique of Paris, 4 October 1946, in *Semaine religieuse de Paris*, no. 4828 (16 November 1946), pp. 756-7.

ment by powerful minds, capable of expressing them vigorously.

You must think rightly. Our ideas are valuable only if they have been conceived in clarity and submitted to the objective rules of a sound judgment: concern for the real, independence of the passions, absolute honesty. Above all, they are valuable if they can be defended against error and also against popular opinions, which can seduce for a time but, because they do not possess the truth, are proved by experience to be frivolous, feeble and short-lived.

You must think effectively. This does not mean that the rights of truth should be sacrificed to some sort of pragmatism, however well-intentioned. But it means that our thought must step down from the field of the abstract to that of the real; it must always aim at achievement, action and result. And this means that our thoughts must be expressed in our lives, lives so strongly lived that they command the attention and respect of men.

Now, my dear students, every one of you knows that this ideal is part of the tradition of the Institut Catholique of Paris. You all know that it is in the mind and will of your teachers, who themselves draw it from that higher source which is Christ. Each of you knows that it constitutes the climate of this house and that by frequenting it you will inevitably and happily receive the benefit of it.

Every year your teachers take the oath of loyalty to the Church, as they will do in a few moments. When they do this they have only one purpose: to conform their teaching to the teaching of the Spirit of Christ, who is himself the truth!

May the Holy Spirit bless these efforts in common. May that blessing give effect to so many good wills applied to this work! May our united efforts and prayers hasten the dawn of a better future for the Church and for France!

THE CALL OF THE WORLD[4]

Dear Students,

The world is in anguish, and you are calmly dedicating yourselves to your studies. These studies, disinterested as they are, seem to cut you off from suffering and to settle you in the world of ideas or scientific facts. Yet your hearts are too wide to remain indifferent to the calls which reach you.

The call of poverty which strikes at nearly all classes and makes the daily bread an obsession. The call of a society in utter turmoil, where everything seems to be questioned and nothing seems stable. The call of a justice which revolts against the profits derived from economic disorder by unscrupulous traffickers. The call of a freedom which is our dearest treasure and seems to be menaced from all sides.

You want to be yourselves, with all your might, outside all partisan spirit. Now, it seems as if events were so developing as to risk leading us to lose that freedom of life and thought which is the glory of our France and in which your faith can flourish.

God's expectation

In face of these appeals, your generosity refuses to be inactive. It shocks you, to be wrapped up in your studies or your security. Every decent feeling revolts against what might seem to be escape or evasion.

This morning I want to call you all to action. You must be the creators of a new world. Do not forget what our Lord said: 'You are the salt of the earth; but if salt has lost its taste, how shall its saltness be restored?' What an amazingly explosive force you could be in this tired world, if every one of you were entirely faithful to the gospel!

In a moment you are going to communion, to become one

---

[4] Sermon at the Easter Mass for students at Notre-Dame, 14 March 1948, in *Semaine religieuse de Paris*, no. 4899 (27 March 1948), pp. 332-4.

with Christ. Will you not be communicating with the soul of Christ, with his will, even to the gift of yourself, to save the world? Never forget that the fate of Christian civilization, even the fate of the world, lies in your hands.

You are like our Lady at Nazareth, on the day of the annunciation. A new presence of God among men can be effected, but it all hangs on one condition: that you say 'Yes'. Will you be able, like Mary, to express that acceptance with all your being? 'Behold, I am the handmaid of the Lord; let it be to me according to your word.' For the name of the Lord and his word will only be procaimed if you are faithful, transparent witnesses.

You know that there are many men about you for whom it is as if Christ had never been born. They have not yet known that revelation of God which changes everything in a life; to them the demands of justice and community which flow from the gospel are a dead letter. It depends on you whether Jesus and his word will reach these souls. Will you remain asleep?

Woe to you if you betray the love of God! Remember Israel according to the flesh, which was rejected because it did not recognize him who came in the name of the Lord. You too are called to make known God's message to the world. Will you, at least, be faithful?

Live as men who must be judged and render account of the talents they have received. When one can see the process of events as your archbishop sees it, when one reckons up the balance of the Christian forces in France, one perceives that your task is immense, and that no one in the world can do it but you. Do not disappoint God's expectation!

Competence and charity

Well, what are you going to do? First, you must not fail by neglect of your present duty, which is to acquire a scientific or technical competence, the pledge of your future service.

But you must not, for all that, limit yourselves to scholastic ambitions or to obtaining a post.

A Christian student ought to do something better than merely prepare an easy future for himself. But ought he to engage at once in social action or political contests? Service in the earthly city is a task which you cannot evade, when the hour for it comes, without being unfaithful to the precept of charity. However, a more urgent duty is required of you, and if you do not perform it today, your service of tomorrow will not be Christian. It is the life in God by faith.

Of all the distresses which weigh on men today, the worst is ignorance and forgetfulness of God. Physical misery is all-engrossing, but still more tragic is the misery of a soul for whom all ends in night. And for that misery you alone can provide the remedy. How? Not so much by propaganda and technical skill as by prayer. Learn to interrupt the pressure of your work for a few minutes every day and be attentive to God, in silence. Learn to read the gospels or St Paul's epistles. Let your soul be modelled on the word of God. Have a desire for genuinely Christian thought. May the light of the Lord shine through your secular studies and illuminate for you the foundations of a Christian world.

Then learn how to act by charity. Charity is not that sentimentality which moves us for a moment and excites a certain pity but remains inactive: it is a wide opening of our soul to the Spirit of God.

Remember that in your search for God you are inter-dependent. In common you have received the word of Christ, in common you have to live by it. Let your Christian communities in your schools or faculties be bound together by the charity of Christ. Banish whatever formalism is still left in them. Do no try to wear masks among yourselves.

United as Christians, live together by one single passion: Jesus Christ. Helping each other in your hopes and in your weakness, learn to contemplate our Lord with the same eyes. Then, in the midst of the love of Christ, they will set on fire whatever touches them.

The world of today is eager for what is genuine. No words will carry conviction to it unless they are supported by the witness of a life. If your communities are true, straightforward and poor, nothing can resist their witness.

Drive out from your hearts all pride, all Machiavellianism. Do not seek for success or effectiveness. Seek only God. When you have found him through Jesus Christ, all things shall be yours as well.

'APPROACH YOUR GENERATION WITH CRITICAL SYMPATHY'[5]

My Dear Friends,

What a large number of you have come to this Mass of the Holy Spirit! You have made an effort in order to come, and that proves that you are seeking God. But perhaps many of you are perplexed at events and changing ideas. You wonder if you will be abreast of your time. You are always being told that you are responsible for your generation and those to come. You find the load on your shoulders very heavy. But in fact you will perhaps come to find that you are not all alone; you form one community around the eucharistic mystery. That community has not yet reached the brotherly unity of the pilgrimage to Chartres, because this is the beginning of the year, but still it is a like-minded community of Christian students. Thus combined, you will be able to see more clearly and make a good start. It is to help you in this that I come to you today.

And because I am even more concerned than you with the events of the day, I need all the forces of the diocese: I need you. I need your youth, so spirited and so full of a

[5] Sermon at the students' Mass for the new academic year, in the church of the Sorbonne, 21 November 1948. *Semaine religieuse de Paris*, no. 4933 (27 November 1948), pp. 1124-7.

will for salvation. True, I am also a little anxious about it, for sometimes it would go too fast, not caring where it goes. You feel this strongly, too; you are attracted, divided, pulled about in almost opposite directions. So you wonder how to return to unity without ceasing to be yourselves. You will achieve it—and this will be my instruction for the year— by making a Christian judgment on the world.

Judging the world?

You often speak, and rightly, of commitment, of accepting responsibility for the world. How can you succeed in this without 'thinking as Christians'? That is your duty. As intellectuals by profession, you must show your interest in the problems of the day by an act of the intelligence. You have to make the diagnosis of your time, to make a valid judgment on it.

At first sight this seems simple. You could even say that in your conversations, in your reviews, you do nothing else. But here I want to put you on your guard, for there are two ways of judging. Never choose the first, which consists in judging from externals. Doctrines or events which are not known or are judged only by appearances, are condemned or exalted, without check or appeal. Judgments are pronounced which are superficial, applying only to details, or pharisaical, condemning without intelligence or charity. You know how strongly Christ spoke out againt the Pharisees. Why? Because they were liars, that is, unjust and inaccurate and because they were moved by passion. They did not judge 'in spirit and in truth', but at the prompting of their interest, their whims or their hates. I know how your generation hates any sort of pharisaism. But are you sure you never fall into it yourselves, unconsciously? Don't you sometimes arrogate to yourselves the role of arbiters, laying down that some scientific hypothesis or some development in history does not square with Christian doctrine or morals? You de-

clare that some solution—philosophical, medical or social—
is incompatible with Christianity: are you sure of it? Is not
what you are comparing sometimes just the caricature of one
or the other? Often when we judge some theory to be false
or certain persons to be dangerous, it is because they do not
agree with our tastes, our prejudices or our interests. Many
examples, some very topical and very burning, could be
quoted from the field of scientific research or of social structures.

A critical sympathy

You must never, then, be narrow or contemptuous censors.
The Christian judgment I want you to practise is an objective and calm judgment. What is required of you is to
approach your generation with *critical sympathy*.

It must be a *sympathy* which urges you to see things from
the inside, to understand not only formulas but intentions.
Use your intuition and try to make it coincide with the
problems. Take an effective part in the questionings and
heart-searchings caused by the present evolution, in all
domains. Realize that other men, who have not inherited
your faith and have started from very different horizons,
can arrive at solutions which you had not foreseen. Be fair:
consider the burden of their heredity and the influences
which have shaped them. Just as we have to rid our judgment of the prejudices which deform it, so we have to 'go
to the truth with our whole soul'. That principle, the golden
rule of all scientific exploration, must also be your watchword.

But at the same time you must take care to keep this
sympathy *critical*, not to let it exalt itself unduly. You will
learn to pick and choose, to test your enthusiasms by the
facts. You will not be too quick to condemn, and you will
not cling dishonestly to positions you feel to be wrong. You
will make use of the opinions of others and be able to take

advice and follow the judgment of the experienced. Will this cause you to lose your youth and originality? Not in the least, any more than the torrent loses its force when it is channelled to become a source of energy. So, then, in the very heart of your passion for the truth, you must guard your self-control. You read the papers and reviews, and you conclude that this or that evolution is part of the current of history. But are you sure that it is not some temporary, local ebullition, doomed to be soon forgotten? And even supposing that history confirms some theory or some experiment, are we therefore bound to follow history slavishly and not, rather, to make it and bend it in the direction of Christ?

My dear friends, you see what a serious thing it would be to commit yourselves without knowing where you are going. It is not only your own life and ideas which are at stake; you run the risk of compromising Christianity and the Church.

Judging in the Church

Thus you are going to promise, this morning, to open your hearts, to put yourselves honestly in the stream of what is being thought, what is being done, what is being prepared. You are going to adopt a spirit of welcome, to be ready for every new acquisition of knowledge or right living. But only on condition that you always belong to the Church. For you are not just some vague, indeterminate kind of thinkers. Without losing any of your legitimate autonomy of thought, you are, in fact, since your baptism and your confirmation, penetrated and inspired by the Word of God, which is sown in every soul and present to it. Of that truth you are the responsible trustees. You do not bear it alone, but in solidarity with all the Christians of the world, and above all in strict but never humiliating dependence on the infallible and enlightening magisterium of the Church.

There, my dear students, is the condition of a true Christian judgment. Nobody forbids you to advance. On the contrary, the Church calls you to go ahead. But nobody, on the other hand, authorizes you to go off as skirmishers or anarchists. No one of you is an impenetrable sphere: each is a cell which lives by the other cells and causes them to live. You belong to the Church. You are her children. You live by her grace and her blood. Never think that you will be any the less men because you are more faithful to the Church. Never think that you will become a person by cutting yourself off from her who helps you to become one: the Church, who is your mother. Be fully persuaded that there can be no union with the world without union with God. For to want the world without first being attached to God is to be lost for ever in the 'great all'. On the contrary, it is by yourselves living by the life of God that you will rediscover the true guiding lines of the world, those which from all eternity have been foreseen by his creative will, those which at every moment of time explain and uphold the universe.

There we find, in the last analysis, the true and profound Christian judgment. It is the judgment which conforms to the very judgment of God on men and on things. But this judgment is not given to all; at least, they do not obtain it without patience and effort. It needs all the Christian asceticism, all the slow practice of the virtues, and above all the inner life. My dear friends, it is in proportion as you live by Christ, by the seven gifts of the sacraments and above all by the eucharist, it is in proportion as you live your Mass, and rule your day by prayer, that you will have the right and the ability to judge truly. It is through looking in on yourselves in order to be cleansed from your faults, but above all it is through living more intimately by charity with the three divine persons who have made your soul their temple, that you will become capable of that penetrating, love-inspired diagnosis which will give peace to your intellects and light to those who consult you.

In conclusion, you might take it as a practical resolution to read slowly two hymns from your Missal: the *Veni Creator* and the *Adoro Te*, the latter composed by that great saint and thinker, St Thomas Aquinas. Every line will show you that the condition of all intellectual and spiritual progress, for you and for your generation, is to deepen youselves in faith and charity. If you want to overflow, like a river, in fertilizing irrigation, you must first open your souls to the replenishing streams of God, to his light, his power, his grace. Then and only then will you be able to judge the things of this world, for you will have first learned to taste the things of God—*dulce sapere*—and taught your souls to live by him —*Praesta meae menti de te vivere*. Grant, O Lord, that our souls may live by thee! Amen.

EFFECTIVE PRESENCE IN THE WORLD[6]

Dear Students,

This Passion Sunday invites us to enter into the drama which is at the heart of Christianity. During the Easter retreats many of you have come to learn that the Christian is one who agrees to die with Christ in order to rise with him. Stamped with the seal of Christ by your baptism, you have to pass through the mystery of his passion, his death and his resurrection, in your lives.

But this personal transformation is not enough. Christ offered himself for the redemption of the world and every Christian shares in the duty of spreading abroad the redemption which in Jesus Christ was accomplished once for all. You must be the redeemers of the world of today. To guide your resolutions, in this Easter Mass which has brought so many of you together, you must try to understand better

[6] Sermon at the Easter Mass for students at Notre-Dame, Passion Sunday, 1949, in *Semaine religieuse de Paris*, no. 4952 (9 April 1949), pp. 347-50.

what your share has to be in the redemption of the world around you.

Untroubled irreligion

Two striking features seem to mark the world in which you live and which, with Christ, you have to redeem. As soon as the Catholic goes out of his Catholic milieu, he finds himself faced with non-believers. This is nothing new, but in our days it has a particular character. A great many men settle down in a state of untroubled irreligion. It is not merely Christianity that they reject, but every religious idea. The invasion of all life by technology, the material energies brought into play, are such that materialized man thinks he can no longer be fully man unless God does not exist. And the blasphemous announcement that 'God is dead' is not simply the work of isolated teachers, but the basis of life for many. It seems that all concern about religion has left them, and they claim to find sufficient reason for existence in a wholly secular life. In your contacts with them you have perhaps been surprised to find, not hostility, but simply a cold indifference. At most they are interested in Christianity as one may be interested, for its records, in some extinct form of life. The very appeal of a religious life seems for many to have finally withered away.

Such is one of the characteristics of the contemporary world, which it is good for us to realize, not so as to be cast down by it, but to find out what our responsibilities are towards it.

The life of faith

If it is true that we are to be redeemers of this world, so estranged from God, our duty is to find the appropriate remedy. What will that be?

It consists, first, in a *profound life of faith*. In this world, for which only the earthly and the human exists, you must

I

affirm, by your conviction and your life, that there exists a transcendent plan of the love of God for mankind. You must say, by all that you are, that beyond the immediate appearances a work of God is going on, that his kingdom is being constructed, that his presence is at work. You must bear witness, each of you, to the call of Christ in your lives.

You know that this is no game, no vague, sentimental religiosity. Your generation is too realistic to be content with that superficial view. If your soul, in the words of the psalmist, is athirst for the living God, you must be prepared to purify yourself and be converted in order to seek God and to find him, as he wills to be found, in prayer, adoration and total self-abnegation before his will.

But living faith is also a transformation of all life, and you have often heard those searching words of the gospel: 'The gate is narrow and the way is hard, that leads to life....' (Matt. 7:13). You will be prepared to stay honest in a world where, as they say, 'anything goes'; you will stay pure in a world where vice is flaunted. Your personal life will have to be intensified, if you are to hold your ground in a world which no longer has faith, and if you are to save it.

But even more than that, you must form what might be called *islands of spiritual resistance* in the midst of this world, in which the intensity of fervour, prayer and generosity will be so great that it can not only hold fast against all attacks, but, by a gradual contagion, can put before those who surround you, and cannot ignore you, the problem of the religious and Christian meaning of their existence, can discover God at work in their lives and induce them, like you, to open themselves to his love.

Earthly tasks

There is another feature which seems to dominate the indifferent world around you, that in which you will live tomorrow.

Many men have lost interest in Christianity and religious values because all religion seems to them useless. To be concerned about God and one's soul does not pay. 'The world is constructed without Christianity,' they say, 'and to accept the Christian values and submit one's life to them, far from improving it, seems to retard its progress. Its structures develop without them and in spite of them. In an age when everything is judged by efficiency, the religious life is devoid of interest, it belongs to a bygone stage of human history.'

To this error, this temptation, you must reply by accepting in yourself and for the world all the consequences of the redemption wrought by Christ. First of all, of course, it is a question of preparing for eternal salvation, but it is also one of transforming this present life. Nothing should be indifferent to the Christian, all the earthly tasks must be assumed by him. And wherever you can set your hand to work, your role is unique. The grace given you is charity; that is, inseparably, the love of God and the love of your neighbour.

In all the social structures, in all human undertakings, it is possible, and it is a duty, to introduce a little of that charity, gradually to work it into social life, into economic, political and even international life. Only by this means will the earthly city, to whose building you have to contribute, become a rough draft, a foreshadowing, of the city of God.

For this task, this redemption, the Church, in Christ's name, counts on you. You will have to continue and improve the experiments of your elders. You will need competence, imagination and boldness.

Competence first. The object of your studies is not simply to enable you to find a job. They should place you at the service of the earthly city. Tomorrow your technical knowledge will cause you to excel on the professional level in the service of your brethren. But in the present, beyond your own subject, cast your eyes around you, be at the call of the world, its problems, its difficulties. Widen your minds and your hearts so that tomorrow you will be able to play your part.

Next, show proof of your imagination. At a stage of your life when nothing is yet fixed, faithfully drawing your inspiration from the principles and tradition of the Church, try to be creators, constantly at grips with the new facts of the world which is always in process of becoming.

And carry out your ideas with boldness, without flinching, not like anaemic, feeble creatures, but like men raised above themselves by grace. Be able to dare, like one who draws his strength and energy from God. 'Whatever anyone dares— I speak as a fool—I also dare,' said St Paul (2 Cor. 11:21).

In the presence of God, in the presence of the world
Don't you think, dear friends, that if the five thousand of you present this morning were to listen to this appeal, something would be transformed? Through you, the ransom of the world would be carried out and the indifference of the world around you could no longer plead the excuse of your lives as an additional justification. It would have to recognize that the kingdom of Christ, which is not of this world, is already succeeding in transforming this world here below, and that to live in the Christian way is the sole pledge of its salvation.

This is a vast programme. Already you are carrying it out in part: your various groups are helping you to cultivate and intensify your faith. Its crown will be the fine manifestation of Christian loyalty which you are preparing and which will be, as in past years, the pilgrimage to Our Lady of Chartres. But it is absolutely necessary not to stop there. Your various groups, according to your faculties, schools or local bodies to which you belong, must become more and more alive, if your presence with God is to be asserted in that world which wants to do without it.

Catholic Action asks you to preserve, in your university

circles, and tomorrow in all your professions, the lasting concern for transforming and improving the conditions of your life. It is Catholic Action which will make all honest souls see that living in the *presence of God* supports and encourages living in the *presence of the world*.

Thus you will really take part in the redemption and will yourselves be redeemers. You will share the aims of the Pope, who calls on the whole Church to intensify her prayer this Passion Sunday, so as to cure the impiety which defiles our age, by opposing it with a more powerful remedy. I know that this progress is hard to carry out. You are overwhelmed with cares of all sorts, examinations to prepare for, worries about finding steady jobs and the uncertainties which hang over the future. There must be days when you are tempted to live as you please, but the call of Christ and the Church finds an echo in you. Never before, perhaps, have Christian conditions of life been so like those of the primitive Church. The world today needs you. Let yourselves be wholly grasped and penetrated, and promise our Lord in this Easter Communion freely to involve yourselves with him in the redemption of the world.

THE ROLE OF INTELLECTUALS

These messages to students should suffice to convince us, if that were necessary, of the high place Cardinal Suhard gave to thought and ideas. In the same spirit he often agreed to preside over or to close the Semaine des Intellectuels Catholiques Français.

THINKING ON A WORLD SCALE[7]

From 11 to 18 April 1948 the Syndicate of Catholic Writers and the Catholic Centre of French Intellectuals held crowded meetings in the Mutalité,[8] on the theme 'Intellectuals and the charity

[7] *Semaine religieuse de Paris*, no. 4905 (8 May 1948), pp. 478-81; and in *Les intellectuels devant la charité du Christ*, Editions de Flore, pp. 7-12.

[8] A famous conference hall in Paris.

of Christ'. On Sunday 18 April the Cardinal presided over the closing session.

Catholic writers, French Catholic intellectuals, I want to thank you twice over.

I thank you for having spoken. Our age is blamed for its verbiage, its publicity, its noise. Faced with such an invasion of books and broadcasts, which break into our homes and bring us only sounds or words, we can desire but one thing: silence.

But you, gentlemen, on the contrary—and it is no small merit on your part—by speaking you have consoled us. You have spoken in order to say something—something which no one says any more. You have broken the silence. You have overcome that 'great fear of men', which you quoted one night, that fear which weighs so heavily on our souls. At a time when so many thoughts can no longer, dare no longer, be expressed, you have proclaimed publicly, bravely and loudly, so as to be heard from afar, the truth which sets us free.

But next, gentlemen, I want to *thank you for having thought.* This is not always so evident as not to deserve special mention here. One of the great dangers of culture, and of those who lay claim to it, is to make use of it, to dress up in it. A mortal danger: for brilliance or subtlety then takes the place of substance and progress. You have not accepted that counterfeit. Before speaking, you have kept silence; before communicating your discoveries to an audience, you have pondered them slowly, in solitude. Obviously you have not the monopoly of this method of procedure; it is the condition of all intellectual life. But what is original and new in your work is its object and its method.

The 'problem of the world'

Its object is what we may call the 'problem of the world'. It is an immense object, since it comprises the fundamental

question of the future of man on the whole planet; yet it is
a precise and limited object, because it is chosen, from among
the tangled skein of human difficulties, as that which sums
up and expresses them all. We have seen this double character taking shape during the last week. The wide extent of
the problems proposed, commanding at once the chief
avenues of thought and the most acute and topical practical
questions, has been absorbed in the simplicity, unity and
high moral tone of the response. This consists in affirming
everywhere the primacy of mutual love which is the complete
identity of the primordial demand of human progress and
the essential teaching of Christianity: charity.

Is it so common to see expressed, in terms of science, and
by experts, so universal a law and so clear a programme of
universal human action?

This synthesis on a world scale is due to the *method* employed. The essential vice of contemporary knowledge is its
multiplicity. As no individual intelligence is now capable of
covering it all, culture is split up into countless specializations.
It is true that some bridges have been built between certain
branches of knowledge, because of their close connection, but
who can discover the relations uniting all these fragmentary
investigations without exception? Who can call this multiplicity back to unity? Up to now, gentlemen, you are the
only ones I have seen who are resolved to assume this task
and to undertake this gigantic synthesis of a world coming
into being.

Work and culture
What you have achieved counts in God's sight and already
makes its weight felt in the balance of divine justice. But
you must go further. These two titles, 'Catholic' and 'intellectual', are a heavy burden. It would be both culpable and
naive to resort to them for some external and artificial credit.
Such a borrowed front would confer no prestige on Christian

thinkers. They will command respect quite otherwise, by the force and honesty of their investigation. Only in so far as they are scholars and creators will they be listened to and followed.

So you will understand that the Church will be very exacting in your regard. Today she asks two things of you: to think broadly and to think quickly.

To think broadly: that is, to place yourselves boldly on the scale of the universe. Do not be content to follow: go in front. Do not be merely disciples: be teachers. It is no longer enough to imitate; you must invent. Look in on yourselves and imagine what responsibilities you would lay on the coming generations if for a long time, through a timidity which is neither human nor Christian, you had compromised the world's chances of evolving to its full perfection and its redemption.

But to that end—and here my appeal is urgent—you must *think quickly*. The days are past when culture was worked out, drop by drop, in the alchemist's laboratory or the cloister library. We have discovered speed, but it has escaped our power, and now it is we who have to pursue it. We have released a movement which will stop, we know not when or where. The one thing we are sure of is that it is more and more rapid and that we are panting to keep up with it. Those who admit only the world's fatalist dialectic have no choice but to fear it. It is not so with the Christian. His thought goes faster and farther than any imaginable evolution, for it does not run after the development: it precedes it, it is ahead of it. It is for you scholars, philosophers, to remember these anticipations and to make use of them. You are *ahead* of the movement, because you have the thought of God, and that is eternal like him. Biology and atomic science can change many things; they will never affect the essential idea of God on man and nature.

So, be confident: work, each on your own ground. The

same effort is not required from all Christians. You who are specialists and thinkers by vocation have the task of rigorous investigation and discovery. You, as educated Catholics, have the task of popularization and diffusion. These results will be obtained only by the effort of all together. This session proves that you have understood this. It owes its success largely to the close collaboration between Catholic writers and the Catholic Centre of French Intellectuals.

This success points the way to the future and involves it. What has been done, you will do again, and better still. And I do not hesitate to say this publicly: I hope that these discussions and contacts may be renewed from now on, and become a regular institution. What the Semaines Sociales and the Congrès des Oeuvres[9] are in their respective spheres, this Semaine may become on the level of speculative thought.

May this wish be the conclusion of these meetings, in which we rejoice to welcome so many eminent foreign representatives. Their presence, and that of so many delegates from the provinces of France, is a sign of the importance of these gatherings which are founded on the gospel. And we may end on a note of hope. May those isolated thinkers, who perhaps doubted their mission and effectiveness, find in these fraternal contacts encouragement and a reason to persevere! And if they have ever felt near to losing heart, faced with a world often deaf to their message, let them remember that after love the greatest gift which they can give to their fellow men is light, and that their true way to be redeemers is to pierce the darkness!

HOW DOES A CHRISTIAN THINK?[10]

Next year, from 9 to 15 May, the chosen subject was: 'Contemporary philosophies in relation to the faith.' Etienne Gilson pre-

[9] Congress of Catholic societies, etc.

[10] *Semaine religieuse de Paris*, no. 4959 (28 May 1949), pp. 551-5; and in *Foi en Jésus-Christ et monde d'aujourd'hui*, Editions de Flore, pp. 9-14.

sided at the inauguration, at which the first paper was given by Etienne Borne. Emmanuel Mounier and Gustave Thibon were among many who took part in the debates.

On Sunday evening, the 15th, at the closing session in the church of St Odile, François Mauriac spoke on the theme 'Does the Christian belong to the world?' Before the singing of the Credo, taken up by five thousand people, the Cardinal drew the conclusions of the Semaine.

Gentlemen,

It is a great satisfaction to your archbishop to be present at this closing session of your magnificent Semaine. It is no ordinary manifestation which you have organized; your meetings and your discussions have been of a genuinely high quality.

It is sometimes the fashion to look back with regret on certain great periods of Church history, the patristic age or the Middle Ages, which produced so many masterpieces of Christian thought. Your work lessens that regret: we are living in a great epoch in which the Catholic intellect is playing an increasingly important part. One after another, masters of thought, who are also staunch believers, have put forward their point of view on the faith in the world of today. We are witnesses of an epoch in the life of the Church which may be compared with those of the theological Summas and the great doctors.

You have spoken finely of the faith. Will you allow your archbishop, by way of conclusion, to return to two very general aspects which underlie all your expositions? What I mean is this: a Christian must think in the light of faith, and a Christian must think with all his human reason.

In the light of the faith
To think in the light of the faith means above all, surely, to place in the centre of one's perspective him who is the living Word communicated to the world—Christ, the Word of God. He did not come to bring us a sum of artificially con-

structed doctrine; he is someone, 'a person', whom men heard, whom they saw with their eyes and touched with their hands. His living word was like a seed planted in the immense field of the world, and since then all human thought, every reflection on man's condition, must be referred, more or less directly, to him who is the revelation of God. It is true that Christ our Lord, in his teaching, seems to have given answers to human problems only to meet particular occasions. But by a sort of condensation there has been stored up, round his life, his teaching and his work, a vast dogmatic and moral synthesis, of which he is the stimulus and the centre.

The mystery of Christ, culminating point of the wisdom of God, has gradually produced a whole new vision of things and, since his coming, that light which is Christ in his Church illuminates all mankind to the depths. To live by the adherence of faith in Christ, and in the Church, is the only way to confer on the human intellligence an attitude which is wholly true, totally objective towards God, towards men and the world, a vision which perfectly balances all knowledge, which enables the understanding to see all things in their relation with the infinite. By faith in Jesus Christ human thought is basically eternal, definitive: it conveys, at least in germ, complete clearness of sight.

But faith is not only unifying; it is a safeguard, a support of the natural truths themeselves; it sustains and fortifies them in personal life as well as in the life of nations and of all civilization. This is a commentary, still to be developed, on that saying of St Augustine: *Credo, ut intelligam*—'I believe, the better to understand.' And that is true until the last day and the final progress of mankind, under the power of faith in Jesus Christ.

With all one's human reason
The Christian must therefore do all his thinking in the light of the faith, but at the same time, if he is not to fail in his

essential task, he must *think with all his human reason.* And it is this second aspect that I should like to emphasize. It needs only an elementary notion of the faith and a cursory knowledge of the Church's attitude throughout the ages to show that Christianity, so far from restricting human thought on earth, has always been its promoter and defender. Christianity is the teacher of free reason, and the Church has taken her stand against tendencies which would have reduced faith in Christ to a blind adherence, destructive of the intelligence. Just as our Lord did not conceive the role of the Church in the world to be that of a theocracy dominating the temporal, so he does not offer us a faith which would be a kind of imperialism of thought, imposing by authority all that has to be said in human fields.

You know, better than anyone, that while there is an interaction between faith and reason, and while Christ and the Church have an eminent role in education and the use of the understanding, it is none the less a more imperious duty for every Christian, and more specially for the Christian intellectual, to study all problems with a more vigorous intellectual daring, a freer scientific objectivity. The faith must never be a school of timidity or narrow-mindedness. If the Lord is the *Word,* that is not in order to suppress or fetter all research and all intellectual progress, but to be able, from the very centre of human intelligence, to enlighten and elevate all things.

God has his silences, which leave to human effort its proper field. Christ our Lord did not will to take away from reason its power to know and to govern itself by its own effort. As you know, we do not find in the Gospel *ready-made* answers coming down from heaven, imposed from outside, in the fields of the sciences, philosophy, social doctrine, art or civilization. From this it follows that we are called to a slow process of elaboration. Christ did not wish to anticipate the slow, necessary labour of the centuries.

So I would also like to warn you against an ever recurring danger, the temptation to construct premature, *a priori* syntheses. We do not know—often for a long time—at what precise point some judgment of our reason must be reconciled with some dogma of our faith. The works of God are deep and take long to penetrate. It took centuries for men to understand something about universal gravitation. Is it surprising that the deepest mystery of mankind's story, the point of junction and interpenetration of the natural and the supernatural, does not at once give up its secret?

It would not, then, be in accordance with our faith to blind our eyes to the *difficulties* of our personal effort by being content with over-simplified solutions: by saying, for example, that the fact of being a Christian solves all problems, that if only mankind were more virtuous, if only the whole world were Christian, all class-war and all wars between men would cease. There are human factors, economic and social, there are discoveries in the realm of thought, which we have no right to ignore or misunderstand. But all these problems must be penetrated in their own order with all the light of which our intelligence is capable. Christianity does not abolish all difficulties, but it helps us to face them and often enables us to overcome them.

The role of time

I urge you, therefore, to great patience in your work. The *time-factor* is indispensable. We must not anticipate Providence, either on the intellectual or the moral level. Along with faith in Jesus Christ, the patient humility which you learn from your various disciplines is the golden rule of all confrontation with the world today, in its mental, social, economic or artistic structures. Moreover, this patient humility is linked with an unfailing confidence. Little by little, Christ leads his own to the full truth. When he wills, he will cause the luminous, fruitful solution to flash out, at a moment in the history of his immortal Church, as he has done in times past.

We may, of course, wait for one who, like St Augustine or St Thomas, will provide, in a vast synthesis, a Christian view of the world which will enlighten the ages. But the ways of God are unsearchable, and what was once the work of a great saint and a great genius, around whom the thought of whole periods was crystallized, will perhaps—if Providence judges it best in the future—be a work of another sort, a collective work, for example, on the actual scale of human progress. In any case, that synthesis will be the outcome of many different labours, and it is to their slow cultivation that you are dedicated.

Christ was the origin of this work; it is he who will again be discovered at its conclusion. When you have toiled and even suffered much for the truth, you will be astonished to see, at the end of these discoveries and this progress, Christ waiting for you. He has seen higher and deeper than all the work of your life and generation. He was at the beginning. He was present at all that effort and he is still at the supreme peak, higher and further than all your dreams.

There is a saying of St Paul, in his Second Epistle to Timothy, which I commend to your reflection in conclusion. Late in his life and at the end of his busy career he states with joy and satisfaction that he has kept the faith: *'Fidem servavi'*, he writes to his disciple. Was it then so difficult for that apostle of Christ, who had vowed his life to him, to keep faith in his Master to the end? We find in these words an indication and an encouragement. St Paul never underestimated the constant effort demanded by Christian faith: it means being open to God, welcoming God, it means submitting to Christ. But through all the intellectual difficulties and the numerous problems which arise in the complexity of the world, a constant effort is called for, to keep unfailing trust in the light, which is the word of the Lord Christ, and to be perpetuated in his Church. This effort is called for to enable us to grope our way through the darkness of the world and its problems and to cast some light on it, while each person is grafted on to Christ and the Church.

After a long earthly pilgrimage may you be able to give that testimony which will also be a great thanksgiving: 'I have kept the faith.'

9. A MISSIONARY'S TESTAMENT

It is October 1948. A new year of apostolic work is beginning. The Cardinal is seventy-four, and he feels it. His priestly golden jubilee is approaching, and he fears that date: he feels it is a sort of confirmation, an inevitable consecration, of old age. When proposing or replying to toasts and the like, he often admits; 'I cannot hide the fact that I am growing old. But that is not important; the essential thing is that none of you around me is growing old.'

He often advises his secretary, when preparing the text of his speeches, to insert the psalm verse: *'Junior fui, etenim senui'*: 'I have been young, and now am old.' Then he corrects himself, and has the sad words deleted.

WHAT OUR APOSTLES EXPECT OF US[1]

On 10 October, the feast of St Denys, patron of the diocese, he meditates on the apostolate of martyrdom. This precious page is all the more intesting in that it is the very last of his private diary.

This 10 October 1948. On the evening of the feast of St Denys, particularly well observed. What our apostles want from us:

That we should appreciate the role they have been holding ... and that, in that appreciation, we should take account of the benefit of the faith and of all the wealth it comprises, but also that we should appreciate the way in which the faith reached us.... And in that way, this is what I see:

The doctrinal truth which they assimilated in its integrity (the real message of Christ). That is their first merit.

I see the mission received, and the receptivity of that mission, which comes from the apostle.

[1] Private diary, 10 October 1948, last pages.

I see the undertaking of that task, with all that it comprises of disinterested and personal dedication.

I see the concern to save souls, and the soul's horror at the sight of idolatry (indifference, false ideology).

I see the concern to pass on that truth to souls, in such a way that it will become their conviction and their life.

I see the effort they need in order to control themselves and keep calm in the face of the colossal mass of paganism.

I see the effort of imagination to discover the point where entry can be effected and souls can begin to be penetrated.

I see the concern to find the means to approach souls and make the necessary contact with them (meeting in some bar, or the house of a non-believer).

I see the willingness to take risks, together with prudence and dash.

I see the willingness to encounter obstacles, whatever danger arises, even peril of death.

I see all the risks of persecution (mockery, disappointments, attacks, slanders).

All this is what makes up the apostolate, and he who has not experienced it is not an apostle in the highest sense of the word.

Therefore, it would restrict the benefit of the apostolate to see it only as the 'enunciation of the truth', however genuine and integral. That is an aspect not without merit, but above all there is the 'subjective aspect' of the apostolate, which forms part of the gift and must be kept in view.

What our apostles expect of us: that we should give thanks to God ... in their person. *Mirabilis in sanctis,* 'marvellous in his holy ones', for everything in them is in them through God. . . . That this thanksgiving should be continued, for it is through all his work and at every moment of his life that the apostle must give thanks, for himself, and for the Christian community, which is the Church.

The martyrs. Pride at having the *martyrs* for founders.

In blood Christ founded the Church; by the blood of the martyrs she is watered and kept alive. Nothing great without the martyr.

'WOE TO ME IF I DO NOT PREACH THE GOSPEL!'[2]

It is now December. The jubilee celebrations are approaching. They mark simultaneously the fiftieth anniversary of his ordination and the twentieth of his episcopal consecration. Pius XII has just sent him a long autographed letter, marked with genuine good will (20 November).

On 5 December, Notre-Dame is in festal array. Hangings and canopies, velvet carpets and curtains.... There is an atmosphere of grand ceremonies, much red and purple, gilt and uniforms. Cardinal Gerlier is there, with Mgr Roncalli the Nuncio, eight archbishops, nineteen bishops, numerous religious superiors, abbots and prelates, representatives of the civil and military authorities and the legally constituted bodies, ministers and ambassadors, while a vast number of clergy and the whole people of Paris pack the choir, the nave and the aisles of the cathedral.

The pontifical Mass begins. After the singing of the gospel the Cardinal, seated on the throne, hears a long address of homage read by Mgr Leclerc. Then he leaves the choir and crosses the basilica, escorted by all the clergy.

He is now in the pulpit. In front of him, filling the five aisles of the cathedral, a huge crowd looks up at him. He begins by thanking all those present, the official persons, the clergy, his fellow workers, his friends. He speaks of his past, recalls his childhood, traces the stages of his life, Rome, Laval, Bayeux and Reims. Then suddenly his tone changes. He is speaking to the whole of Paris. The jubilee, the protocol, the lights and the incense—all these, it seems, have ceased to exist for him. He has done with memories. He has before him the Paris of today, the people for whom he is responsible, and heart to heart, as never before, he speaks to that people:

My brethren, it is on you now that I gaze, full of love and gratitude. You represent the whole people of Paris, in which all social classes, though separated by daily life, are but one

---

[2] Extracts from the sermon preached at the Cardinal's jubilee celebrations, 5 December 1948, in *Semaine religieuse de Paris*, no. 4936 (18 December 1948), pp. 1200-2.

of the days of mourning and the days of joy. Those who
do not really know you may find you light and easy-going.
But I know well who you are, and what you are worth. You
are true Frenchmen, an instinctive reserve makes you hide,
under a mask of laughter or mockery, your sufferings and
still more your passion for all that is noble and lovely. Today,
when certain reserves are dropped, I want to tell you simply
that I love you and I count on you!

To prove this, and to give you a lesson to carry away from
this jubilee—so many of you here, and so attentive!—I want
to explain to you what I have tried to do, and to sum up the
intentions which have guided my episcopate. For this purpose
I ask you to place yourselves in thought with me in front of
the Basilica of Montmartre, and to look out from there. As
far as the eye can reach, Paris! Paris, the 'completed' city,
and the inhuman city; Paris, city of grave disorders and
city of saints. Under these smoking roofs some six million
inhabitants live and die, love or quarrel, pray or despair.
See the vast city which God has entrusted to me as my portion! And why? To save it! To save Paris means two
things: to save souls, and to save the city.

To save the souls of Paris

To save the souls of Paris: that, my brethren, is the first
task. It is for that multitude that I shall have to answer on
the day of Judgment. Do you realize, then, the agony I feel?
It haunts me, it is a fixed idea which never leaves me. When
I go round the suburbs with their dreary factories, or the
brightly lit streets of the centre, when I see that mass of
people, some refined, some destitute, my heart is torn with
pain. And I have not far to seek for the subject of my meditation; it is always the same: there is a wall separating the
Church from the masses. That wall must be levelled at all
costs, to give back to Christ the crowds who have lost him.

But how is it to be done? My torment would be endless

if I were alone. But I am not alone; priests, religious and faithful Christians of Paris, I know that you are one body with your archbishop.

Our first weapon will be holiness. Without that, no redemption is possible. Until we are saints we shall save nobody. Never confuse the apostolate with propaganda!

What will this apostolate be? It will be a missionary apostolate. Some people are afraid of that word. They suppose that everything which has proved itself in the past must be dropped in favour of some new formula, unique or compulsory. No! The Church does not impose on her sons either a monopoly or a dictatorship. She simply asks you not to work as skirmishers, but in intimate liaison with the hierarchy, for concerted action.

This will be carried out on three levels. On the territorial level it will be the parish. Far from wrapping yourselves selfishly in your privileges, you will do all you can to become a great fraternal community. You will turn resolutely towards all the non-believers, to love them, to accept responsibility for them and to help them to find Christ.

Through Catholic Action you will act on your various spheres of life. Where the priest can no longer penetrate, the laity have found the way, in the factory, the university, the world of entertainment. Imitate them. Because Christians are everywhere, Christ is everywhere, and the Church is present to the world. This, with the 'promotion of the laity', is the incalculable result of our Catholic Action movements.

Finally, in co-operation with these militants and with the parish, some little communities of priests and lay people, witnesses to Christ in the midst of the masses, constitute a new experiment in evangelization. That is why, while acknowledging the indispensable and primary role of our diocesan seminaries, I attach such importance to that 'Mission de France', the institution and idea of which has been so magnificently understood and supported by the Assembly of Cardinals and Archbishops. That, too, is the reason why I have been glad to entrust to some of our priests, pioneers of the advance guard, our 'Mission de Paris'.

Thus on all fronts I call on you to march forward, and to march all together. For there are not two categories of Christians with some as professionals of the apostolate, and others as passive spectators of a changing world. You are all called in conscience to take part in this advance of the Church.

To save the city

To save the city, my friends, means first of all to save the souls of its inhabitants. But it also means to save the city, that is, to assume responsibility for it as it is, with its past, its future and the complex problems of its present. If I leave these aside, if I am not concerned about them, I am failing in half of my mission; for as soon as these problems arise on my territory they become themselves my 'subjects'. 'Woe is me if I do not preach the gospel!' cried St Paul. After his example, and in your presence, I repeat that terrible cry. For to preach the gospel means today not simply to preach the gospel aloud in a public place; it means to assume in Christ the burden of that civilization which is so rapidly emerging; to baptize its new structures, to consecrate to God a world which is seeking its unity. Besides the redemption of persons, there is, as we sing in the liturgy of Holy Saturday, the 'redemption of things' and the conversion of society to the empire of Christ the king.

In this domain, therefore, I here put out to you, Catholic intellectuals, scholars and writers, a serious appeal. The hour has come when you hold in your hands the fate of civilization and the future of history. Your role in regard to the forms of the future is immense. Do not leave to others the task of working them out under pagan mystiques. This is not the time to imitate, but to create, to invent, to do! Construct laboratories, open research centres, group together all intellects and all minds of good will. Apply sure rules and sane judgments to these ideas on the march. It falls to you, very largely, to be the artisans of the Church's rise—or the witness of her decline.

All together

When these responsibilities seem to overwhelm me, I hear in my heart the voice of Christ answering me, as he did St Paul: 'My grace is sufficient for thee', and peace returns. But also, my brethren, I am not alone in this diocese on its road to eternity.

I am upheld, not only by the laity, whose courage and worth I can never praise too highly, but by my priests. In a sense, because Christ has made their hands all-powerful, they alone can fully help me to bear the weight of this redemption. They alone, because they are the continuation of the God-Man on earth, can be the source of life and the soul of the missionary movement.

But these priests, so few for the task, are taken from among men. Their vocation is not an abstract call: it strikes its roots deep into the human condition. It comes from God, but very often by passing through you, who as parents are listening to me. On your response depends, to a great extent, the response of your children. So, if one of them confides in you his desire to be a priest, do not quench the new fire; understand that there are stiflings which are worse than death, there are gifts which are worth more than life. If our Lady had not spoken her *Fiat,* Jesus, at least in the central plan of redemption, would not have come to save us. Christian parents do not shut your hearts to the messages from heaven; think of those on this earth who await their salvation from your sons.

TRUTH AND CHARITY[3]

If God had not called him home on the morning of 30 May 1949, the young, once again, would have been addressed by the Cardinal that day. The thousands of students gathered in the cathedral square of Chartres awaited his coming in vain. While they joyfully sang the High Mass of the pilgrimage, they did not yet know that their archbishop had left them. So the words we are about to read were never spoken. No one can ever know in what tone, with what feeling, they would have been uttered. And so, no doubt, for all who love Cardinal Suhard, they will remain the last testament murmured to each one, the private confidence and the last avowal of a life consecrated, in faith and kindness, to the service of truth and charity.

My Dear Friends,

For three days you have talked about charity, and you have put it into practice in that atmosphere of brotherly friendship and respect which every year astonish all who witness your pilgrimage. But it is now that you are really *living* charity. For to us Christians it is not a mere theme for reflection, but a living reality, the most personal of things.

Be conscious of that privilege. In spite of the fatigue of your already long morning, offer your wills, open your souls to the gifts which this presence makes to you, as an answer to your prayer and an end to your waiting.

As I see you thus assembled in silence and longing for a bread more real than the bread of the journey, you seem ready—ready to be recollected and to respond. Let me tell you, however, in a few words, simply the words of a father, of a possible rift in your apparent unity.

There is reason to fear that some of you, at least, are dividing God as it were into two different realities: on the one hand the God of the intellect, on the other the God of the heart. I want to remind you, so that you may meditate on it during this Mass and your thanksgiving, that our God is at once the God of truth and the God of charity.

[3] Unpublished. From Fr Bouëssé's papers.

God is the Spirit of love

When St John (4:24) writes that 'God is Spirit', you readily admit it, as the crown of all that you have learnt about the world and man. This statement confirms all your scientific and philosophical reflections; it seems to you, and rightly, the fulfilment of all the groping hypotheses which pass before your eyes when you retrace the history of human knowledge.

But when the same St John, in his first epistle, tells you that 'God is love' (1 John 4:8) you do not accept this astounding definition so unanimously. One might even say that those three words, *Deus caritas est*, produce two great families, as it were, among you: that of the 'fideists' and that of the 'rationalists'. The former find it quite natural that God should be love. They have always been taught so, but more, they have always *felt* it. And they think of God solely as the one whom they love, and who loves them. That is not, of course, where they are wrong. Their mistake is to reserve the God of love only for what the heart can grasp, and to deny the right of the intelligence to prove and enlighten in this field. And that is partly the motive of the opposite attitude of some of your fellow-students, even sincere Catholics: they mistrust love. When they hear sermons, or read in spiritual authors, about an appeal to *love*, when they are advised to *trust* in divine Providence, they draw back, they are on their guard. They think these exhortations are more sentimental than rational, and pertain to direction of conscience or pastoral exhortation, but not to critical thought. They believe in God; they fear the 'good Lord', even giving this common term its fullest and most theological sense.

My dear friends, you should not be looking at those about you; it is not to others that these false ideas of God should be ascribed. It is you, each one of you, who are concerned. And no wonder, for everything in our time conduces to this regrettable separation. In the thirteenth century St Francis of Assisi went through towns and villages, crying out those words you know: 'Love is not loved!' Today we should have to say: 'Love has lost its rights, love is no longer legal tender!'

You will not expect me, here and now, to give proof of what is all too obvious. Simply ask yourselves this question: are human contacts, are international treaties, are agreements between employers and employees, regulated by love? Is it brought into account? Are not almost all the collective or even private acts of mankind dictated rather by self-interest, fear and the will for power?

It is the task of the Church, and therefore of all Christians, to restore love to common currency, to give it its primacy of place. The more technology is perfected, the more is love indispensable, if the world is not to be transformed into an insoluble labyrinth, or a field of battle. But the particular duty of you students in this common effort is to bring love back into the world in a *rational* manner, to re-establish it by thought; it is to show that love is not an ecclesiastical *invention*, an edifying consideration or a soothing balm, but the highest of all values. It is your part to make charity accepted in the world, not only by *hearts*—still so rich in generosity, after two thousand years of impregnation by the gospel—but by *minds*. How can you succeed in reconciling *truth* and *charity* in the eyes of your contemporaries, affected as they are by three centuries of rationalism? In two ways.

It is love that creates the world
The first will be theoretical. You will show that the world is not intelligible, has no meaning in its history, except through love.

Only the free and boundless love of a God as wise as he is good can account for the origin of the world: man created by God for happiness. Only that 'prevenient' love can account for man's 'end': the 'recapitulation' of all things, in Christ,

for the glory of God. You will also prove to the most exacting critics how far the intellect, in order to develop fully,
needs to find in everything the signs of an intention and a
will, ordered to the Good. 'Woe to the intelligence which
does not turn to loving!' You will adapt that cry of Bossuet
to your argument, but you will also reverse its terms: 'Woe
to the love, the charity, which does not turn to understanding, to seeing, to contemplating!'

In this twofold manner you will recover the wealth of
authentic Christianity, as it was understood and lived by
those benefactors and men of genius, the great mystics. Your
God and theirs is both pure spirit and love, both the light
of the understanding and the assuagement of the heart:
Deus meus et omnia: You will be able to adapt and apply
to yourselves St Paul's recommendation to the Ephesians,
Veritatem facientes in caritate': 'doing the truth in love'
(Eph. 4:15).

To this love you must also give a name, its true name.
Let it not be an abstraction, but Someone. I am certain—
from the very fact of your presence in this cathedral, which
for you all is both a goal and a starting-point—that on this
point you admit no equivocation. As Christians, you know
by your faith and by your life that the charity spoken of
by scripture is that same love, infinitely higher than our
human affections (though it takes them over and transforms
them), it is that divine gift, greater than faith and hope, as
St Paul says, and more lasting than they, for 'Love never
ends'. It is that gift, generous, purified and purifying, made to
one's neighbour for the love of God, of all that one possesses,
all that one is. There are not several loves; all charity comes
to us from the Father, by the Son, in the Holy Spirit. There
is no other source, in earth or in heaven, but this overflowing, ever-new love. All other loves in this world are either
its image, or its rough copy, or its degradation. Your charity,
my friends, will not seek its models in some esoteric philo-

sophy or some religious exoticism, in favour today and forgotten tomorrow. You will have only one example, one measure, for your love of God and man: the words, the life and
the death of Jesus Christ. Your charter will be his supreme
testament; your strength, his living presence in the eucharist.
From him you will draw the capacity for a self-giving ever
more complete, ever more stripped.

It is love which gives love
To give yourselves! This is the second way of proving love
to your non-believing friends. They will judge you by your
actions, by what you are, far more than by your reasonings.

But this movement of the soul, unique in its current,
unique in its final object, can be extinguished or tarnished,
lost in the sands, or else it can spring up into eternal life.
It can grow and be made perfect. And so, my dear friends,
after your arduous hours on the march, when all selfishness
and divisions were left behind on the road, in this hour of
true union and virile desire for God, I repeat to you the
eternal command, that which 'no ingratitude can end, no indifference can tire': 'Love the Lord your God with all your
heart and with all your soul and with all your might'; love one
another for the love of God, as Christ has loved you. Do not
fear that your legitimate dignity as men will suffer from
your loving in this way; in it you will find freedom and
reason. Read St Paul again and hear him: 'Let your charity
abound more and more' in you; let it remain 'poured out
in your hearts'. And: 'Who shall separate us from the love
of Christ?' (Rom. 8:35).

And yet this love will be attacked, both around you and
in yourselves. Be ready to defend it by spreading it; love
proves itself by loving. To defend it by justifying it, in the
name of a 'dialectic' which has had no need to wait for
others, in order to give—so brilliantly in its humility—the
peremptory proof of its wisdom and its well-doing: the dia-

lectic of love. To those who scoff at you for being led by
what they call the enervating influence of the gospel and
the beatitudes, show by your high culture that a man can
love without being a dupe, and spread charity while radiating intelligence. To those who make sad shipwreck on the
beacons they have themselves lit, you will show another light,
warmer and gentler, which never goes out. To those who are
choking in a closed universe, in a world shut in on itself,
you will open the gates of wide heaven, the path of the stars!

And if your generation, intrigued by the success of a life
which combines scientific rigour and technical efficiency with
faith in God and trust in men, if these classmates, still outside our mother the Church, question you on the secret of
your victory, you will be able to answer them, with a humility equalled only by your thankful joy, that what gives us
our strength, what gives us our certainty, is that 'we have
believed the love God has for us' (1 John 4:16). So be it!